CW00349568

ABOUT THE AUTHOR

A scholar and author focusing on politics, religion, and security studies, Dr H.A. Hellyer is a nonresident Senior Fellow at the Rafik Hariri Centre for the Middle East at the Atlantic Council in Washington, DC and an Associate Fellow in International Security Studies at the Royal United Services Institute in London. He writes about and comments on current events in the Arab World, Europe, and Muslim communities worldwide are regularly for international media networks such as CNN, the BBC and Al-Jazeera, and he is the author of several hundred op-eds for publications including *The Washington Post*, *Foreign Policy*, *The New York Times*, *The Guardian*, *The National* (Abu Dhabi), and *Daily News Egypt*.

Prior to joining the Council, Dr Hellyer was a nonresident Fellow at the Centre for Middle East Policy at the Brookings Institution in Washington, DC and Research Associate at the JFK School of Government at Harvard University. He also served as the first Arab world-based Senior Practice Consultant at the Gallup Organisation, where he analysed public opinion data in a variety of countries in the Arab world and the West. During his tenure at the University of Warwick (UK) as Fellow and then Senior Research Fellow, he was appointed as Deputy Convenor of the UK Government's Taskforce for the 2005 London bombings, and served as the Foreign & Commonwealth Office's first Economic and Social Research Council Fellow as part of the 'Islam' & 'Counter-Terrorism' teams.

Alongside his analytical career, Dr Hellyer has held positions at noted institutions including the University of Warwick, the American University in Cairo, and the Oxford Centre for Islamic Studies of the University of Oxford, where he authored several books and monographs & has contributed more than twenty-five book chapters and journal articles to various presses. His publications include *Muslims of Europe: The 'Other' Europeans* (Edinburgh University Press) and *Engagement with the Muslim Community & Counter-Terrorism: British Lessons for the West* (Brookings Institution Press).

Dr Hellyer's degree in law was read at the University of Sheffield School of Law, with an advanced degree in international political economy at the University of Sheffield's Department of Politics. He completed a multidisciplinary PhD at the University of Warwick as an Economic and Social Research Council scholar, and researched Islamic thought with traditionally trained specialists in the UK, Egypt, Malaysia and South Africa.

www.hahellyer.com

ADVANCE PRAISE FOR *A REVOLUTION UNDONE*

'Egyptians made their own history in 2011 with a revolution that inspired the world. But its story since those momentous eighteen days has been both complex and controversial, defying tidy definition. H.A. Hellyer is eminently qualified to inform, and interpret the punishing years since 2011 which have polarised Egypt and left many searching for certainties. There's an academic's rigour, a pollster's precision, and a journalist's compelling anecdotes in his chronicle of Egypt's "unfinished revolution." Committed to the principles of that peaceful protest, he doesn't shirk from holding everyone to account: from the revolutionaries who failed to follow through; the Muslim Brotherhood which fell from grace and power; and a military which played a pivotal role throughout. Egypt's story is still being written. But five years on, this book puts down an important marker.'

Lyse Doucet, Chief International Correspondent, BBC

'Attempting to follow the extraordinary tumult in Egypt has often felt like wading through a dense fog. It takes an assured and skilful navigator to plot a constructive path through the gloom and shine a light where it is needed most. Hellyer is just such a navigator: thoughtful, perceptive and above all committed to the promise of revolution, even as he spells out with intellectual honesty and historical nuance where those fighting for a more democratic Egypt have gone wrong. His analysis is an antidote to lazy stereotypes and reductive binaries, and today it is more important than ever.'

Jack Shenker, former Egypt correspondent for
The Guardian; author of *The Egyptians: A Radical Story*

'H.A. Hellyer has written an inimitable book. Specialists and general readers alike will benefit hugely from the accounts exquisitely related by an insider and a fair observer in one. Hellyer's organic link to Egypt and consciously impartial perspective produce a unique combination that we should appreciate, as many of the books published on the subject tend to lean towards one view or one side. His writings have long made clear his consistent and balanced insight—and in this book, Hellyer lets no one off the hook, calling all to account.'

Hassan Hassan, Associate Fellow of Chatham House; author of the
New York Times bestseller *ISIS: Inside the Army of Terror*

'*A Revolution Undone* represents the most authoritative, thoughtful, and nuanced account to date of Egypt's 2011 revolution and its aftermath. The book is replete with the kind of unique insight that emerges only from direct proximity to the events it describes. Hellyer's is a voice of studious integrity, allowing the book to achieve the near impossible when it comes to analysing Egyptian politics today: balance and perspective. A bold, defining, and—ultimately—hopeful statement on the Arab Spring that should be read by anyone interested in the future of the Middle East.'

Peter Mandaville, Professor of International Affairs at
George Mason University; author of *Islam and Politics*

'Throughout the tumultuous events of 2011–2015, H.A. Hellyer has been a lucid but hardly dispassionate analyst. Now he has written a book presenting that period that draws on the same assets as his contemporaneous analyses: he writes from the heart but without losing a touch of his clear-headed thinking. Those who remember only a confused tumble of events will find a sure guide, but even those who recall these events well will learn from his book.'

Nathan J. Brown, Professor of Political Science and International Affairs at
George Washington University

'It is hard to imagine a better qualified analyst of recent Egyptian history than H.A. Hellyer: a British political scientist of Egyptian heritage, conversant in the modern history of Islamic thought, equipped with the most credible public opinion polling, well-connected with a broad circle of activists and diplomats, and a Cairo resident who personally lived through the upheavals of both 2011 and 2013. Hellyer started out cautious about the first protests in 2011 but he came to identify what he calls Egypt's "revolutionary current" as its best hope, and his honest and probing account of those events will be a great resource for future students of that history.'

David D. Kirkpatrick, correspondent for the *New York Times*
and its Cairo bureau chief from 2011–2015

'H.A. Hellyer has written a deeply knowledgeable and personal set of reflections on the Egyptian revolution and its grim aftermath. It is impossible to read this book and not come away with a sense of the spirit that drove the young people of Tahrir Square in the early days of 2011, and which drives many Egyptians still. Many books have been written with the words "Egypt" and "Revolution" in their titles, but this is the only one worth reading.'

Tarek Masoud, Sultan of Oman Associate Professor of International Relations at
Harvard University; author of *Counting Islam: Religion, Class and Elections in Egypt*

'*A Revolution Undone* combines in the most revealing of ways both the author's participatory observations and his analytical skill in tackling questions of politics, religion and human rights. This is a persuasive analysis of the structural realities hindering democratic governance in this most populous country in the Middle East.'

Amr Hamzawy, Associate Professor, Department of Public Policy and Administration
at the American University in Cairo; author of *A Margin for Democracy in Egypt:
The Story of An Unsuccessful Transition*

'To see Egypt through H.A. Hellyer's eyes is to observe with rare immediacy the turmoil, excitement, lost hopes, and ultimate uncertainty since the heady days of protest in 2011. Engagé but never one-sided, affecting but also clear-headed, he powerfully demonstrates how an Islamist right and authoritarian military have each tried to highjack the post-Mubarak order. That this will be a successful revolution in the long term depends, in this eloquent and unflinching analysis, on whether the precipitating search for dignity is not betrayed.'

James Piscatori, Professor of International Relations, Durham University

'Hellyer combines an engaging personal memoir with insightful and balanced analyses to present a clear portrayal of the Arab Spring revolution in Egypt. His account departs from the all-too-common treatment of the major elements as monolithic, and instead, provides an understanding of the complex mosaic of Arab Spring politics in Egypt. One strength of his analysis is his coverage of the evolution of coverage of the changing political scene. As he shows, observers played important roles in constructing the various narratives of the revolution. In the growing library of books on the Arab Spring, Hellyer provides a refreshingly intimate perspective that will be of use to all interested in twenty-first century political developments.'

John Voll, Professor Emeritus of Islamic History, Center for
Muslim-Christian Understanding, Georgetown University

'Part personal narrative, part contemporary history, H.A. Hellyer's *A Revolution Undone* provides a brilliant, gripping account of Egypt's 2011 revolution and its aftermath. Told from the unique perspective of someone who lived through and bore witness to these historic events, the book is most notable for its analytical and moral clarity. Ultimately, the author's conclusion is an uplifting one: the young revolutionaries who flooded Tahrir Square may have failed to change the political order in Egypt, but the idea of the revolution continues to inspire and have resonance in that country and far beyond.'

Stephen R. Grand, Executive Director, The Middle East Strategy Task Force,
The Atlantic Council; author of *Understanding Tahrir Square*

'At a time when many have already written off the Arab world's ability to transition to pluralistic societies, A Revolution Undone presents a more nuanced analysis about the region that offers balance, empathy, and above all, hope. Written by a pre-eminent scholar and analyst deeply-embedded in the region, this book is a must read for anyone seeking deep insights into the Egyptian uprising, its aftermath, and its possible trajectory.'

Marwan Muasher, Vice President for Studies, Carnegie Endowment for
International Peace. Formerly Foreign Minister and Deputy Prime Minister of
Jordan, he is the author of *The Arab Center: The Promise of Moderation*

A REVOLUTION UNDONE

H. A. HELLYER

A Revolution Undone

Egypt's Road Beyond Revolt

HURST & COMPANY, LONDON

First published in the United Kingdom in 2016 by
C. Hurst & Co. (Publishers) Ltd.,
41 Great Russell Street, London, WC1B 3PL
© H. A. Hellyer, 2016
All rights reserved.
Printed in the United Kingdom

The right of H. A. Hellyer to be identified as the author of
this publication is asserted by him in accordance with the
Copyright, Designs and Patents Act, 1988.

A Cataloguing-in-Publication data record for this book
is available from the British Library.

ISBN: 9781849046848

This book is printed using paper from registered sustainable
and managed sources.

www.hurstpublishers.com

To Darah and the next generation:

Your heart was in Tahrir long before most people had even heard of it—and without you, I wouldn't have written this. This book is for those from among the next generation that you and I will raise. May they absolve themselves from our generation's mistakes—and build a future better than the one we could provide.

To my mother:

There will never be good enough words to describe your sacrifices for your family—but may you be given good enough reason to be proud of your son.

CONTENTS

CONTENTS

ACKNOWLEDGEMENTS

There are a number of people and institutions that ought to be acknowledged for this book. The first are the various publications that I wrote for between 2011 and 2015—*The Guardian*, *Foreign Policy*, *The Washington Post*, *Mada Masr*, *The National*, *Al Arabiya*, *Al Jazeera*, *Al-Monitor*, *Salon* and others. It was in their pages that I first explored many of the themes of this book, and without them I probably wouldn't have been able to sit down and finally put my ideas together—hopefully, in a coherent and sensible form.

I went to a number of places to discuss the themes in this book over the course of four years—ranging from university campuses in the UK, to think tanks in the US, policy circles in governments across Europe and the US, discussion groups in Cairo and elsewhere in the Arab world, and more. Sometimes these discussions were challenging, but they were invariably useful, and I am grateful for those opportunities. The place where I wrote the most was in a study provided to me by the Azzavia in Cape Town. I'm indebted to the folk of that wondrous place for granting me that solitude and that support.

I should note that my bibliography is a 'selected' one, with only the most pertinent publications included. A much more extensive bibliography may be available on my website, www.hahellyer.com/ARevolutionUndone, and I hope to continue to develop that bibliography over time.

Some people read the book (or parts of it) at various stages of its development and gave wonderful comments, insights and critiques. They include John Voll, Shafiq Morton, Hafsa Halawa, Basil el-Dabh, Jack

ACKNOWLEDGEMENTS

Shenker and Miriam Berger. They also include scholars and observers who encouraged my work such as Tarek Masoud, Peter Mandaville, Lyse Doucet, Nathan Brown, Amr Hamzawy, James Piscatori, Andrew March, and Stephen Grand; to all of them I offer my appreciation. Michael Dwyer, Alasdair Craig and Jon de Peyer at Hurst were patient with me—it's been a pleasure working with them. It ought to go without saying that the good things in this work are likely due in no small measure to the efforts of those whom I have mentioned. Nevertheless, any errors and mistakes belong to me and me alone.

I had good friends who encouraged me to write this book. I can't list all of them here. But my wife, Darah, was always there to support me and urge me to move forward, even though it took me away from her and our wonderful family. I cannot thank her enough—but I can at least dedicate this book to her, and to our children. May the latter build the future well, without making the mistakes our generation is guilty of.

A NOTE ON TRANSLITERATION

There are established academic transliteration conventions that mean that 'Mursi' ought to be a more appropriate rendering than 'Morsi', and 'Muhammad' rather than 'Mohamed' or 'Mohammed', along with diacritics. I normally advocate such conventions. In this book, however, I have come to a compromise position between following the most appropriate academic convention and trying to avoid distracting the reader in a book that is meant for a wide audience. Transliteration will follow, as much as possible, the style of the *International Journal of Middle East Studies*, but without diacratics and italicisation.

Where authors have published under their own spelling, I will respect that for the purposes of faithfully representing their work. I have kept to alternative spellings for proper nouns that have become so widespread, out of concerns the reader might be misled unintentionally (such as 'al-Jazira' instead of 'al-Jazeera' or 'Omar Sulaiman' rather than 'Umar Sulayman', but Khalid Sa'id rather than Khaled Said). I use 'al-' rather than 'el-', and only when citing a complete name (so, for example, 'Muhammad al-Baltagi', and 'Baltagi'). Where the name is of an Egyptian, I use 'g' rather 'j' for the letter 'jeem', even if I personally feel 'jeem' ought to be used.

GLOSSARY

People

Abd al-Fattah al-Sisi	Former Egyptian military officer who, as defence minister, overthrew President Muhammad Mursi on 3 July 2013
Abd al-Mun'im Abu al-Futuh	Pro-revolution and left-leaning Islamist politician and former Muslim Brotherhood member who unsuccessfully ran for president in 2012
Adli Mansur	Egyptian judge who served as a figurehead interim president after the ousting of Mursi
Ahmad Maher	Revolutionary and co-founder of April 6 Youth Movement, jailed in 2013 for violating the anti-protest law
Ahmad Shafiq	Former Mubarak confidant, who briefly served as prime minister and narrowly lost the 2012 presidential elections in a runoff to Mursi
Ala'a Abd al-Fattah	Prominent Egyptian revolutionary and political activist, jailed under Mubarak, the Supreme Council of the Armed Forces, Mursi, and then Sisi for violating the anti-protest law
Amr Hamzawy	Liberal politician and former member of parliament active in the revolutionary uprising
Amr Moussa	Egyptian politician and diplomat, who served as the secretary general of the Arab League and unsuccessfully ran for president in 2012

GLOSSARY

Bassem Youssef	Egyptian political satirist who was highly critical of Mursi, and then left Egypt following pressure put upon him after the post-Mursi political dispensation
Bassem Sabry	Highly respected Egyptian journalist and commentator on the revolution, who passed away in 2014
Emad Effat	An Azhar Shaykh who earned the name 'Shaykh of the Revolution' after his death during a protest in 2011
Essam al-Erian	High-level member of the Muslim Brotherhood and the related Freedom and Justice Party, imprisoned in 2013
Hamdeen Sabahi	Egyptian Nasserite politician and Mubarak critic, who unsuccessfully ran for president on a pro-revolution platform in 2012, and again in 2014
Hasan al-Banna	Egyptian founder of the Muslim Brotherhood
Heba Morayef	Human rights activist and former director of Human Rights Watch in Egypt
Hossam Bahgat	Human rights activist and journalist, founder of the Egyptian Initiative for Personal Rights
Husni Mubarak	Ruled Egypt for three decades until his forced resignation on 11 February 2011
Gamal Mubarak	A wealthy businessman and Husni Mubarak youngest son who many feared was being groomed to succeed his father
Khalid Sa'id	A young Egyptian beaten to death by police in Alexandria in 2010, sparking a popular pro-revolution Facebook page, 'We Are All Khalid Sa'id'
Khairat al-Shater	Muslim Brotherhood senior leader; initially the Freedom and Justice Party candidate for the 2012 presidential elections until being disqualified;

	currently in jail after having been arrested in in 2013
Muhammad al-Baradei	Former Egyptian politician and Mubarak-critic who founded the pre-2011 National Association for Change and briefly served as vice president in 2013
Muhammad al-Baltagi	Leading Muslim Brotherhood and Freedom and Justice Party member, currently in jail after having been arrested in in 2013
Muhammad Hussain Tantawi	Egyptian general who headed the Supreme Council of the Armed Forces, which ruled after Mubarak's ousting
Muhammad Mursi	Former Muslim Brotherhood member elected president in June 2012, who ruled until his ousting and imprisonment by the military in July 2013
Omar Suleiman	Mubarak's former 'spy master', politician and diplomat, who briefly served as Egypt's vice president in 2011
Sayyid Qutb	Muslim Brotherhood member whose mid-twentieth-century writings influenced subsequent strands of political Islamism
Wael Ghonim	Internet activist, former Google employee and entrepreneur who founded the influential 'We Are All Khalid Sa'id' Facebook page

Organisations

Al-Azhar	Centre of Islamic study, based in Cairo. The Grand Shaykh of al-Azhar is a political and religiously influential position in Egypt
April 6 Youth Movement	Pro-25-January–revolution youth movement; started in 2008 in support of worker protests
Cairo Institute for Human Rights Studies	Independent Egyptian human rights organisation started in 1993

GLOSSARY

Constitution Party	Political party founded in 2002 by Muhammad al-Baradei
Egyptian Initiative for Personal Rights	Independent Egyptian human rights organisation started in 2002
Egyptian Movement for Change ('Kifaya')	A grassroots coalition of political groups opposed to Mubarak's rule and founded in 2004
Freedom and Justice Party (FJP)	Muslim Brotherhood-affiliated party founded in 2011 and banned in late 2013
Gama'a al-Islamiyya	Egyptian Islamist group that waged an insurgency against the government in the early 1990s
Mada Masr	Independent progressive news website launched in 2013
Muslim Brotherhood (MB)	Islamist movement with branches in countries worldwide
National Association for Change	Non-ideological group of Mubarak critics, founded by al-Baradei in 2010
National Democratic Party	Mubarak's political party, disbanded after the 25 January uprising in 2011
National Salvation Front	Coalition of political parties opposed to Mursi's rule, formed in 2012 after his constitutional decrees
Noor Party	Main Salafi political party, started after the 2011 uprising
Revolutionary Socialists	Pro-revolution Trotskyist political party, active before and after 25 January 2011
Supreme Council of the Armed Forces (SCAF)	Egypt's highest military body, which ruled the country for fifteen months after Mubarak's ousting
Tamarod	Anti-Mursi movement that petitioned and mobilised for end of Mursi's rule in 2013
Ultras	Groups of football fans with a history of clashing with police and who were active in the uprising in 2011 and subsequent protests

TIMELINE

25 Jan. 1952	Egyptian police clash with occupying British troops, an event that decades later would be commemorated annually as Egypt's National Police Day
1954–70	President Gamal Abd al-Nasser ruled Egypt
1970–81	President Anwar al-Sadat ruled Egypt
1981–2011	President Husni Mubarak ruled Egypt
2004	Founding of the Egyptian Movement for Change (Kifaya)
2005	Egypt holds allegedly fraud-ridden presidential and parliamentary elections that bolster Mubarak
2008	Founding of April 6 Youth Movement and Mahalla labour protests
2010	Egypt holds another round of allegedly fraudulent parliamentary elections
June 2010	Khalid Sa'id murdered by police officer in Alexandria, sparking an anti-regime campaign
14 Jan. 2011	Tunisian dictator Zine al-Abidine Ben Ali ousted after a month of protests, sparking what became known as the Arab Spring
25 Jan. 2011	Anti-Mubarak protesters take to the streets on National Police Day calling for the president's removal and an end to emergency law

TIMELINE

28 Jan. 2011	'Friday of Rage' in which protestors take hold of Cairo's central Tahrir Square as protests spread and police retreat
2 Feb. 2011	Bloody 'Battle of the Camels' between revolutionaries and alleged paid Mubarak thugs, who entered Tahrir on horseback and camels
11 Feb. 2011	After eighteen days of protest, Mubarak announces his resignation and the Supreme Council of the Armed Forces assumes power. Protestors begin to leave the square
19 March 2011	Constitutional referendum, supported by the Muslim Brotherhood and military and opposed by the revolutionary camp, passes
9 Oct 2011	Egyptian security forces run over peaceful protestors in the Maspero Massacre
Nov. 2011	Muhammad Mahmud Street clashes in Cairo between military and anti-SCAF protestors
Dec. 2011	'Cabinet clashes' break out in Cairo after the military tries to disband an anti-SCAF sit-in
Nov. 2011–Jan 2012	Muslim Brotherhood wins big in parliamentary elections
1 Feb. 2012	Port Said massacre, in which seventy-four, mostly Ultras football fans, are killed
April 2012	Court annuls first Constitutional Assembly
May 2012	First round of presidential elections
June 2012	Supreme Constitutional Court dissolves parliament, while the military issues several decrees strengthening its powers
30 June 2012	The Brotherhood's Mursi announced winner of presidential elections
12 Aug. 2012	Abd al-Fattah al-Sisi becomes defence minister, and Muhammad Hussain Tantawi is retired
21 Nov. 2012	Mursi issues decree dramatically expanding his powers

TIMELINE

4 Dec. 2012	Clashes break out between pro- and anti-Mursi protestors at the presidential palace
22 Dec. 2012	New constitution, backed by the Brotherhood, passes in a referendum
April 2013	Tamarod anti-Mursi movement begins petitioning for early presidential elections
30 June 2013	Massive anti-Mursi protests calling for early presidential elections
3 July 2013	The military, led by Sisi, ousts Mursi and assumes power
8 July 2013	At least fifty-one pro-Mursi protestors killed in clashes with the security forces at the Republican Guards headquarters
14 Aug. 2013	Egyptian security forces violently disrupt pro-Mursi sit-in at the Rab'a al-Adawiyya mosque, leaving an estimated thousand dead
Nov. 2013	Anti-protest law enacted
May 2014	Sisi elected president.
Jan. 24 2015	Shaima' al-Sabbagh, supporter of the 25 January uprising, and activist in the Socialist Popular Alliance party, is killed by Egyptian security forces while commemorating the January uprising in a peaceful march near Tahrir Square

PROLOGUE

Landing in Cairo... again

On Wednesday 1 December 2010, I step off Egypt Air flight MS778 from London Heathrow, arriving in Cairo. It is a flight I have taken many times—and I do not imagine this trip will be much different from others. Indeed, the very point of it is to embark on a period of predictability and, above all, tranquillity.

A familiar stroll awaits me as soon as I disembark: I walk through Terminal 3 of Cairo International Airport, and receive the usual interrogation at customs. 'Interrogation' is perhaps a strong word. In truth, it is a humdrum of quick questions, as I break the mould of the typical arrival. My red passport identifies me as a British national, and my last name is clearly English in origin; the customs official, nevertheless, becomes dumbfounded as he and I converse in Arabic, and my first (Arabic) name becomes the topic of debate. He asks, 'Where is your father originally from?' Depending on my mood, I either answer the question simply, which prolongs the conversation a great deal, as he digs through subsequent generations of my father's ancestry—or I let him know what I know he really wants to know:

'My father is English, but my mother is Egyptian'.

This answer, at least in part, indelibly defines this book.

Multiple identities

That question at the airport raises a familiar theme in my life. I was about five or six years old when, as a pupil at Hill House in London, I came home to ask my father to clarify something a fellow pupil had confronted me with. 'The Thames is longer than the Nile!' I had been told. My father, as I recall, looked puzzled when I repeated the assertion to him—he was very consciously (one might even say proudly) an Englishman, but he found the claim absurd, considering the Nile is about nineteen times longer than the Thames.

Nevertheless, that day was perhaps the first time that I was confronted by the fact that I was not only an Englishman, but also an Egyptian—and not only an Egyptian, but also an Englishman. Both that child and that Egyptian customs official thirty years later were far removed reminders to me that my perspective, as I began to write and comment on political affairs, would be informed by two very different worlds.

In both of those worlds I was, and remain, simultaneously a native and a stranger—and it is precisely this frame of mind that has preoccupied my own analysis of Egyptian affairs. On a personal level, my interaction with Egypt has been Western and Arab; English and Egyptian. My father is an Englishman from Rowfant in West Sussex, and I inherited a very particular type of Englishness indeed. It was an Englishness formed by a rural, even provincial origin—but also an Englishness that found its political voice born within transnational solidarity movements, such as the Anti-Apartheid Movement, the national executive of which my father served upon. He was a member of what was then called the 'Red Guard' of the 'Young Liberals', the youth group of the forerunner to the Liberal Democrats in the UK. The Red Guard went against the traditional Liberal line, campaigning along lines more usually associated with the radical left, particularly in its opposition to the Vietnam War and apartheid, and its advocating of the Palestinian cause.

But I had an Egyptian and Arab heritage as well, which was in many ways more cosmopolitan and diverse than my Englishness. My Cairene mother defined it—she of mixed Egyptian, Sudanese (Ja'alin Abbasi) and North African (Sanusi) heritage. But if there was an English political voice that indelibly impacted me as a child, my Egyptian political voice really crystallised when I first walked in the Square of Liberation (Tahrir Square) during the revolution of 25 January 2011. I didn't 'become' Egyptian then, but certainly the intensity of what I learned about politics in more than a decade as an Englishman before 2011 was comparable to the force of what I learned in a few years as an Egyptian after 2011. With time, I learned how to incorporate the latter experiences into the former—but their clout and fury certainly produced a tremor within my system of thought. I've no doubt it was for the best—and one way or another it defines much of this book.

Navigating the elements

Many times in the years since I stepped off that plane in December 2010, that varied background played into how I explained, to myself and to others, the different facets of the Egyptian revolutionary story. On a personal level, my being an Englishman in Egypt, an Egyptian in England, a European in the Arab world, an Arab in Europe... well, it would have been hard not to see things a little differently than most observers. It sometimes also caused me to rethink and challenge—perhaps too critically at times—what I found in the predominant narratives in both the Arab and Western media on events in Egypt. My own reading is undoubtedly flawed, but hopefully my recognition of those flaws influences how I try to peel away the different layers with a critical eye, rather than fall into the trap of hasty assumptions.

That revolutionary story of 2011–15 has, after all, been subjected to an inordinate amount of reductionism—whether in terms of narrative, or in terms of analysis. The results often appear unsatisfying: why would it make any sense to condense the events of those years into a battle between 'liberal' and 'Islamist', 'secular' and 'religious', or even 'Muslim Brotherhood (MB)' and 'army'? Over the course of this book, I hope to expose the oversimplification of those cognitive frames—cognisant that I have my own references.

It is not a simple story. The 25 January revolutionary uprising was the deathblow to Mubarak's presidency, and ended with his resignation eighteen days later. The 25 January awakening, on the other hand, is a quite different story—one that has taken many a turn since 11 February 2011, and which defies straightforwardness and demands delving deeper.

In order to take a comprehensive view of the Egyptian revolution, I have tried to avoid falling into a single ideological camp. There were times when I wrote things that were sympathetic to the MB, and there were times I considered them to have been opportunistic at best in terms of the revolutionary struggle. It's due to that kind of perspective that I have had the sordid pleasure (hopefully not too much of one) of being described as the 'Godfather of Zionist traitors to Egypt' in one breath, and as an 'Islamist bigot from Qatar' in the next. In the academic world, my homes in political theory are more often than not among liberal writers. But having critiqued their shortcomings in various ways in the Egyptian political context, I have also had harsh criticisms about many self-proclaimed 'liberals', who exhibited regrettable tendencies after the military takeover in 2013, while still resisting the simple portrayal of all Egyptian non-Islamists as simply unprincipled. Perhaps that set of contradictions is precisely the unexpected contrast it ought to be—in a fashion that might also be typical of the Egyptian revolution itself.

Confronting the binaries

I have always thought of the writer's occupation as one that deals with power—not simply the power of one's own words, but also the imperative of focusing one's own power of criticism on those in power, rather than on criticising the powerless. That is not to say that the powerless are always right, but that the function of the genuine writer is to call to account, and it is the powerful that deserve most to be called to account. That was true of the Supreme Council of the Armed Forces when it ruled Egypt from the front; it was true of Muhammad Mursi when he was a president for a time; and it will be true for all those in authority. Indeed, it sometimes applies to criticising those who have momentary physical power—or ideational power, as did the 'revolutionary trend' of 2011 and onwards—but those with material capacity and power must always take precedence in this regard.

But beyond this calling, and my role as an analyst in Western think tanks, the perspective that permeates the following pages is that of an entrenched witness, on whom the revolution had a profound effect. Besides being a Western, English commentator, I am also an Egyptian of the 'City Victorious', or al-Qahira, who grew to be deeply invested in the 25 January Revolution. I toyed for a time with writing a detached book that would ignore the deep connection I have built with the revolution—but I held back from it. This book therefore aspires to the genre of political writing typified by George Orwell's *Homage to Catalonia*, dealing with perhaps parallel issues and themes in the context of the Egyptian uprising and its aftermath.[1] Egypt in 2011–15 had a profound impact on my understanding of these themes and the political arena, that reminds me of Orwell's own experience during the Spanish Civil War, and his engagement with different political trends therein. I do not mean to imply that my writing holds a candle to Orwell's—he set a standard that is difficult to match—only that the impact of that short period in his life in Spain fundamentally affected him in multiple ways. When the Egyptian revolution disappointed me, it anguished me personally; when it showed resolve, it gave me inspiration and hope. My interaction with this story ranges from the depths of power in the nation's capital, to the streets where the revolution was at its most raw. I analysed from the sidelines—but I was also caught in the tear gas with protestors.

As I wrote this book, I felt obliged to confront the two predominant narratives at work in understanding the Egyptian revolution, critiquing them both, and to some degree rejecting them both. The binary equation that Egyptians and non-Egyptians alike are often falsely presented with is simply this: favour the military and the deep state over the fascist MB, or favour the MB over the fascist military and deep state. In the early years after the 25 January uprising, the choice between those two binary framings has taken geographic shape. To favour (even reluctantly) the pre-25-January–2011 status quo is the preference of much of the West, as well as certain Gulf states, as an expression of support for stability and continuity over chaos and uncertainty, as well as a distinct apathy (or even full blown opposition) towards any sort of reform. The MB found support generally within the Muslim world and a certain sub-section of Western intelligentsia, where it has been able to present itself as the upholder of Islam and Muslim autonomy—and its members as modern freedom fighters against the tyranny of the autocratic state.

These binaries have been at the forefront of many narratives—but they explain little about the country's traumatic, and yet often quite inspiring, transition after those eighteen days in early 2011. Over the past three years, a number of narratives have been written looking at the revolution of 25 January, but invariably they have focused on the revolution as either a chance for a particular political group (such as the MB) to take its rightful place as the representatives of the Egyptian state, or as a failure. Neither perspective is useful, and I do not intend to simply add a third, turning the binary into a trinity.

One of the lessons I have seen illuminated time and time again during Egypt's post-Mubarak transition is that there are always alternatives to the most obvious paths of action that are in front of us. Egypt showed it was not ready for those alternatives—but that does not mean that Egyptians are forever doomed to be stuck with the choices they made. Because the on-going pace of change in Egypt makes it clear there are always other options. They are not always easy ones, to be sure, but they exist, and understanding what the different alternatives are provides the observer with a far clearer picture of what is actually happening in the country. Egypt is Egypt: while it is inevitable that there will be forces in different countries that will view it only through the prism of their own national interests, I do not take that stance in this book. The world remains interconnected and interdependent no doubt; but precisely because of that reality, each country ought to be evaluated on the basis of the independence and autonomy of its own people, which was my only concern in dealing with Egypt in this book.

The years after the beginning of the Egyptian awakening—and, indeed, that of many in the Arab world—were traumatic ones. Many masks were dropped, and yet there were still those who continued to believe in the ideals of the 2011 'dignity revolutions'. Those 'marginal mavericks' of the *midan* (square) stood on principle—particularly those principles based on '*bread, freedom, social justice, human dignity*' (the slogan of the revolution)—and they can be criticised for being ineffectual. But, ultimately, when it comes to loyalty to the original values of the Square of Liberation (*Midan al-Tahrir*) in 2011, one would be hard pressed to describe any other group at present as being a worthier candidate for fealty.

Yet, when the world looks at factions in Egypt, they needn't look at the marginal, maverick middle to support instead of the MB or the army. Rather, they ought to consider the principles that these revolutionaries uphold—and ask themselves whether, indeed, the binary choice between one camp or another is not best put to one side, and a choice between principles entertained instead.

PROLOGUE

In the world of academia, there were two main proponents of approaches to the Arab world in the 1980s and 90s. The first was the neo-conservative-friendly Bernard Lewis, the British-American historian who promoted the 'clash of civilisations' thesis that was later popularised by Samuel Huntington, and who was deeply supportive of Israel in the Arab-Israeli conflict.[2] The second was the progressive Edward Said, who was a key intellectual contributor to post-colonial studies, and a towering scholarly figure of the Palestinian resistance. Said criticised both the corrupt, ineffectual Fatah of the Palestinian Authority, and the religious right wing of Hamas—two elements that arguably correspond to the Egyptian deep state and the MB. He never failed to argue intellectually and peacefully in support of the Palestinian cause and against the Israeli occupation, and in so doing he eventually formed a 'democratic third force' in the form of the Palestinian National Initiative that included the likes of Mustafa Barghouti and others. That is a model of some worth to consider—keeping in mind that it has, thus far, failed to be capitalised upon. But good ideas do not necessarily become successful in and of themselves: they need to be properly deployed, with strategies and tactics that match the challenges of the day.

Living through a perspective

In the following pages I draw on the research I've developed in my academic career in the UK and Egypt, but also on the public opinion work that I did as a senior practice consultant at the Gallup Organisation, writing mostly on Egyptian affairs after the revolutionary uprising. My academic perspective is informed by the work I did at the University of Warwick prior to the revolution, and the work I did with colleagues at Harvard University after the military removed Muhammad Mursi in 2013. It is a perspective born out of intense engagement with government as a think-tank specialist at the Brookings Institution in Washington, D.C., and later the Atlantic Council, and the Royal United Services Institute in London. My engagement with government preceded the Egyptian uprising, but intensified after it, in the Arab world, Europe and North America. Again, mine is not *the* perspective—it is *a* perspective, one that I lived through and experienced.

PROLOGUE

During these past years, I've written several hundred pieces of commentary in media including *Foreign Policy*, the *Washington Post*, the *Guardian, Mada Masr, Daily News Egypt*, and others, examining and looking at the revolution through what I understood to be its own eyes—eyes that believed in its promise. Those were eyes that filled with tears; eyes that felt pain when that revolution was betrayed; eyes that could not help but glisten with anger, because of the outrage when people were killed with impunity.

I am thus in the position of being able to rely on an established set of writings in the public domain, which serve as good reminders to me as I try to recall how I thought about the events at the time. But they're also useful in terms of allowing me to reconsider those views now, as I periodically bring in details that I never felt were quite appropriate to put into those sorts of media, personal and private as they were. My intention is to make this work primarily a chronological narrative of analysis. The information provided will be based on first-hand experience as well as the testimonies of my contacts in the political forces in Egypt from the pro-MB camp, the revolutionary sector, international diplomatic actors, and the international analyst community.

Telling this story and offering these reflections are as important to me as writing the analysis embedded within it. As I lived through these events, I often thought that we are used to being presented with the 'good' and the 'bad', with as little time as possible being dedicated to identifying the grey areas between. But this entire epoch in Egyptian history is as much about the grey as it is about the 'good' and the 'bad'—the Egyptian revolutionary uprising might have been all about the good, but it was soaked with grey.

Chapter 1 delves into the eighteen days of the 2011 revolution, the period's major actors, and their connections and divides. Chapter 2 parses the politics of the revolutionary groupings and the MB, providing an initial overview of their opportunities and constraints. Chapter 3 dissects Egypt's hesitant transition from revolutionary uprising to some trying to rebuild and democratise, focusing on major events and pitfalls in the first two post-revolutionary years. Chapter 4 provides an overview of the MB and Islamism in Egypt and specifically analyses the role of religion in Egyptian politics post-2011. Chapter 5 takes on the election of Muhammad Mursi and the tumultuous year of the Brotherhood's rule.

PROLOGUE

Chapter 6 analyses the demise of Mursi's presidency and the forces that contributed to the country's polarisation and ensuing counter-revolution. Chapter 7 deals directly with the Rab'a al-Adawiyya massacre and violence and unrest following Mursi's ousting. Chapter 8 analyses politics in the Sisi-era, the establishment of a type of security-apparatus regimen, and the consequences for Egypt's revolution deferred. Chapter 9 provides concluding lessons for Egypt going forward.

Many voices as one

A few weeks after I stepped off that plane in December 2010, I suggested in an Arab newspaper, *The National*, that revolution was precisely what the Egyptian nation did not need.[3] Yes, I wrote that the Egyptian nation did not need a revolution. I published that piece on 24 January 2011, and I discuss it later on in this book. A few days later, I was in Tahrir Square—and those eighteen days of uprising that began on the 25th were the promise of a revolution. My intellectual and rational edifice of reluctance to endorse a revolutionary idea, especially against the backdrop of a state that I believed had obliterated civil society, came crashing down. To put it another way—I didn't think a revolutionary uprising could take place in Egypt without immediate huge costs, and very little benefit. I was wrong. I've never been happier to be wrong.

The title of this book, *A Revolution Undone: Egypt's Road beyond Revolt*, was discussed carefully and at length with my publishers. A revolution 'undone' is one that began, but which was never completed—and that is true of Egypt's. The Egyptian revolution wasn't demolished and destroyed—that's a finality that can't be diagnosed yet, just as the effects of revolutionary events cannot be adequately ascertained until years later. But, certainly, the Egyptian revolutionary uprising hasn't yet led to a revolution being accomplished—and counter-revolutionary events also took place, fighting hard against changes that had been begun. Nevertheless, the road of Egypt beyond the revolt, despite the winding and curving of it, remains one informed by that revolutionary uprising of 2011. Where it will lead remains unknown, as are the eventual impacts of the uprising itself. There is no finality or conclusion—there remains continuation and development.

PROLOGUE

Will history record in twenty years from now that the revolutionary uprising was but a blip on Egypt's historical record, and that the counter-revolution successfully erased its consequences? Or will history note a sequence of events that began with the uprising, and led to Egypt's path being irrevocably altered, for the better, in the long term? That is a choice for Egyptians—and that choice is a continual one. In 2016, it seems pertinent, indeed, to look back, and see how those choices have worked themselves out thus far—especially at a time when the history of those choices is being rewritten for a variety of political purposes. For me, this offering is also a way to step back, after having been so continuously consumed with Egypt. After all, as the French say: *il faut reculer pour mieux sauter*. You have to step back, in order to jump further.

PART 1

THE REVOLUTIONARY UPRISING

1

THE EIGHTEEN DAYS OF TAHRIR

My father-in-law, with whom I was travelling past Tahrir Square in a taxi, carried on home. He was not opposed to the protesters in the square but he was able to resist the urge to tell the taxi driver to stop, in a way that I was not. I asked him if he would go back on his own, and I would make my own way back. He said, 'it's your choice'. I left the taxi, started walking from Qasr al-Nil bridge, and headed into the square. That was 2 February 2011.

I remember that when Shaykh Emad Effat, the Azhari scholar, was killed after the uprising, a number of his more famous statements were collected. One of them was: 'The first time I entered Tahrir Square (during the revolutionary protests) was the first time I saw Egypt.'

I know exactly what he meant.

I

On 24 January 2011, many Egyptians I knew were already dismissing what had recently happened in Tunisia as unlikely to reoccur in Egypt. Indeed, many of them considered such a repeat as impossible. I agreed: I thought that the Tunisian uprising had been a fluke, and I did not think it was possible that it could take place anywhere else in the Arab world. Frankly, I thought it would be an awful idea if it did.

I penned my thoughts in this regard for a popular English-language newspaper in Abu Dhabi, *The National*.[1] The gist of my argument was fairly straightforward and, I'd like to think, thorough. It was also broadly wrong—although perhaps right in certain particular ways. My views on revolutionary activity in the Arab world—particularly Egypt, which I knew the best—could have been summed up in two points. The first was that I was concerned that the breakdown of any authority establishment, whether in the Arab world or elsewhere, regardless of the oppressive or repressive nature of that establishment, could lead to more chaos and tension than it might resolve.

Revolutionary activity, as I conceived of it at the time, had to lead to some sort of bedlam if it was to be successful in producing any real change. That kind of turmoil was unpredictable—and I feared it would lead to a worse situation, particularly if it involved an armed insurgency, as I suspected it would.

Secondly, any revolutionary movement would have to rely on civil society essentially picking up the slack in the aftermath of any overthrow of the state. My fear with regards to Egypt in particular, but also elsewhere, was that the decades of autocratic rule and repressive governmental practices meant that it was impossible to consider that there would be any civil society to depend on. The Mubarakian state had systematically and completely, in my estimation, ensured that civil society was not only dead but had been stamped out of existence.

If the state were to collapse—which is what I presumed any revolution in Egypt would lead to—then society at large would collapse. In Tunisia a strong civil society element reasserted itself during and after the uprising, but I could not imagine this would be possible in Egypt. I remember that the day after Mubarak was pushed from power, a friend I had made in Tahrir Square told me of how he'd tried to organise residents in his neighbourhood to collect garbage—an endeavour that had been circumscribed by the authorities. The logic, he told me, was that if he could organise for that, there was no telling what else he could organise for. Even picking up trash was a threat to this kind of repressive state.

As I said, I was both wrong and right.

II

When the protests began, I was certainly not much of a believer. As I mention above, I, like most inside and outside of Egypt, did not think too much of their potential. In retrospect, that was a great advantage of the original protest movement because it meant they took the authorities wholly by surprise. For many years, a variety of small, disparate human rights groups and movements had been agitating against the government. The April 6 Youth Movement, which was born out of labour movement protests in Mahalla on 6 April 2008, had capitalised on a number of different activists who were pushing for change—but none of them could have predicted the swell of activity during January and February 2011. The National Association for Change, directed by the former head of the International Energy Agency, Muhammad al-Baradei, and the *Kifaya*[2] movement (officially called the Egyptian Movement for Change), which was a non-ideological banding of critics of the regime, were other groups who also did not expect much to come out of the 25 January protests.[3]

The irony was that neither did those who went to the streets on 25 January themselves. They picked that day because it was Eid al-Shurta (the Festival of the Police or 'Police Day'). The event marks 25 January 1952, when Egyptian police refused to hand over their weapons to the British in Isma'iliyya. In response, the British Army stormed the police station, resulting in some fifty dead police officers and many more injured. But while the day evokes feelings of patriotic pride for some, that wasn't why protesters chose the 25 January as their day of action in 2011, fifty-nine years later.

If there was one institution in Egypt on 25 January 2011 that did not command the support of more than a sub-fraction of the population, the police force was it. It was the police that represented the direct, ever present, hand of the repressive state against its citizens—because it was usually the police that was the first example of it in any citizen's life. 'Citizen' is probably an unduly strong word since most Egyptians did not really feel much in the way of 'citizenship'. They were subjects, but not subjects of a monarch they loved and respected. They were more like conquered inhabitants, and their conqueror was the repressive police state that existed prior to the 25 January 2011. That police state was responsible for a great deal of the torment of many Egyptians—and one of them was a young man called Khalid Sa'id, who was beaten to death by police officers in Alexandria.[4] I never knew Khalid Sa'id. But one thing was clear: his death, and the treatment he received at the hands of Egyptian police, touched young Egyptians in a way that was very particular. His death symbolised something for them in that it could have happened to any one of them.

When a small group of activists decided to go to the streets on that day, most of them did not have the audacity to think they would get as far as they did. They did not expect Mubarak's departure or millions in the streets. But after Tunisia they dared to think it might be possible for there to be some sort of shift—and they were willing to try.

There had been protests before. Small ones, isolated and disparate. Few people expected the 25 January protests to be much different, except in one respect: the regime would take few chances. The police, it was assumed, would clamp down immediately, the protests would disperse, and that would be that.

Except, of course, that was not that at all.

III

Protests have a long history in Tahrir Square. An academic colleague, as I wrote this book, reminded me of this—that even as far back as 1960 he attended rallies in Tahrir that were meant to express support for then-Egyptian leader, Gamal Abdel Nasser. The occasion was Nasser's return from the United Nations, and even those of the *fellahin* (country provincials) seemed to have a sense of Nasser's achievements on the world stage.

Nevertheless, the protests did not begin at Tahrir Square. Their first focal point was in front of the most hated building in Egypt, the Ministry of Interior, which oversaw, and continues to oversee, the police force. The demands were modest by most standards, but radical in the Egyptian context given the prevailing political climate. The protesters aimed to decry police brutality; they insisted on the resignation of the interior minister, the repealing of the emergency law and the institution of term limits for the president. In retrospect, the demands were hardly revolutionary—but in the Egypt that existed on 24 January they were certainly radical. The fulfilment of just one of those demands would have been hugely significant. Indeed, Mubarak might have saved his presidency very easily and quickly. Instead, he resisted—and an earthquake took place.

The protesters were, predictably, set upon by the security services. But they did not disperse. They played a game of cat and mouse and, to everyone's surprise, managed to regroup and set up camp in Tahrir Square. That square, one has to remember, was hardly a positive place for anyone in Egypt—it stood on the edge of the infamous *Mugamma*, the main administrative building for the Egyptian bureaucratic machine. But in the space of a very short time, the square became the symbol of a movement that would make history.

The protesters managed to get into Tahrir Square. They held it for a short time before the police cut communications and invaded the square with force of arms. But the security forces did not manage to keep Tahrir empty for long. The protesters kept agitating to take back the now recognised symbol of the uprising—it had not yet turned into a revolutionary uprising—and on the 'Friday of Anger', 28 January, Egyptian protesters re-took Tahrir Square. And they never lost it, until the fateful day that they left it voluntarily.

Those first few days were, arguably, the most pivotal in the conversion of the 25 January protest into the 25 January revolutionary uprising. Yes, there were other days in the eighteen days of uprising that were deeply significant—the day of the Battle of the Camels for one, or the day Wael Ghonim, one of the administrators of the 'We are all Khalid Sa'id' page, was released after being detained by the state, and spoke on television.[5] But the days of 25–28 January made the uprising a reality. The charge into Tahrir Square from Qasr al-Nil bridge, with the iconic images of protesters praying on the bridge and being pummelled with water cannons; the state's cutting of communications; the international attention; all of this happened in the first few days. And it made all the difference.

I was not in the square in those early days. I had not yet become a believer in the idea that change could actually happen—or that if it could happen, it could be for the better. That came a couple of days later. By that time, however, I was personally invested in the security of my own neighbourhood. A few days into the uprising, the regime, in preparation for the 'Day of Anger' called for by the protesters, cut the Internet. It obviously had other plans for its subjects. First, it withdrew the police from the streets, as in the first few days of the protest: their spirit had been utterly broken. They retreated on 28 January after protesters had charged them near Tahrir Square, and then fully occupied the square. A presidential order—importantly, not an order from the interior minister—then led to the army being deployed in metropolitan areas, but not before a completely disgraceful act took place. A number of prisons were opened and prisoners released.[6] The shock and horror this caused when the citizenry found out was immeasurable: would Mubarak's regime really unleash common criminals on us, I wondered?

In light of those types of threats, a truly astounding thing took place.

IV

Beyond Tahrir Square and the other *mayadin* (squares), there were other autonomous zones in Egypt during the uprising. As noted, the government had called for the police to go home and instituted martial law. At the same time, thugs aligned with pro-government forces were loose on the streets, terrorising people—and prisoners had been let out of jail. I remember that first night on the 28th clearly, and how surprised I was when I went out onto the street to stand guard in the southern Cairene suburb of Ma'adi—instinctively to protect my family from escaped prisoners and delinquents who roamed free amid the police vacuum—and found that I was not alone. There were many of us. Most able-bodied men descended onto the streets around their homes and within their neighbourhoods and began to institute new codes—indeed, new laws—to protect themselves and their communities. Around Cairo, temporary *ligan al-sha'biya* (popular committees) sprang up. We were bound by similar fates and fears.

That was Egypt in the first eighteen days. Many Egyptians felt a renewed sense of purpose and engagement that went far beyond the squares that were shown on international television and that so inspired the world. I cannot emphasise enough the shock that Egyptians were going through, and the incredible resilience they showed. The people that Egyptians normally turned to for protection were the ones they blamed for this insecurity, and many feared the whole of Cairo would erupt into anarchy and turmoil, with the entire city looking more like Mogadishu in Somalia. And there were instances of a breakdown of order: police stations were attacked and ransacked; in some isolated areas shops were broken into, particularly during the first twenty-four hours after the police withdrew from the streets. But Cairo didn't suddenly become bedlam.

We formed checkpoints, and established teams to check cars coming into our neighbourhoods. Some would scrutinise the drivers' licences and others would search the cars. We had no legal authority to do this, but we deemed ourselves to be acting in accordance with natural law, and no one that we stopped objected. No one was threatened in any way—on the contrary, everyone acted with good manners—and everyone, including those in the cars, knew that it was in the interest of us all that we assumed those positions of authority. We were not chastised for these extra-legal actions; rather, we were applauded by all who came onto our streets and into our districts. That in itself was something: we truly recognised that these were *our* streets and *our* districts. I'm not sure if that was really the case prior to the uprising, given the all-encompassing nature of the Egyptian state.

Certainly, we were carrying clubs and homemade weapons. On the other hand, the police force had been carrying guns and worse. They had been feared, yes, but they hadn't been applauded.

Our cooperation was immediate. We established roadblocks in the street, and searched vehicles coming into the neighbourhood. We fashioned weapons out of clubs, blocks of wood and pipes. We even delivered escaped convicts, whom we had caught, back to the army. It was almost comical how brave people had become, from the old man who scared everyone with his bellowing voice to the party animal from a nearby street who turned into what I can only call an Egyptian Rambo (with far more decorum, I must say), complete with a buck knife and tattoos.

Most notable, though, was the civility with which we treated each other, both those on patrol and those we stopped. There was no abuse, rudeness or ill will. When cars were stopped and searched, everyone behaved with the utmost politeness and respect. People brought out tea and coffee, sweets and biscuits, sandwiches and crisps to keep the neighbourhood patrol fuelled. Old squabbles were absent. In their place was camaraderie and good nature. We were truly a multinational, non-sectarian force. In Tahrir, Christians stood guard while Muslims performed their prayers. Non-Egyptians joined Egyptians to defend their collective streets. As the nights went on, more piled into the streets, bringing their children to show how people protected their neighbourhoods together.

As we stood guard, something else emerged: a collective sense of mission. We were all in this together, regardless of class or background. This was something unusual in the area I helped defend, where the gap between rich and poor is wide. But on these nights, class standing disappeared—if only temporarily. It just wasn't relevant anymore. This was one of the key reasons why I embraced the uprising.

There were those who worried about stability and the safety of their families, and who would never have supported an uprising for those same reasons. But when reports arrived of how the government was responding, the unifying feeling was one of revulsion. Everyone I spoke to held the government directly culpable for the unrest we defended against, and for the years of repression that had preceded it.

People around me wanted two things: security on their street, and the whole of Egypt's government to change. For a long time Egyptians had been told these two demands were mutually exclusive. But the people of Egypt didn't seem to be convinced of that anymore—not back in those heady days of 2011.

But sometimes, there were those who did not applaud—and in the absence of their applause, we also found strength.

V

He was the driver of one of many cars we stopped that first night of the 'popular committee' in our neighbourhood. Foolishly, I did not take his national identification card and his car registration, which would have identified him and his occupation—I just asked him to open the trunk of his car. He opened it with pleasure, and was about to drive off, when Muhammad, one of my neighbours, recognised him.

'Oh, hello. Wait a minute, aren't you the police officer we saw here yesterday?'

Bashfully, he replied, 'Um, yes.'

Muhammad responded, in a tone of righteousness, 'So, no work for you today?'

None of us wanted to see a cop. None of us wanted to see one ever again. A few days ago, the police were both the mainstay of our security and the annoying bane of our lives. Far too many of them perpetrated abuse. But tonight, the police were not a mix of good and bad. Tonight, the police were the ones who had obeyed an order to come off the streets, and deserted their posts. It was the police who had left us to the mercy of the escaped convicts and looters, who were out in their thousands across Egypt. It was the police that we suspected of being part of the same larger establishment that opened the jails in order to terrorise the wider population into submission.

One has to remember that the foundation of the social contract in the Arab world was that the state provides security from internal and external aggressors. This formed the basis of Islamic governance for centuries, from the very first Muslim community in Medina in the seventh century, up until now. Beyond that, in fact, the state was not meant to do very much. Historically, and through to the past hundred years or so, the state had been a very minimal presence in Muslim societies. What was far more powerful was civil society. It was civil society, through foundations and trusts, that lit the streets of Al-Andalus (Muslim-ruled Spain and Portugal); it was civil society that provided the schools and the mosques; it was civil society that provided free, clean water. Then came colonisation, which dealt a crippling blow to the traditional basis of society in the region. And then after the ravages of colonisation came the independence movements, which had learnt well, or rather badly, the awful lessons of statecraft from the colonial regimes, and which we will come back to later.

This has all led to the point where in the twenty-first-century Arab world, if you have any civic problem then you expect the state—and not civil society—to sort it out for you. And in exchange for the deal, you tolerate pretty much anything and everything from the state—just so long as you have security and peace of mind.

No more, it seemed. That's why Muhammad spoke to the police officer like that. The fear had gone. As the world was reporting: Egyptians had tasted freedom and they weren't about to lose its taste easily.

'Umm... well, I was working a bit yesterday', replied the cop nervously.

Muhammad decided to let him off. 'OK. You can go.'

As we stood at the roadblock, someone took a picture of the officer. He immediately reacted, forgetting which time he was now living in: 'Why is he taking pictures of me?'

Muhammad shrugged and said, 'Ask him.'

And then, I think, the man remembered. This was January 2011. The people were no longer afraid of him. Maybe for the first time, he felt the same fear that he had tried to instil in so many. He drove off, like a bat out of hell.

VI

As I alluded to earlier, my mother is from Cairo. Fortunately for me, she was not in Cairo during the eighteen days. 'Fortunately', because many who went to Tahrir Square had to hide that fact from their parents. One of the many jokes in the square was that Mubarak had better stand down quickly, because the parents of the protesters would soon find out where they were. Mine were not in Egypt at the time, so I had far more liberty than most to move about without having to have much of a cover story. Yes, even those of us in our thirties and forties were concerned about such things. Egyptian mothers can be pretty fierce.

The first time I went into the square, it was a few days into the uprising. That day was interesting. My father-in-law had wanted to go to Mohandaseen on an important errand, so I went with him. I can't remember if I went with him just to ensure he was safe, or to see for myself how the city was. I'd like to think it was both. Either way, it was pretty safe out there. It was daytime—around midday—and thus there were no checkpoints, army or otherwise. On the way back, we drove from Mohandaseen through Zamalek, and then crossed the Qasr al-Nil bridge.

As we drew closer and closer to the Tahrir Square side of the bridge, my heart started beating harder and harder. In an eerie sense—and though it sounds utterly naïve to say it—it called to me. I know that sounds peculiar, but surely anyone reading this will understand. Tahrir was better known to the world than to many of us in Egypt, because all we had was access to incredibly skewed sources of information. I knew, nonetheless, there was something very special about that square—and as I saw us drawing closer and closer, I turned to my father in law and said, 'I can't. I have to go.' He didn't approve—entirely out of concerns for my safety, I am sure. But he didn't try to stop me. I asked the cab to pull over. I jumped out, and walked towards Tahrir Square, for the first time since the revolution had begun. It was 2 February.

Some indescribable force had grabbed me from the car, and I decided to venture in. I say 'venture' because, until this point, I had not been given much of an opportunity to actually see very much of the square. My family did not have a satellite dish—we purposely tried not to have any television in the house—and as such we were at first confined to radio (which was invariably state radio). We then dug out an old mini television set from my university days, and hooked it up, which gave us state television. As we quickly understood that we were watching pure propaganda, we ceased to rely on the television as a source of news[7] and came to see it as more of a barometer of how concerned the regime was about the protests, which we could judge by the preposterous material it fed us.

That day, however, I walked into the square myself. I waited in line with scores of other people, not all of whom were in favour of the protests. Nevertheless, even those who seemed to support Mubarak wanted to see this strange exhibition of 'people power' in the centre of Cairo. For a generation of Egyptians, the very notion of gathering in such large numbers for any sort of cause was anathema; such was the Mubarakite state. The 'curtain of fear' had been that strong—but now it had been ripped to shreds. Even those who had been opposed to that curtain coming down were curious as to what its destruction might lead to.

That was more than a week after the revolution began. I think I will forever be saddened that I did not spend more time in that square from the first day—and forever grateful that I was granted the opportunity to be there at all. As I got into line, just across the street from the Arab League—a building which represented so much of the bankrupt politics that the square was revolting against—I could little but wonder what lay ahead of me.

I would say most people who went to Tahrir went in solidarity. But there were many who went out of curiosity, and there were many who went even though they opposed what the square actually stood for. I remember so clearly being in line that day, and two people in the crowd who were arguing about whether or not it was the correct cause. A middle-aged man, who had brought his child, and had him hoisted onto his shoulders, argued with another, rather jovially, about the legitimacy and integrity of Tahrir. But they were all there. They all wanted to wait in line and to see what Tahrir was about. I remember thinking then, as I do now, how wonderful it was that two people could actually argue about politics in the open in Cairo, without fear of reprisal or retribution. We might take such things for granted in many other countries, but in Cairo that wasn't a given at all.

As I think back now, I wonder if that child was the child who was killed later that day when pro-Mubarak thugs stormed the square, and killed so many people in the infamous Battle of the Camels.[8]

As I drew closer to the checkpoints—there were several of them on the edge of Tahrir, near the entrance to the Arab League, but on the Mugamma side—I was stopped, and asked for identification. I had my British passport—the only passport I ever had—and showed it to the gentleman. And yes, I thought of him as an incredibly dignified gentleman because he behaved with such cordiality and generosity of spirit. He searched me and patted me down but he was just so utterly apologetic as he did it.

I was amazed. I've been through Cairo's airport many times, and while I have never been searched in such an invasive fashion before, I'd never thought that being stopped and searched could be such an unobtrusive experience. I find most airports to be rather intrusive in the way they stop and search—but in Tahrir I didn't feel any of that. After another person searched me, again apologising for having put me through the bother of being searched, but insisting it was for their sakes as well as my own, I couldn't help but stop and kiss him on the forehead. God bless you, I thought.

One of them said, 'Welcome to Egypt'. It was as though God had placed words of profound truth upon his lips without him knowing it—for, indeed, that moment I felt as though I had finally arrived in Egypt for the very first time.

I have a very subjective viewpoint of that first visit to Tahrir, of course. But it's a subjectivity that is born out of having been in Tahrir during the eighteen days of 2011, and seeing what was there. It was not, as some now try to retroactively say, an imaginary utopia—it was real. At its core, in my opinion, was the ability of people to engage with their differences, with respect and dignity, without needing the heavy-handed authority of the state machinery to ensure civility.

As I passed through 'security', I saw posters on my right that said 'Cleanliness is half of faith'. It's an old saying, narrated by a companion of the last Prophet, relaying his exact words. The message was clear: for us all to remain cognisant that this was our land, our home, our territory, and because we had a sense of ownership over it, we ought to respect it and keep it clean. I was deeply impressed as I saw people walking around, picking up rubbish, and hoping to keep Tahrir clean. And indeed, it was one of the cleanest places I'd been to in Cairo. Later protests in Tahrir have been different: the concept of its cleanliness was unique during this occupation.

Tahrir was a fascinating, if unintended, sociological experiment. I remember many arguing after the eighteen days of occupation that sociological studies would have to be made of how the square had functioned because it had defied so many expectations. Order was kept in a way that was truly organic, and even beautiful, though unsustainable on a long-term basis. But it was sufficiently rigorous enough for me to consider Tahrir a precinct of law, rather than the unruly turf the Egyptian media claimed it was. There were zones. As I entered, the Nasserites (socialist Arab nationalists), I think, were up there on the right, kind of centre-ground in front of the Mugamma. The centre of the square, of course, was totally covered in tents and signs, where different political forces and trends slept and rested, and talked and discussed. But no one was there as a political force *per se*, trying to dominate the narrative of what was happening. Yet they were there and they were identifiable.

I could see, for example, that on the western side of the area in front of the Mugamma there was a group of Azhari preachers, decked out in their quintessential style, with the *imama* (turban) and the *jubba* (cloak). They were making *du'a*—supplicating for the victory of the cause. Religion was never absent in the square, despite the notion that some out of the country held that the protestors were a bunch of ultra-Westernised secularists. Religion was as much a part of Tahrir as the pluralism which defined people's relation to religion. Those stories of Copts protecting Muslims as they prayed weren't false or exaggerated. When Copts carried out their own services, Muslims also stood watch over them. Pluralism was in that square. There is much to say about religion in the square, and how religion was instrumentalised in it and through it. But that is for later in this book (see Chapter 4).

Across the street from the Azhari preachers there was another crowd. I saw Nawal al-Sa'adawi, the age-old Arab feminist, arguing and discussing with a bunch of young men and women. The discussions weren't acrimonious, even while they might have been infested with disagreements—but they were discussions I could never dream of having in public before the revolution. Not like that. We would have been too afraid. But not in Tahrir.

I walked around and I thought to myself: this is the Egypt that I always thought existed, but had until now never quite seen. It was an Egypt of many different things: of different trends, world views, genders; of religious people and non-religious people; of those veiled in the *niqab* (the face-veil that some observant Muslim women wear) and of those not veiled at all; of Muslims, of Christians, and so on.

Thus, the words of Shaykh Emad Effat (the Azhari scholar who was killed—or martyred, as his supporters would say—in the midst of a clash with the security forces),[9] quoted at the start of this chapter, so described exactly how I felt. In a very real way, this was the first time I had seen Egypt. And it had come naturally—organically—not because of academic workshops or social awareness programmes. It had come because a group of people had wanted freedom, had fought for it, and had established something unique that was their own.

It was such an opportunity. When, five years later, I look back on that day and others like it I realise how much Egypt, the region and even the world has lost. In 2016, it is easy to forget that in those days of 2011 the Egyptian uprising was affecting the social consciousness of people in southeast Asia, people in North America, people in Australia—movements and mobilisations for all kinds of things, inspired by Tahrir Square. Now, the memories of those days are fading.

But it was real. It was not a mirage, despite how some now like to make themselves comfortable in feeling (because they don't need to search for anything different to the squalor and Faustian pact they've embraced).

Those days were special. I've never really been able to put it all into words—or really explain it sufficiently well to do it justice, and show how it affected my own life. But it did.

'This is the Egypt that young Egyptians are taught actually exists, even though they've never actually seen it.' Those were the words that kept buzzing in my head as I walked around Tahrir Square. It showed the best of what Egyptians could be.

Later that night of 2 February, I saw the uglier side of Egypt. Because, you know, Egyptians can be rather disappointing, too. About thirty minutes after I'd left Tahrir, pro-Mubarak thugs stormed the square on camels and horses. Raging street battles then ensued long into the night as protesters confronted these regime-aligned thugs. It was like a cheap scene from an old 1940s blockbuster movie, but it was deadly. It also could not have been won without the contribution of Muslim Brotherhood (MB) members who came out (unofficially) to support the uprising that day, as well as the rag-tag warriors of the Ultras, largely young football fans with a storied history of clashing with police. Both these groups would later, to varying degrees of success, call upon their contributions that day to argue for their post-uprising legitimacy.

In the end, that day eleven people were killed and 600 injured, and I think the first one to be reported dead was a young boy, maybe ten years of age, who had been struck on the head by a stone. I was on patrol that evening on the neighbourhood watch. When I heard the news, I relayed the sadness of it to those on patrol with me. The response was deeply depressing, but utterly enlightening.

'What was he doing there? His father should bear the blame,' was the refrain.

I was stunned. Shocked that anyone could be quite so callous as to blame a man whose son had just been killed by renegades, in all likelihood supported by the state, for the crime of… what, precisely? Visiting a public square, entering an unarmed protest in the centre of Egypt's capital city, for the simple purpose of showing his son that, yes, Egyptians could be free in their own country, and unafraid of the powers that be?

It seemed that for some Egyptians, some people's absence of fear of the authoritarian order was a reason to be fearful. The notion that Egyptians deserved better than that Orwellian 'Big Brother' reality was beyond them. That, in itself, was a tragedy—unhappily, a tragedy I would witness many times over.

I had not expected the protests would effect real change—not till quite late in the day. But they did. The protests were not particularly popular to begin with—but as the days went on, more and more Egyptians began to steer towards them. Indeed, in the weeks after they had ended, some eight out of ten Egyptians claimed they'd supported the protests according to Gallup polls.[10] Of course, it didn't have to be that way. The regime could have played its cards far more deftly, which might have resulted in the protests becoming quite unpopular. It certainly appeared that it could go that way early on, but the belligerency of the regime towards what Egyptians gradually came to see was just a cross-representation of Egyptians at large, was extraordinarily counterproductive. The protesters were tenacious, to be sure, but they were also joined by large sections of society, more so than in any previous protest. They had the regime to thank for that. Mubarak's speeches were too little, too late, and the actions of thugs backed by his supporters, including at the infamous 'Battle of the Camels', instigated a great deal of sympathy for the protesters among Egyptians who initially had little interest in revolution.

That mass of public support was important for two reasons. Firstly, it established a sense of massive popular legitimacy for the ending of Mubarak's presidency. That was important, because to end Mubarak's presidency in this fashion lacked a legal basis. This needn't have been the case: Mubarak could have signed executive orders to ensure a legal grounding for his departure, but he didn't. Indeed, his resignation was the subject of a (failed) court case by one of his acolytes later on.

Secondly, the popular backing caused Egypt to come to something of a standstill. Businesses were closed; thugs were looting in certain areas; a nation-wide curfew was imposed; workers' strikes were happening all over the country; urban areas saw massive protests and there were solidarity marches in major squares all around Egypt. That temporary cessation of normal life cost the country millions of pounds, and was unsustainable. The country's institutions knew it: critically, the Egyptian military knew that if the protests continued for much longer, the ramifications for Egypt's economy would be tremendous, and they'd have to pick up the pieces. Beyond economic damage, there could also be substantial civil unrest—and while one can claim that Egypt's uprising already constituted civil unrest, it was far more restful than what might have come to pass.

There was another factor that few took into account. The Egyptian military was hardly a revolutionary force. Regardless of how it played the scene in 2011, it likely had two main concerns, neither of which was about the deficiencies of Mubarak's presidency or the need for radical reform of Egypt's institutions. The first was, as mentioned, that the protests were beginning to destabilise Egypt. The second related to internal unrest already prevalent within the army about the prospect that Egypt's next president would be Mubarak's son, Gamal Mubarak, whom the military top brass had little respect for. No one would ever publicly go on record to admit this was a factor, but it is difficult to believe that the army did not see the protests as an opportunity to ensure that the project of Egypt becoming an inheritance of the Mubarak family would be forever set aside.

Finally, a basic public relations coup took place. The protest movement managed to hold on for a significant amount of time in the square, and while it was incredibly important that the protests were successful all around the country, the focus on Tahrir was tremendous for a single reason: the media. The world was focused, via the media, on the protests in Tahrir Square. The world watched it—day in, day out—and that placed enormous pressure on political leaders, which in turn placed pressure on Egypt's own leadership. With all these factors coming into play at the same time, Tahrir managed to achieve something that, truly, few thought was possible or had planned for.

VII

Within Egypt and beyond, it was declared that Tahrir Square and the protesters were signs of a 'Facebook revolution'—that a 'social media revolution' was upon the masses. The narrative went something like this: young Twitterati from the upper-middle class organised Egyptians to go around the country and protest. They had the tools of the twenty-first century, and were able to connect to each other as they went from place to place.

It is a nice, simple equation. But it is not entirely accurate. The social media arena in Egypt certainly played a role[11]—perhaps even a critical role—but Egypt's uprising, for much of which the Internet was cut, was not a 'Facebook revolution'. At least, not according to all the data that actually exists on the protests.

The data makes for interesting reading. In 2011, the Gallup Organisation (now simply 'Gallup') carried out several nationally representative opinion surveys in Egypt. Unlike most polls that relied on either only urban areas, or the use of interviews by telephone, Gallup's surveys were carried out nationwide, and always through face-to-face dialogues. Throughout 2011, the answer to the question 'Did you support the protests that led to the removal of then-president Husni Mubarak?' was resoundingly 'yes'. It varied somewhat through the year, but as I mentioned before, about eight out of ten Egyptians claimed to have supported the protests when asked, through repeated surveys, in 2011.[12]

Clearly, however, not all of those who supported the protesters actually participated in the protests. Nevertheless, those who did were not an insignificant proportion of the population: in March 2011, when Egyptians were asked if they had participated in the protests, 11 per cent answered in the affirmative. While those who said they took to the streets were most likely to be young, educated and male, the demonstrators included the entire demographic spectrum. Most importantly, their average household income reflected that of the public at large. In a country where the deepest political divides often fall along class lines, the protesters managed to attract the participation of a broad cross-section of the population, transcending traditional economic differences.[13]

On an anecdotal level, that is what I saw myself in Tahrir Square. The pictures that were seen on the world's television screens were authentic. Eventually, Tahrir Square was so full of people who were there consistently over that period of time that, as we have seen, an almost autonomous zone existed therein. The military did control access points, but beyond these the protestors were in charge. The mini-state they set up within Tahrir Square was one that called for no arms (and so they patted down everyone coming in), insisted on social justice (thus people were feeding each other), and required respectful relations between all people, regardless of religion or class. Interestingly enough for students of libertarianism and the philosophy of law, none of this was compulsory, except for the no arms rule—and where respectful relations were transgressed in a way that caused danger, the people in the square would cordon off the offending party, peacefully but quickly.

This image, however, was far from what state media presented— foreign instigators and the MB wreaking havoc—when it covered the protests at all. By the time of Mubarak's fall, Egypt's media had become a relatively cacophonous space,[14] as light liberalisations enacted over the 2000s enabled the rise of privately owned television channels and newspapers, often each with an associated online presence. Circulation numbers are suspect, but *Al-Masry Al-Youm*, the first private newspaper launched in 2005, had likely eclipsed *Al-Ahram*, Egypt's storied newspaper of (a certain) record. Still, the cards remained stacked against an independent press: state media maintained an upper hand on licensing and publishing production, while the businessmen behind Egypt's new media ventures never structured them as sustainable and independent money-making enterprises. Rather, the privately owned media, the bad along with the good, became a new arena for Egypt's biggest businessmen to leverage for personal gain, with journalism ethics and the rights and needs of journalists relegated to the politics of a rich few.[15]

This is all to say that while new media was no doubt vital to the making of the revolution, it too came with ingrained limitations. By 25 January the number of Egyptians on the Internet and using social media was continually on the rise, but still not approaching anything like a majority of the population.[16] Indeed, a Gallup poll showed that only 8 per cent of the Egyptian population at large got their news from Facebook or Twitter in early 2011—social media was not then, nor is it now, the core information medium for the average Egyptian. The numbers were higher for protesters, but while Facebook, Twitter and YouTube networks spread and built support for the now-historic call to protest, helping to bridge gaps and build a new political culture,[17] the effect of this ought not to be overestimated.[18] When the government cut Internet and communication lines three days later, people still mobilised and did so using 'old' on-the-ground news-gathering networks: friends, families, neighbours, strangers. Those who managed to keep tweeting, or did so in the months and years after 25 January, are important parts of this story: politics everywhere, after all, remains an elite affair. But for every tweet in English providing a hot take are thousands more perspectives unheard by and lost to the West. Egypt's Internet regulation, moreover, still remains a messy affair, furthering certain kinds of Internet uses and cultures while inhibiting (and criminalising) others. The characterisation of 25 January as a 'Facebook revolution' (thereby seemingly fulfilling false prophecies about democracy, technology and other issues) might have immediately made Egypt more palatable to an outside—particularly a Western—audience, but in the long term has also distorted real-time developments and their embedded causes and consequences.[19]

VIII

Several years on, more than a few Egyptians wonder: did they make the right choice? Was the 25 January uprising, that became a revolutionary moment, the right choice? As time went on, the Gallup surveys captured a good deal of that feeling: while 76 per cent of Egyptians in April 2011 thought that conditions for themselves would improve as a result of Mubarak's resignation, only 51 per cent thought so in September of the same year. If there is one lesson to be learned from the years after the uprising, it is that a critical mass of Egyptians generally favoured and prioritised a sense of stability above all else. The revolution might have been capable of being the bedrock to a new stability based on the principles of Tahrir Square—but it never fulfilled this promise. The uprising gave rise to a revolution, but it also brought out into the open two main poles of power, neither of which was interested in the revolution except to further their own interests.

Yet, the question of 'did Egyptians make the right choice?' in terms of the revolutionary uprising is framed in a rather misleading manner. It suggests that there was a choice, and that ought not to be taken as a given. That is something we shall return to.

What was, however, a choice that ought to be examined here is how the uprising unfolded internally. Here, the protesters did have a choice. They could have turned into wanton vandals and rioters, or they could create new potentials for space to action. By and large, they chose the latter option. The eighteen days were not an utopia all around Egypt— there was violence that led to the burning of police stations, for example, as the symbols of torture and oppression. Some shops were broken into, far away from any of the protest sites, by those who took advantage of the absence of the police forces. But the eighteen days did not turn into utter mayhem. On the contrary. A few months later, the London riots were the next example of 'public disorder' that occupied the world's television screens—and they were far more tumultuous and frenzied than what transpired in Egypt. Egyptians chose a different path. Months later, I commented in a public speech that Egyptians had to give Mubarak due credit for what Tahrir Square became, because had Mubarak not been so utterly stubborn and short sighted, Tahrir Square would never have materialised into the remarkable counter-reaction it became.

The catastrophe was what happened after the eighteen days. I remember clearly where I was on the eve of 11 February, the day Mubarak was removed. Sitting in a café ten minutes away from Tahrir Square, I was waiting with friends for Mubarak to give his speech. It was due at 9pm on Thursday night, and we waited for forty-five minutes for him to make his appearance. The restrooms were constantly engaged, as the stress of simply waiting for this man, the ruler of Egypt for some three decades, to give what was expected to be his farewell speech, proved physically challenging for even our bowels and bladders.

If Mubarak had given that speech ten days earlier, he might have rescued his reign. At that point his speech, which we later learned was pre-recorded, only served to rile the emotions of the protesters. Mubarak offered some concessions, but refused to resign, and that refusal was met by a huge swathe of disappointment among the protesters.

That disappointment turned to anger and then to resolute determination. One of my friends in the café told me, 'OK, that's that then. Tomorrow, we are ready to die.' Not to kill—but to die if necessary.

Shortly after Mubarak's speech, it was announced that the army's leadership would make its own declaration. They never did. But the following day, it was all over—or, at least, something was. Just not what most were led to believe at the time.

The last time I was in Tahrir Square during those eighteen days was on 11 February. I had been home, after having been prepared to march in Tahrir all night the day before. The news came through: the stone-faced vice president and spy chief, the infamous Omar Suleiman, had announced Mubarak's resignation.

I made my way, as quickly as I could, to Tahrir Square. Just before I was about to enter, a good friend called me from the United Arab Emirates (UAE), where he was staying. He was an Egyptian-American, and only a few months before, had told my wife that he was utterly opposed to any movement to pull down Mubarak, out of fear that the result might be catastrophic. That evening he called me and asked, 'I've been in a meeting for the last hour. Is it true? Is he really gone?' I replied, 'Yes. It's true. And I see Tahrir Square in front of me.' He went silent. He then murmured a prayer—a prayer not out of fear of what was to come, but of gratitude for what had been possible.

'Can I ask you for a favour? Can you please get a copy of *Ahram* for me tomorrow?' *Al-Ahram* was Egypt's national newspaper, and for the first few days, reflecting the state line, it did not cover the protests in print at all. By 11 February, *Al-Ahram* had tentatively changed its colours and, indeed, that copy was a sight to see: 'The people brought down the regime' was the headline.

'Of course,' I replied. And then I walked into the square, and was greeted by young and old Egyptians chanting: 'Raise your head high— you're Egyptian.'

The Supreme Council of the Armed Forces removed Husni Mubarak from power, as it became clear that his very presence as head of state was an immediate source of instability for the country. With his depar- ture, the immediate impetus for the crowds of protesters to remain vanished—which was the point. Nearly all of what was to become the 'revolutionary camp' departed the squares of Egypt on 11 February after celebrating Mubarak's removal. That was a choice they made— and it would be one that would come back to haunt them.

2

THE PLAYERS EMERGE

The revolution is not a single event—it is a process. The revolution did not end on 11 February 2011, but many forces did start to try to deflate it from that point onwards. The irony was that many of them had said they were in support of the 11 February deposal of Hosni Mubarak. If the eighteen days were a marriage of convenience, the divorce came very quickly.

Conversation with an activist, Cairo 2011.

The revolutionary moment in Egypt catalysed around the 25 January protests, with a great deal of work having gone into it from long before. Various youth movements, human rights groups, labour collectives and others had laid down the groundwork for something to happen. That is not to say they planned a revolution on 25 January—it took them by surprise. But they had helped to create the conditions that made a revolution possible.

The question on 12 February, as the revolution moved past its first milestone, was clear: who were the forces in Egypt's political arena that could aid—or hinder—the revolution? Over the following years, their relative strengths and commitments became evident.

I

Let's start with the most impotent political force after the eighteen days, which, ironically, was the most important one during the eighteen-day uprising. The term 'revolutionary' was used as almost a short-hand during that period, but it applied to more or less anyone who claimed they supported the key goals of the revolution. The 'revolutionary camp' found its nucleus in certain sectors of society prior to the uprising actually taking place.

It remains a term oft-applied but difficult to define. For me, the revolutionaries were those who rejected certain positions throughout the first few years after the uprising. They rejected the regime of Mubarak, and they rejected an alignment with the Supreme Council of the Armed Forces (SCAF) in order to get power. They rejected the instrumentalisation of religion for partisan ends, and they rejected authoritarianism, which gives the state and its institutions a near-sacred standing. They affirmed the pluralistic spirit of the eighteen days, and affirmed a civil polity, in which the fundamental rights of all are upheld, and genuine reform occurs to fulfil economic and social justice for all. As noted, terms are often contested, and many may consider 'revolutionary' to mean something quite different. When I use it, however, it is both a term of negation and one of affirmation. This is my reading, which informs the words that follow.

Political parties, whether from the non-Islamist elite, or the Islamist current, were thus not, it ought to be pointed out, a part of the 'revolutionary nucleus'. On the contrary. Foreign media and analysis also often conflated 'revolutionary' with 'liberal' or 'secular', terms that in Egypt and Arabic don't have the same history or present context as in the US or Europe. What was prominent, nonetheless, was a small selection of political movements, foremost among which were the April 6 Youth Movement and the Revolutionary Socialists. The former had been founded in the spring of 2008 to support the workers' strike, called for in Mahalla, an industrial town in the north of Egypt, with about half-a-million inhabitants. That original labour action arguably laid down a critical part of the groundwork that led to the 25 January revolution.

It's important to mention what April 6 was not, as much as what it was, because that, in turn, explains a good deal around what the revolutionaries at large were. April 6 was not a political party, but it did mobilise, particularly through the use of technology. As previously mentioned, the 25 January uprising was not a 'social media revolution'—to call it that would be to tremendously underestimate the breadth of Egyptian society that it managed to attract. But the revolutionary camp in general, and April 6 in particular, certainly used social media a tremendous amount to organise and mobilise.

April 6 was also not an Islamist movement, but it is somewhat misleading to call it 'secular' without unpacking quite what that kind of label means in an Egyptian context. Certainly, it did not promote the politicisation of religion for partisan ends, but the movement was correspondingly not made up of opponents to religion. In this regard, April 6 was a quintessentially Egyptian movement, in that it appealed to very typically Egyptian youth: Muslims and Christians, with generally strong religious identities. There was not a deep ideological component to April 6, expressed through common political ideologies such as socialism or conservatism or something else. April 6 was far more fluid in that regard. Its focus was on civil rights, social justice, and many of the topics that would become focal points of the Egyptian revolution, but it was rather loose and eclectic in how it addressed those issues. In a way, one might argue, they were ideologues without an ideology. Their key figures were what made the movement: people like Ahmad Maher, Asma Mahfuz, Waleed Rashed and others.

The Revolutionary Socialists, also fairly instrumental in mobilising for the 25 January protests, were rather different. If April 6 was characterised by an absence of formal ideology, the Revolutionary Socialists were dogmatic in how they related to Trotskyism, a strand of Marxism. In that regard, the Revolutionary Socialists had an advantage over many others within the broader revolutionary camp, in that they had a very clear political identity from the first day of the revolution, but this also meant that they were less able to appeal to a broad section of the population. Even while some Revolutionary Socialists would use religious slogans at marches and the like, their actual stances on religion put them at odds with a society that deeply valued religious identity—in a way that Marx never would. Some of them, nonetheless, were tremendously well connected to technology, and became conspicuous throughout the Western press both during and after the uprising. These included figures such as Hossam Hamalawy, Gigi Ibrahim (who became a Revolutionary Socialist after the uprising) and Tarek Shalaby.

The roots of 25 January ran deep and wide. Another important instigator was the *Kifaya* movement, started in 2004. *Kifaya* brought together public intellectuals and everyday Egyptians opposed to Mubarak's corrupting ways and the then-likely prospect that the ageing dictator's son, Gamal, would takeover next.[1] Related petitions, protests and organising sessions pushed the boundaries of permissible speech and political action, something on which the 25 January movement relied. Around this time, student activists organising protests against the 2003 Iraq War and Israel's actions in the second Palestinian Intifada and 2009 Gaza War—both also roundabout ways of criticising Mubarak's policies—enabled the formation of new networks and the use of new tactics in dealing with Egypt's security forces. The Muslim Brotherhood (MB), meanwhile, was also testing its political muscle through contesting (and, significantly, often winning) seats in the 2005 parliamentary elections and professional syndicates.

Going beyond political movements, which were only one aspect of the revolutionary camp, there were civil society groups and organisations. However, civil society had been severely limited due to the restrictive climate of the pre-revolutionary Mubarak period. The participants of the major civil society groups were drawn far more from the elite than those of the April 6 movement, although it was perhaps less elitist than the Revolutionary Socialists. Human rights organisations and civil rights activists were part and parcel of the revolutionary uprising during those eighteen days, and consistently remained a part of the revolutionary camp thereafter. They did not provide much in the way of mobilisation but they did provide a certain intellectual resource, which was part of the bedrock of the January uprising. Some of the more prominent organisations in that regard included the Egyptian Initiative for Personal Rights and the Cairo Institute for Human Rights Studies, but there were many others who were less well-known. On an individual basis, there were also prominent human rights campaigners and advocates, involved through their organisations as well as independently or through political groups. They included the likes of Hossam Bahgat, Heba Morayef, Bahey al-Din Hassan and others. The sad irony in relation to this particular section of the revolutionary camp is that other human rights organisations in Egypt, who claimed to support the revolution at its outset, then quickly became partisans of the new ruling elites. To describe that as a bitterly felt experience within the human rights community would be a gross understatement.

There were also intellectuals, media personalities and bloggers, some of whom were active before the revolution, and some whose activities were born through it. These included Wael Ghonim, the Google executive; Belal Fadl, a writer and playwright; Ahdaf Soueif, a noted novelist; Amr Hamzawy, a political science professor and liberal politician; Rabab al-Mahdi, a famous academic; Bassem Youssef, the 'Jon Stewart of Egypt'; and many others. They had tremendously varied political ideologies: some were socially conservative but politically liberal, while others considered themselves on the left, without being socialists. The span of that pro-revolution core was fairly expansive.

Finally, there were individual activists—solitary figures who did not consider themselves to be members or representatives of existing groups or movements, but who carved reputations of their own. The most famous among them was Alaa Abd al-Fattah, a left-leaning activist who had been imprisoned under Mubarak for his pro-democracy activities—but again, there were many others. Since the beginning of the revolutionary uprising through to the present, new figures have come to the forefront in ever-increasing numbers.

The question was never whether or not a revolutionary uprising had taken place. It had, and these various sectors of the revolutionary camp were at its core, sustaining it during the eighteen days of uprising, and then maintaining a revolutionary trend afterwards. The question was whether or not that trend had critical mass at any point after the toppling of Mubarak at the hands of the military establishment—and the truth is that it did not. The revolutionary camp was the force that carried the most weight during the eighteen days, and it was the force that had the least impact thereafter. It was the most potent force during those early days, and the most impotent after them.

Admittedly, that's something of a generalisation—but the gist of it is important. Certainly, there were a number of 25 January revolutionaries who decided after the toppling of Mubarak that the struggle had to shift from the street to the ballot box. They joined a variety of newly formed political parties, and worked assiduously to develop them. Some even ran themselves for parliamentary seats in the fresh elections called in 2011. But the revolutionary camp as a whole was unable to make that shift quickly or effectively enough in the aftermath of the 11 February ousting.

The first test of that was within a month of the removal of Mubarak. The military custodians of Egypt opted to put forward a referendum on certain constitutional amendments—a referendum that was, by and large, rejected by the revolutionary camp. As will be discussed in greater depth below (see particularly Chapter 3), most revolutionaries were concerned that the roadmap suggested by the military would result in far less radical change than Egypt needed, and they insisted that instead of amendments, a completely new constitution had to be drafted in advance of a referendum. They were right, but they failed to organise and mobilise effectively for a proper alternative against the referendum, which both the SCAF and the MB supported. This was the first sign of trouble ahead for the revolutionaries, as well as an important warning about the MB's fickle loyalties and pragmatism in the quest to gain and retain power. Ultimately, public demands for 'stability', and the backroom interests pushing this narrative, won out.

The referendum thus took place on 19 March. Impressively, over 77 per cent voted in favour of the constitutional changes, and the revolutionary camp was put well and truly in its place.[2] The revolutionary allure of 25 January had faded fast in the face of people's immediate needs and political intrigue, with the revolutionaries now handicapped by their lack of support and failure to organise outside the transient *midan*.

I recall being profoundly struck by a conversation that I had with a middle-class security guard who worked in my Cairo neighbourhood. He told me, struggling to be as polite as he could, that supporters of a 'no' vote 'will leave this country if the going gets tough. We, on the other hand, have nowhere to go. We're stuck here. We're not going anywhere. And what's most important to us is stability, so we can get back on our feet.'

The military and its allies had successfully pitched the constitutional amendments as a path to 'stability'—an equation which would come back to haunt the revolutionary camp again and again. But this wasn't altogether dishonest of the military, because the revolutionary camp had not provided, in any shape or form, a competitive alternative that could be sensibly articulated and easily understood by the vast majority of the population. Their hearts may have been—and may continue to be—in the right place, but from the moment Mubarak was pushed from power, their lofty ideals were never translated into a cohesive programme that the population could realistically believe in.

Edward Said correctly notes that speaking truth to and criticising power is a duty in the public sphere, regardless of who holds that power. The revolutionaries, nonetheless, were seldom subjected to that type of scrutiny. If they ever held power in the formal sense, it was always far less than that held by other forces, warranting less attention.[3]

During the uprising in 2011, the revolutionaries gained a certain type of power. Their theoretical perspective, though imprecise, became manifest through popular mobilisation. With that, they were able to fundamentally disrupt the workings of the state, provoking and forcing it to change direction, resulting in the removal of Mubarak. At the same time, they also missed the opportunity to harness and develop that power. They had considerable political capital at the time of the 2011 referendum. But, though they generally mobilised for a 'no' vote, they provided little in the way of a plausible alternative, and they lost the vote. Their failure to properly express a well-developed political vision meant they missed a key opportunity to set the agenda of the post-Mubarak period.

A year later, the revolutionaries had the option of coalescing around a single candidate for presidential elections. It is likely that such a candidate would have prevailed. Instead, the revolutionary vote was split, leading to a runoff between Mubarak's last prime minister, and the non-revolutionary MB. Some will claim the revolutionaries played a critical role in that runoff, by ensuring the former regime candidate lost. That is true, but the very occurrence of such an abysmal runoff would have been impossible had there been a single, pro-25 January revolution candidate, or even a coherent response to the subsequent runoff and the election of the MB's Muhammad Mursi as president.

The criticism cannot stop there, for even if the revolutionary trend had been able to successfully establish a coherent platform, it still would have had to deal with the problem of communicating it to the vast majority of Egyptian citizens. In early 2013, I participated in a public debate hosted by Tim Sebastian (previously of the BBC's *HardTalk* programme) on the topic. My opponent was a representative from the Constitution Party, a relatively new party set up by Muhammad al-Baradei, the Egyptian politician and former head of the International Atomic Agency. The motion was simple: 'This house believes the Egyptian opposition has wasted its chances, and let down the people.'[4]

It was not particularly difficult to win the debate. The Constitution Party and the other components of the wider 'National Salvation Front' (more on this in a moment) had not only failed to construct fully developed political platforms, but had also comprehensively failed to engage with Egyptian citizens. These parties were elite affairs, and they dealt rather lazily with the wider Egyptian population, despite numerous criticisms from both friend and foe. When they did get out of their comfort zones in the upper-class neighbourhoods of Cairo and Alexandria, they invariably were incapable of connecting efficiently with those that they sought to convince.

That was the story for those who actually sought to become involved with organised, regular political forces. A large proportion of the revolutionary camp—perhaps the largest—did not get involved with political parties, and stuck with street mobilisation. In essence, there is nothing wrong with that tactic: popular mobilisation has been a tool of political movements since time immemorial. The problem with this part of the revolutionary camp is that 'the protest' ceased to be one among several tactics—and instead became a strategy in and of itself.

To be sure, Egyptians have seen how effective protests can be many times in recent years. Protests can promote a sense of solidarity among those who participate. And, indeed, the protests in Egypt over the last few years have achieved that, prompting those within an embattled revolutionary movement to realise that they are not alone. In the months after the removal of Mursi in July 2013, the first protest that was held by the revolutionary camp gave its participants a necessary reminder of this. It was a time when the political atmosphere in Egypt was toxic beyond belief, and I remember that day in Tala'at al-Harb in downtown Cairo that, even though there were not huge numbers of protesters, those who were there felt that at least they were not alone. That, in itself, is a type of accomplishment in certain contexts.

But a successful mobilisation is one that actually produces results, and in this regard the revolutionary camp has been unable to point to more than a few successes. In part, this is because it has been unable to use 'the protest' in conjunction with other forms of political activity. A typical example is the extra-judicial decree of then-President Muhammad Mursi on 22 November 2012, a decree that caused a wave of mobilisation against his government due to its unilateral declaration that until a new constitution was agreed upon, the president would be immune from all legal challenges. Protests began, almost spontaneously, in Tahrir Square, as well as outside the presidential palace. The momentum was clear, but Mursi and his government ignored the protests. Then, the revolutionary camp and other opponents of the Mursi government were given an opportunity: the government put a newly written constitution out to referendum. The protests showed, clearly, that there was a sense of dissatisfaction with the government—and a 'no' vote would have dealt it a blow.

Instead, the protests dissipated, with no cohesive leadership behind them. The organised political opposition coalesced into the National Salvation Front, which had some revolutionary supporters within it but which was also tainted by figures that had been close to the Mubarak regime. More than that, the front had not led or mobilised any protests—on the contrary, the front was following the protesters. They were not leading but were simply trying to keep up with the public mood. When they had the opportunity to issue calls for a 'no' vote in the 2012 constitutional referendum, they dithered until only two days before the vote was due to take place, eventually issuing a position against the document, albeit far too late for any impact to be felt as the vote took place.

The result (on a low turnout of 30 per cent of registered voters)[5] was hardly a staggering victory for the government and the MB. Yet, it was a massive defeat for the organised political opposition and the revolutionary camp. The MB and its allies could only bring out 20 per cent of the population to vote for them, but the opposition could only muster 10 per cent.

Again, it bears repeating, protest has a role in any healthy political system. And in Egypt from 2011 to 2013, the protest of the revolutionaries was a tool for agitation, which in turn did have some minor effects. But when the protest became the main tool of the revolutionary camp, it ceased to have the same relevance. Protest is meant to capitalise on public sentiment—not to invite a counteraction that is even more damaging than the current situation. Far too often, this is precisely what happened: protests would be called for which did not capitalise on more than the feeling of a tiny segment of the population, and worse still, they would engender opposition and anger from far wider sections of the populace. When this happens, protest damages rather than advances the goals of the movement.

This focus on protest had caused some to criticise, and even attack, the revolutionary camp for contributing to the 2013 military ousting of the MB's President Mursi. As the argument goes, the revolutionary camp, by not sufficiently engaging in formal, regular politics, strengthened the notion that electoral politics was not what Egypt needed, and thus opened the way for the military to suspend the results of the ballot box in 2013. Indeed, by calling for early presidential elections in 2013, the revolutionary camp was essentially inviting the military to overthrow the government, and set Egypt's democratic experiment back.

It's an interesting argument, but it is somewhat difficult to make stick. As already noted, the revolutionary camp did not have much political impact throughout 2011–13. It was two pro-revolutionary figures, Amr Hamzawy, a liberal politician and former member of parliament, and Abd al-Mun'im Abu al-Futuh, more left-leaning and a former MB leader, who had first advocated early presidential elections. But it was neither them nor the revolutionary camp that turned the call into a popular mobilisation that was then joined by non-, and even anti- or counter-, revolutionary forces.

A few days before the 30 June protests took place, the revolutionary camp showed it had become at least partially split on the issue. Looking back on 2013, there was no revolutionary voice that pushed back against a call for early presidential elections—yet that was the only point of consensus. The revolutionary camp was not united on the call to mobilise for the 30 June protests, nor was it unanimously supportive of the decision by the military to remove Mursi a few days later. Lina Atalla, a noted pro-revolutionary journalist, enunciated clearly the divisions over the mobilisation of the protests in her article 'Back to the Margins', published by *Mada Masr* before the protests began. The piece admitted that the protests, before they had even been initiated, showed signs of being infiltrated by powerful counter-revolutionary forces, and as such were dangerous.[6]

That did not mean all protesters who supported the 30 June call were counter-revolutionary. On the contrary, there were many who had supported the 25 January revolution, who now supported protests planned for 30 June, but were also explicitly opposed to military intervention of any sort. In late June, before the protests began, a group of pro-revolutionary political figures[7] and movements declared as much at a public press conference. When Mursi was removed on 3 July they certainly did not shed many tears, but nor did they unanimously celebrate with gusto.

Nevertheless, there were some pro-revolutionary activists and figures who did celebrate on 3 July—and not simply due to the removal of Mursi. But they were vicariously naïve about how things would be after the military returned to Egyptian politics. Eventually, either they left the revolutionary trend altogether, becoming indistinguishable from those supporting the state and the military leadership, or they subtly reversed their positions. It is difficult to calculate the proportions that all these sections constituted within the revolutionary trend. Many revolutionaries had either stayed home altogether, or had participated with express opposition to any military role whatsoever. There were others that essentially left the revolutionary trend altogether, and became part and parcel of a new, pro-military tendency.

With all of that said, there are three points that ought to be very clear. The first is that blaming the revolutionary trend for the 3 July coup is difficult to substantiate, especially when it is readily apparent that the overwhelming majority of revolutionary activists and figures were opposed to military rule, and those few naïve voices that did not immediately recognise the dangers posed by July 3 soon recanted anyway. The second point is that it is immensely important to distinguish between political figures involved in formal politics, and those involved with street action and mobilisation. Both ought to be called to account, but certainly not in the same fashion; responsibility for both is different.

The third point is that even if all revolutionaries had been supportive of a military coup, or even if all of them had joined pro-Mursi protests, the end result would have been the same. The revolutionary camp, as detailed before, had not enjoyed the critical mass to affect the eventual outcome in any significant way since February 2011, with one exception (the presidential elections of 2012). How the revolutionary trend could be considered 'responsible', morally or otherwise, for an action that it did not support is difficult to fathom.

What is also true is that that the revolutionary trend also paid a price for the new political arrangements after 3 July, with many of their number arrested. Repeatedly, the revolutionary camp, through all its different formations, provided loud voices against the abuses of the new, as yet not fully formed, regime—whether those abuses were aimed at the revolutionaries themselves or at those they considered to be enemies. Not all parts of that camp, nevertheless, were loud from the get-go: on the contrary, too many were silent in those early weeks after the coup, despite the immense brutality by the security forces that was visited in July and August of 2013. Others remained steadfast on the principle that excessive state violence is wrong and ought to be loudly and openly opposed at every instance—but not everyone in the revolutionary camp can claim they followed that principle quickly enough, even if they eventually did.

There are good reasons to be critical of the revolutionary trend in Egypt's post-Mubarak political landscape. Had it been better organised, perhaps the revolutionaries could have presented or endorsed a single candidate for the presidential elections in 2012, which would have avoided a run off between a representative of the former regime, and a right-wing religious candidate. Had it been better organised, it might have been able to mobilise more effectively against the constitution of 2012, which in turn might have forced the MB government to become more inclusive. But it also ought to be kept in mind that the revolutionary trend was born of the street. Many of its members never wanted to leave the street, and even decried those who did so to take up a political file. Perhaps it is simply unreasonable to expect that political maturity of that nature could develop in such a short time.

But certainly, the revolutionary trend in Egyptian politics, small as it is, remains a source of great stimulus. It was from within that trend that the Egyptian revolution began. To date, there is probably no tendency that can claim to have always stood 100 per cent behind the principles of 2011—but the revolutionary camp has been the most consistent in standing against human rights abuses that affect all Egyptians. It ought to be held to account, and its proponents should constantly re-evaluate its failings. One hopes that in the years to come, if Egyptians are given the opportunity of a free and open political arena again, it will be from within that trend that a genuinely cohesive and constructive political alternative is derived.

II

For years, the MB was described as a 'moderate Islamist group'. As Islamist groups go, the MB is—relatively speaking—a centrist incarnation of contemporary political Islamism, which is why it was such a huge disappointment in the Egyptian revolution. Disappointment aside, it has also paid an unjustly heavy price. Moreover, it's a price that has caused all of Egypt to suffer. In the midst of the revolution, the narratives around the MB have been revised time and again, both by supporters of the MB and their opponents. Historical revisionism aside, it's important to understand exactly what role this movement did and did not play in the past few years of Egyptian history.

Let us begin with the start of the 25 January revolutionary uprising. One narrative suggests that, essentially, the 25 January movement was weak and feeble and could not bring more than a few people to the streets from the wider public. As such, the MB valiantly took up the cause, mobilising people from day one of the uprising to ensure the revolution succeeded, and was the leading force of the uprising. Recently, this narrative gained credence with supporters of the MB outside of Egypt, and others who were not actually in Egypt during the eighteen days.

On the anti-MB side, one can find a range of perspectives in support of another narrative. Some (particularly in the anti-Mubarak but pro-military private media) suggest that the MB was essentially absent from Tahrir Square and the various squares around the country at the beginning of the uprising. It joined the Egyptian people, according to this narrative, very late, and was essentially inconsequential.

The last of the main historical revisionist narratives is one in which the MB was very much involved in the uprising. In fact, the 25 January uprising was a conspiracy by the MB. (It's worth bearing in mind that this narrative particularly took root after the 30 June protests.) The protesters that were killed by pro-Mubarak forces on the day of the Battle of the Camels were killed, actually, by the MB. As the claims go, there were non-MB forces in the square, but the MB was just manipulating them.

The truth is that at the beginning of the Egyptian revolution the MB was absent. Certainly, it was not opposed to the 25 January protests, and it had engaged with al-Baradei's National Association for Change, an umbrella group for opposition to Mubarak's regime. So it would be difficult to portray the MB in the run-up to the 25 January protests as somehow being aligned to the regime.

In the run-up to the protests the MB, like most Egyptians, also did not take the call to protest very seriously. There are suggestions the leadership met to discuss the protests, especially after what had happened in Tunisia. Nevertheless, when this highly disciplined organisation (at least in 2011) mobilised, it was organised—and there is no evidence to suggest that it decided to mobilise privately, let alone publicly.

Claiming that the MB was a critical part of the protests in the early days would then be quite a stretch: the leadership didn't take 25 January that seriously, although it did not forbid MB members from participating if they so chose to do so. Essentially, it was up to individual members to choose whether or not to participate as independent Egyptians.

At the same time, it is important to understand the perspective of the MB when it came to oppositional practices in the run up to 25 January. The MB was not a revolutionary organisation. Rather, it was traditionally a 'reformist' one, whether one deems their desired 'reforms' to be positive and progressive or not. When the Tunisian revolution succeeded in removing Tunisia's President Ben Ali, the MB put out a press statement calling on Egyptians to reform the system in order to avoid revolutionary upheaval. Naturally, that was not a call of support for Mubarak—it was more an expression of the MB's preference for slow, stable change, instead of sudden change with an unpredictable outcome.

Indeed, prior to the uprising itself, that sort of pragmatism had led to reports from high-ranking former leaders, such as Muhammad Habib, that the leadership of the MB had an agreement with the Mubarak regime. The MB would, as the story goes, not object too vigorously to the turning over of power from Mubarak to his son—and in return, the MB would continue to be tolerated as a political force.[8] It is, of course, difficult to verify such reports, despite the seniority of Habib, who was a deputy of the organisation, and had been expected to become the General Guide in 2010. Nevertheless, the tendency of the MB to engage in pragmatic political moves up until the revolution in 2011 was evident in a regular pattern of behaviour.

It can be concluded, then, that as an organisation the MB did not foment the 25 January protests. It is true that when the protests began, Mubarak's government did attempt to pin the blame on the MB.

However, the response from the leadership was unequivocal: no, the MB was not responsible. Having said this, it is also the case that members of the MB did attend the protests from very early on, but not as representatives of the movement.

To characterise the 25 January protests as 'MB protests', as some forces in the Mubarak regime did at the time, and as MB supporters did afterwards, is therefore somewhat imaginative. The MB was initially a reluctant player—and remained as such for a few days after 25 January. It was a relatively small crowd that went to the streets and within it there was a small group of MB youth members, among the majority who were not part of the MB. The point is that these young people attended the protest not as MB members acting under orders, but rather as young Egyptians wanting change along with their fellow countrymen.

Indeed, according to one of the recorded accounts, the MB leadership had to be convinced even to allow this. According to the account, members of the university division of the MB, which was the structure most representative of the youth, wanted to send an appeal to the Guidance Council to allow them to participate in the protests. The head of the division, Mahmud Abu Zayd, objected since the Guidance Council had already decided against participation. A contingent of the MB youth then tried to intervene directly with the Bureau by arranging a meeting with Essam al-Erian, a prominent senior MB leader. It is said that as a result of that encounter the youth were given the green light to participate in Tahrir as individuals, but not as MB representatives.[9]

Even then, describing the MB youth as constituting the most revolutionary part of the revolutionary movement at large is problematic. The youth themselves were divided. According to one confidential source, there were essentially three groupings of MB youth at the time of the uprising: the leftists, the centrists, and the right-wing. The more progressive were those who contributed to the mobilisation for the 25 January protests early on. Not surprisingly, they were the ones who left the MB after the protests to join the presidential campaign of the more left-leaning former MB leader, Abd al-Mun'im Abu al-Futuh.

The more centrist camp was itself split, with some members deciding to join in on 25 January, and some waiting until the MB leadership was more enthusiastic. The right-wing section of the youth waited until the decisive 'Day of Rage' on 28 January.

In a very short period, the people of Egypt became energised by the 25 January call for change, and momentum gathered in all sectors of society. Looking at the published statements of the MB during January and February, it is clear that the leadership went through an evolution in its perspective vis-à-vis the protests. In particular, the forty-eight-hour period from the evening of 25 January till the evening of 27 January saw the MB change its position more than once, quite dramatically.

On 26 January, the MB's Guidance Council assembled to discuss how to respond to the protests. Publicly, the MB had tried to disassociate itself from the organisation of the protests. Privately, it had let its youth members know that they were not forbidden from participation. The message to the regime was clear: 'we have nothing to do with organising this, so don't you try to pin it on us. You should rather respond to the youth and the people in the streets.'

Protesters called for the Day of Rage on 28 January—the first Friday of the revolution—and different sectors of society decided to join them. This was the beginning of a mass mobilisation of Egyptians—one that, as mentioned earlier, 11 per cent of Egyptians later claimed in nationwide Gallup polls that they participated in. Those same polls show the movement as a broad-based, popular movement that represented all sectors of society and was not limited to one particular faction.

In response to the impressive organic mobilisation of ordinary Egyptians, the MB leadership decided to change their original stance of disassociation from the protests, and formally called for their members to mobilise on the evening of 27 January. From that point on, the MB, as an organisation, was indelibly involved on the side of the revolutionary camp. The regime was fully aware of this. By the following morning, much of the MB's senior leadership had been arrested as a result of their public statement—but many of their members still mobilised and joined the protests.

Jack Shenker of the *Guardian* correctly characterised the MB's initially evasive, if not hesitant, involvement in the protests:

> When the call first went out for mass pro-change protests on 25 January, the Brotherhood responded as it always has to any major anti-government activity originating outside its own sphere of influence—it dithered. With that dithering came a loss of credibility, as the demonstrations gathered momentum and coalesced into nothing short of a revolutionary challenge to 30 years of entrenched dictatorship.[10]

As Shenker indicates, the delay in the MB's official organs coming out in support of the revolution cost the MB: it lost credibility with its own members as well as with the revolutionary camp. Within the MB, younger members were ahead of their leadership, and many of them quickly developed relationships with non-MB supporters of the revolution. That dynamic was to hurt the MB later on, particularly after the removal of Mubarak.

The MB's leadership tried to monopolise the political activity of its membership, something that exacerbated the disillusionment of some of its members. Many of the MB's brightest, such as Abd al-Rahman al-Ayyash among the youth and Abd al-Mun'im Abu al-Futuh among the leadership tier, left the movement shortly after Mubarak was forced from power, regarding the leadership as insufficiently revolutionary on the one hand, and too one-sided on the other. One has to remember, though, that for much of the of the MB rank and file, the organisation has never been a political party. It has always been a movement, and it was preordained to fight for more than its own political power. For the leadership, however, political power was necessary to pursue the movement's goals—and, as such, the movement and the political project (which was to become a political party) were not one and the same. Rather, one might argue, the movement was subservient to the search for power.

Were those young MB members justified in feeling betrayed by the MB leadership? That is another story, which relates to the question of whether the MB leadership truly believed in revolutionary change, or decided to utilise the revolution for its own partisan interest. But even if the answer is the latter, the MB's leadership are not the only ones who can now be accused of that.

Beyond the difficulty of juggling their ideological movement with the pragmatic need to attain political power, the MB had another, albeit slightly less important issue to deal with. The revolutionary camp claimed a monopoly on the uprising, and claimed that the MB only joined in after it became clear that it could plausibly serve the MB's own partisan interests. In January–February 2011 that sort of sentiment was not so sharp, but as events unfolded through the following months and years, that single decision of the MB not to participate officially from day one came to deeply affect the narrative of the revolution.

Of course, the MB could have legitimately claimed that for it to have officially backed the protests would have hurt the protests, allowing the regime to describe them as 'Islamist'. Moreover, the MB stood to suffer a great deal as an organisation, in a way that the more disparate revolutionary camp could not, being less structurally cohesive and thus less of an obvious target.

The reality is that the MB at this point was a deeply conservative, and risk-averse, movement. To join protests of this nature from the moment they were first considered—particularly when they were deemed to have very little chance of success—would have been decidedly out of character. Indeed, there were many outside the MB who felt the same way, and who decided only after several days that the protests were indeed a way to genuinely change Egypt for the better.

Going forward during the eighteen days the MB's role increased, to the benefit of the protests. Mobilisation was important, but mobilisation during the eighteen days was something that went far beyond the MB. It was a national phenomenon, drawn from all sectors of society. In that regard, the MB bears a portion of the credit, as does all of Egyptian society. But it deserves particular mention for its role during the clashes with pro-regime thugs on 2 February, the day of the famous Battle of the Camels. Without the bravery of the youthful cadres of the MB on that day, which was widely observed, I feel it is quite likely Tahrir Square would have fallen. One can therefore only view with irony, pity and bemusement the accusation, which fed into the Egyptian national media's narrative a couple of years later, that the thugs were actually MB units. This is a total fabrication, but one that was easily believed by a portion of the Egyptian population, given the media's representation of events.

As the protests intensified, the political standing of the MB increased. On 6 February, along with other political movements, the MB agreed to negotiate with Mubarak's notorious spy chief, and newly appointed vice president, Omar Suleiman. This was an about-face from the day before, when the same movements had decided to reject such talks—and the change did not go down well. It was a decision the MB would soon regret: the youth movements that remained in the square rejected negotiation on a matter of principle, insisting that Mubarak had to step down and that any negotiations would simply empower a counter-revolutionary push. As the most powerful of the political groups that had been invited to talks, the MB leadership took the brunt of that criticism. Others, arguably, could not claim to be more than figureheads. The MB, on the other hand, could mobilise, and if they had agreed at the talks to stand down in exchange for political favours, it could have dealt the revolutionary uprising a blow—though not an absolutely crippling one since, as noted before, the MB was but one player in protests that were made up of many different sectors of society. Indeed, the MB was not even the most powerful voice, as the leadership itself admitted through several statements when it insisted it was simply one party among many. Nevertheless, their departure would still have been a recognisable loss.

Those fears were well placed, but in the final event the MB did not withdraw its support from the revolutionary camp during the eighteen days. The protests persisted, and the army eventually removed Mubarak on 11 February. At this stage, the messy divorce between the revolutionaries and the MB leadership still lay in the future.

During the uprising, MB leaders openly said they would not run a candidate for the presidency. Soon after the protests finished, they added to this a commitment to aim for no more than 30 per cent of the parliamentary seats in the election scheduled for the end of the year. The MB's reasonableness certainly boosted its reputation inside and outside the country—but along with the earning of political capital came a looming split with the revolutionary camp.

The 'marriage' of the revolutionary forces with the MB during the eighteen days in Tahrir Square was, by all accounts, including my own, an inspiring affair. The respect for pluralism and political difference was staggering—and viewed against the backdrop of Egypt's current polarisation, all the more stirring.

It did not last. In the aftermath of the removal of Mubarak, SCAF, as discussed, put forward a constitutional referendum to establish a 'roadmap' for a transitional process. The amendments were deeply problematic: they essentially allowed for the existing structure of the constitution to remain, while making a few minor changes that would allow for parliamentary and presidential elections, which would then be followed by constitutional reform. The revolutionary camp mostly rejected the timetable, insisting that constitutional reform had to take precedence, particularly over the presidential elections—otherwise a new dictator could easily be elected.[11]

The MB was fully in favour of the proposed roadmap. Their motives were speculated about incessantly. One key benefit to the MB with regards to this roadmap was the fact that it put parliamentary elections first. The MB stood to gain the most from early parliamentary elections, and all the political forces knew that. In contrast, the newer, inexperienced pro-revolutionary political formations, which were extremely slow to organise, stood to lose the most.

As mentioned, while most of the pro-revolutionary forces and figures came out in favour of a 'no' vote to the constitutional referendum held in March 2011, the MB decided to push for a 'yes' vote. Its support for the 'yes' vote was interpreted to mean two things. The first was that it was no longer interested in coordinating with the revolutionary forces for the success of Egypt's revolution. Rather, it considered itself to be the rightful—and the most responsible—actor in Egyptian politics to take Egypt to its next stage (a stage where the MB would find itself in a powerful position). Some even spoke of the 'burden' of power, and MB officials privately spoke of their exasperation with what they dismissed as the 'immature revolutionaries'.

Secondly, the MB's support for the 'yes' vote showed that its interests coincided with those of the military council. That confluence of interests would define much of Egypt's political reality for more than two years—and the destruction of that convergence would define politics thereafter.

An overwhelming majority of Egyptians voted in favour of 'yes'. The MB did not push for 'yes' alone, of course: the military was clearly in favour of the referendum passing, portraying it as a vote for 'stability', and the Salafi networks were also quite supportive of a 'yes' vote. But had the MB not supported that vote, and decided instead to maintain the pro-revolutionary alliance, it's entirely possible that the 'no' side would have won. The vote would at least have been far more disputed. That contestation could have led to more pressure on the military council to push forward a healthier transitional process—something that it is clear that Egypt needed, given what we now know about how that period tragically unfolded.

Moreover, the MB's conduct during the vote was key to how it was later perceived. During the campaign, there were obviously many actors arguing for a 'yes' vote on the basis that it would restore stability, especially after a tumultuous eighteen days at Tahrir. There were also those portraying the referendum as a poll on religion—more specifically, on Islam. This will be discussed in more detail in Chapter 4, but suffice it to say at this juncture that the MB was not shy about utilising religious arguments to promote a 'yes' vote. Mostly, the MB was not avowedly and prominently sectarian at that point—that was more characteristic of the purist Salafi networks who also mobilised for a 'yes' vote—but the MB did show in this instance that it was quite happy to politicise religion for partisan gain.

Consequently, as the year progressed, support for the MB among the broader population increased while its popularity in the revolutionary camp diminished. According to Gallup polls, when Egyptians were asked in April 2011 if they had confidence in the MB, some 12 per cent answered in the affirmative. That number steadily (but slowly) increased right up until the parliamentary elections of December 2011.[12] In September 2011 some 16 per cent of Egyptians polled said they supported the MB's political party, the Freedom and Justice Party (FJP). This increased dramatically to 50 per cent in December. The big shift came not from people who had previously indicated they did not support the FJP, but rather from those who said they were uncertain. In July, 35 per cent of Egyptians expressed uncertainty about the group, one way or the other, but that number dropped to 11 per cent when parliamentary elections approached. 2011 was undoubtedly the MB's best year, in terms of increasing public support and winning over a lot of Egyptians who had previously been dubious about them.

At the same time, the MB's reputation among Egypt's intelligentsia, as well as the revolutionary camp, diminished. There were obviously those who had been opposed to the MB from day one, regarding it as intrinsically unfit for anything but the role of the persecuted. That, though, did not account for all who increasingly viewed the MB as a deeply partisan and narrow movement.

When the MB began its foray into political life after Mubarak's ousting, it focused on its strength as a disciplined, focused organisation. Members of the group were expected to toe the leadership's line, not simply in terms of political opinion, but political organisation too. Now that the Egyptian political arena was open to MB activity, the leadership did not respond by freeing up its members to take action; on the contrary, it closed down internal debate.

We have to remember that the MB was a movement and not a political party. Nevertheless, the movement's leadership treated it like a party—and a very tightly knit one at that. The leadership made two things very clear: first, until decided otherwise, the MB would not run a candidate for the presidency. Anyone running for this office would be ejected. In fact, the leadership went beyond that, stipulating that if any MB member wished to engage in politics, that person had to join the MB-authorised political party, the FJP. Membership of any other political entity would result in expulsion.

These internal dynamics had an external effect. For those who were suspicious of the MB's commitment to the revolutionary cause, this type of 'party discipline' was worrying. If this was how the MB dealt with internal differences and diversity, the argument went, how would the organisation respond to pluralism outside the movement? It did not help matters that those who were expelled from the MB were those members who had most strongly supported the revolution. These internal dissidents wanted to build a wider pro-revolutionary coalition—even if this coalition's political vision differed from that of the MB. The MB's leadership viewed this independence as treacherous.

This was hardly surprising. The MB is an old organisation in the context of modern Egypt: it has existed for some eight decades, and has done so through some bitter and difficult times. Given its history of suffering from repression, it is not surprising that it would develop an internal mechanism that—though it might limit its creative energies—would ensure the survival and continuation of the collective above all else.

Here, though, the MB made a fatal error. As mentioned, the traditional mission of the group was a social one. It was a grassroots charitable movement. The group's leadership had a choice: to restore that aim to the centre of the MB's overarching purpose, or to subject it to the parochial aims of a political party. It chose the latter. Where it could have allowed its members to support whatever political parties they wanted, thus itself staying aloof from partisan politics, the MB leadership chose the opposite course. That decision would seal its destiny.

The MB's rise and fall from grace took place in an astonishingly short time. As we already know, the popularity of the group steadily increased through 2011, even while the organisation lost a great deal of goodwill from other political forces owing to what were seen to be duplicitous actions. After its promise in early 2011 to run for no more than 30 per cent of parliamentary seats, it increased this to 50 per cent a few months later. The MB argued it had no choice owing to a paucity of pro-revolutionary candidates. So when it eventually decided to run a presidential candidate in 2012, in spite of its many previous declarations that it wouldn't (even expelling one of its own members for running as an independent), its public reputation came under review. One has to keep in mind too that the MB was running on a religious ticket, and the consequences of failing to keep its word politically would disproportionately hurt it because of its religiosity.

The relationship between the MB and the ruling elite of the military council, at least during 2011, put the MB in an advantageous position. The military council had made a strategic decision. As a non-ideological institution, unlike Turkey's strongly secularist military, Egypt's armed forces were content to engage with the MB in order to ensure that the street was pacified. For its part, the MB was content to play footsy with the military, in order to get the prize that it had wanted for so long—a place at the table of power via the ballot box. While the revolutionary camp continued its protests against SCAF during 2011 and 2012, the MB was far more cautious. During its own protests, it would often continue to utter support for the army, in stark contrast to the revolutionary protests that expressly called for the downfall of military rule.[13] Furthermore, the MB was exhibiting signs of moving closer to the right-wing religious camp of the ultra-conservative Salafis, specifically in terms of how it promoted its own rhetoric. The purist Salafi political movement became a critical force on the political scene as a result—and questions of the religious establishment at large, by the wider population of both Christian and Muslim religious leaders and institutions, began to be asked within, and without.

3

ON DEMOCRACY AND REVOLUTION

The revolution is not in the ballot box.

Khalid Abdalla, Egyptian-British actor and activist

I

I first saw Khalid Abdalla on television in 2007 or 2008. My wife and I were watching a series called *Spooks*, and he was playing a rather unflattering character (an Arab terrorist) with skill and grace. The next time I saw him was also on television—but this time in an interview being carried by Al-Jazeera, sometime in 2012. I couldn't help but admire his passion, even while I often disagreed with his political idealism. He viewed the revolutionary uprising of 2011 as the vehicle through which political change would be effected, but until the revolution was successful, nothing revolutionary would be possible in practice. 'Regular' politics, if such a thing existed, would have to take over.

Abdalla had a point. The political dispensation of Mubarak had been based on a number of things, and the entire regime had been shaken by the eighteen days of uprising. None of the changes that took place thereafter—whether the military taking over from Mubarak on 11 February, the scheduling of parliamentary elections, or, indeed, any of the major political events that followed the uprising—would have been conceivable without the eighteen days of Tahrir.

It is clear that not all of those who went to the streets during those eighteen days were after the same things. The demand they coalesced around was the removal of Mubarak—and when he was removed, that was sufficient to allow the protesters to claim a modicum of success and go home. But the revolutionary camp wanted far more than simply Mubarak's head: they wanted a restructuring of the Egyptian state; they wanted the slogans of the uprising to be fulfilled in terms of social justice, economic reform, judicial reform and other reforms.

To have assumed that the revolutionaries would see all their demands satisfied would have been tremendously naïve to say the least. But they did have a point, in that Mubarak's removal from office was something that depended on 'revolutionary legitimacy'. Technically speaking, what Mubarak did on 11 February—handing over his presidential authority to the Supreme Council of the Armed Forces (SCAF)—was not legal. He did not have the authority to do that, even if we assume for the moment that he did so willingly and without duress. If there was any legitimacy for the overthrow of Mubarak, it wasn't grounded in law.

However, neither the vast majority of the Egyptian population nor the international community rejected the decision. In Gallup polls carried out after the uprising, 78 per cent of the population voiced support for the protests that led to the resignation of Mubarak.[1] Around the world, there was no country that declared that it did not recognise the new military regime of Egypt because of the way it assumed power. The revolution had driven Mubarak out and the military had opted to stand on the side of the revolution.

II

The legitimacy of the process, nevertheless, presented a legal quandary. With the resignation of Mubarak, the constitution of Egypt was also suspended and parliament dissolved. There was no legal precedent for a transitional process. It was for that precise reason that a week before Mubarak resigned human rights activists in Cairo urged that he sign several decrees before he stepped down.[2] Hossam Bahgat and Soha Abdelaty, both of the Egyptian Initiative for Personal Rights, one of Egypt's most renowned human rights organisations, had a modest plan for transitional government—far more modest than what the military allowed for on the 11 February. And in the end, it all came tumbling down.

In the Bahgat-Abdelaty plan, Mubarak needed to do several things before leaving power. He had to first delegate all his authority to the vice president, via a presidential decree, and then use the same power to lift the 'state of emergency' that had been in operation since 1981. He also had to arrange for an 'independent commission of respected judges, constitutional law experts, civil society representatives and all political movements' that would draft amendments to the constitution, ensuring that presidential elections could take place in a fashion that would be free and fair. The plan included a 'diverse caretaker government', followed by a presidential election, the drafting of a constitution that was commensurate with democratic values and fundamental rights, and an equally free and fair parliamentary election.

Mubarak did none of that. The process was simply handed over—de facto if not de jure—to SCAF. In the vacuum left by the absence of a proper legal transfer of power and authority there were two forces: the institution of the army and popular consent. The Bahgat-Abdelaty plan had great merit, and was far better thought out than the ad hoc set of moves by the SCAF that eventuated—but they couldn't bring their arguments to fruition.

The SCAF knew they couldn't continue ruling Egypt without some kind of legal framework in place, so they simply created one. Their manufactured solution proved to be as malleable in operation as it was in construction. The SCAF's main concern appeared to be simply about maintaining as much of the status quo as they could, something in which they succeeded.

The military did, nevertheless, put itself into an awkward position. The protests had taken them, like most people, by surprise, and the SCAF was wholly unprepared. The military leadership had been generally displeased at the notion of the helm of the Egyptian state being passed from Mubarak, one of their own, to his son Gamal. It had been clear for years that Mubarak senior had been grooming his son, who had not been raised in the military, but rather among the business elite whom much of the military leadership reportedly despised.[3]

At the same time, the decision of the military to engage in the uprising had a number of consequences. Firstly, it established an explicit narrative: the idea that the military had answered the call of the Egyptian people, and had sided with them in the uprising. There was some degree of truth to that. But the military wasn't a revolutionary establishment. The protests had threatened to rock the country and Mubarak had become a liability in the light of the civil unrest within, and the international pressure from outside. If that had not been the case—if the protests hadn't so spectacularly stunned the core of the Egyptian political dispensation of Mubarak—then it is unlikely the SCAF would have engaged at all. Moreover, as later reports would indicate, the SCAF and the military were apparently not so gentle with the protesters after all. There were several documented cases of the military physically clashing with protesters, though this was relatively underreported at the time.[4]

The narrative was problematic for another reason. It confined the SCAF to a particular modus operandi. For the next few years, there would be pressure to put Mubarak on trial for the crimes he allegedly committed in office.[5] The cases eventually raised against him were always prosecuted somewhat flimsily, unsurprisingly leading to a series of verdicts that put him more or less in the clear. The judicial leadership simply had no appetite for assembling a solid case against their former president and finding him guilty. Yet the military could hardly release Mubarak: what would this say about the military that overthrew him? Would it not indicate that they had chosen the wrong side? Instead, then, Mubarak found himself in a limbo of detention, presumably the hope of the military being that he would die of old age. Ultimately, he was not released, but nor was he found guilty. Five years later, the charade of trying Mubarak in an Egyptian court for charges related, amongst other things, to the deaths of protesters during the uprising, was still ongoing.

III

The SCAF put together a team of legal experts that was responsible for formulating amendments to the constitution, which would then be put to a referendum. If the referendum passed, it would then lead to parliamentary elections, followed by a presidential election and a fresh constitutional referendum after a full-fledged discussion on a new constitution. The transitional period would, it was foreseen, only last for a matter of months.

As we have seen, the protests that led to Mubarak's departure were, according to Gallup polls, supported by 78 per cent of Egyptians in their immediate aftermath. It was a massive popular mandate, coupled with support for the military in general. The vast majority of Egyptians supported the military—partly due to its role in removing Mubarak and partly due to its positive portrayal over many years in the media and the educational system. Yes, there were stalwarts of the old regime that opposed the protests, but they would not have been willing to identify themselves, or organise openly after the military had stepped in. The military therefore tried to convert popular consent into legal legitimacy. The constitutional amendments were put to referendum. The vast majority of pro-revolutionary forces rejected the amendments, arguing that Egypt needed a far better roadmap than what was being suggested, but they lost the argument. Of those Egyptians who voted, as discussed, 77.2 per cent were in favour of the military's amendments.

The revolutionaries often spoke of legitimacy not residing in the ballot box but in the revolution itself. On one level, they were correct because without the revolutionary uprising, there would have been no ballot box to speak of. But on 11 February the revolutionaries made the choice to return home from the streets. Had they decided otherwise, it's unclear if they could have maintained the impetus of the mass mobilisation, or if they would have prevailed in any kind of confrontation with the military. Success in such a confrontation is difficult to imagine. The revolutionary camp did not have a clearly laid out plan that would specify what victory looked like—and, more specifically, it did not have an organised leadership that could mediate and negotiate what the revolution should look like in real terms.

In any event, the revolutionary camp departed the scene of popular mobilisation and the military took control of the political arena. If the revolutionaries could argue that their revolution had had popular support (to the extent that the revolution demanded the departure of Mubarak they were correct), the army could point to a new legal document that saw a vast majority of Egyptian voters in agreement—along with the popular support that the military had for itself. The legitimacy of the revolutionary camp might continue in certain respects—but without vast popular support, it would not mean very much in a political sense. In the Egyptian context, revolutionary change required an underpinning of popular support—even a level of support that could approach a popular consensus.

Of course, had the military leadership, led by Field Marshal Muhammad Hussain Tantawi, genuinely wanted to steer the country into a series of reforms, this would have been the perfect time to do so. The military was, in and of itself, tremendously popular and a revolutionary fervour was still in the air after a very popular uprising. The military could have engaged, quickly and easily, in a consensus-based roadmap. It could have been a roadmap that put a reform dynamic into the heart of Egyptian politics and it would still have preserved much of its popular capital. But there was no indication that that was what the military wanted to do.

IV

The constitutional referendum was a milestone. It is the key in understanding how, in the aftermath of the uprising, so much of its potential to change the Egyptian state was lost. The military did not simply put the amendments into effect. It took the opportunity to make further changes to ensure the SCAF was empowered further, with the SCAF regarding itself as the executive and legislative branch of the country at one and the same time. None of this served widespread reform—on the contrary.

It did have a great deal of popular support to back it up, though. While the vast majority of the revolutionary camp still believed in political mobilisation in the shape of protests to effect further change, this became a remarkably unpopular strategy among the broad majority of the Egyptian public.[6] The Muslim Brotherhood (MB), the most organised political force in the country and one that had not been associated with the Mubarak regime, was also not interested in rocking the boat with the military. It made its own strategic calculations, and aligned itself with the military roadmap. It had good reason to.

In the absence of genuine democratic institutions, independent political parties and a fully fledged civil society, the MB had good tactical reasons to associate itself with the military's roadmap. For decades, the MB had built up social capital in Egypt's most needy areas through a variety of social welfare programmes. Different Salafi contingents had done the same on a smaller scale. The MB hoped to take that social capital and convert it into political capital, and it succeeded.

In Chapter 2 we saw that the MB increased their level of support among Egyptians from 12 per cent in April 2011 to 50 per cent by the end of the year. Most of that increase resulted from those who had previously been undecided about the MB swinging behind them.[7] The shift was unsurprising since, apart from the Salafi welfare and religious groups, no other subsection of Egyptian society had invested so much time and effort on the ground. No other group had the social capital that could then be converted into political capital. That was to the credit of the MB. It had been extensively active on the ground for a long time. But it also meant that support for it was not the result of deeply held ideological or political beliefs. It was conditional; it was predicated on the expectation that the MB could deliver.

When Gallup analysed its polling numbers from 2011, it found that voters across the board—whether they voted for the MB, the main Salafi Nour ('Light') Party, or the deeply anti-MB party of the Free Egyptians—all focused on the same priorities. All of these priorities had to do with general, basic, bread-and-butter issues, such as jobs, the economy and security. None of them had anything to do with overtly Islamist agendas.

V

The peak of the MB's popularity came in early spring 2012. If some 50 per cent of the population expressed confidence in it by the beginning of the 2011–12 parliamentary elections, about two-thirds did so by early 2012. That was the peak of the popularity of the MB in Egypt— from a respectable 12 per cent in spring 2011, to a massive 66 per cent a year later.[8] But all good things must come to an end, and while many will no doubt point to Mursi's eviction from power in 2013 as the turning point in the fortunes of the MB, the reality is that it began much earlier than that.

No one quite knows why the MB began to lose its popularity. The only theory that seems to have much validity is that the new parliament, with a MB plurality, finally sat in early 2012 and was immediately the subject of controversy owing to its lacklustre performance. Parliamentary sessions were aired on television and the parliamentarians did not acquit themselves well in the eyes of the Egyptian public. These elected representatives of the people were not occupied, it appeared, with urgent issues concerning the faltering economy. Instead, the media reported on inane debates such as one about whether or not to have the call to prayer inside parliament.[9] MB MPs were not solely responsible, but as members of the largest party they often bore the brunt of the blame.

Prior to the parliamentary elections, the MB courted the public in order to gain its goodwill in votes. After the elections, it withdrew back into its own shell. When it had seemed clear that the protest movement in 2011 was a force to be reckoned with, the MB had thrown its lot in with it. But when Mubarak was evicted from the presidential palace, the MB had gone its own way, and had shown little interest in engaging seriously with the revolutionary forces that had made those protests possible. While most of the revolutionary forces had recognised the flaws in the military-led roadmap of March 2011, the MB had embraced the roadmap, and encouraged voters to see the referendum in terms of religion, with a 'yes' vote being a vote in support of religion and a 'no' vote being a rejection of religion.

The MB, as an organisation, has been a gradualist one for most of its existence. It has usually played the long-term, rather than the short-term, game. At the same time its gradualism has never translated into pluralism. Its focus on the 'long-term game' has not meant that it would be willing to engage in broad coalition-building to bring about a genuinely pluralistic democratic system in Egypt.

Had it been interested in that, the MB might have collaborated with pro-revolutionary forces in 2011, and lobbied against the military council's roadmap. Such an alliance would have been deeply threatening to the SCAF's plans. Had the MB been focused on a broadly pluralistic framework, it would not have expelled young, more progressive cadres simply because they wanted to join political parties that were not the official, mandated Freedom and Justice Party (FJP).

As spring unfolded in 2012, the presidential elections grew closer. The MB had previously declared it would not run a presidential candidate, and had expelled a more liberal-leaning MB leader, Abu al-Futuh, after he announced that he would run for the presidency. But, having originally claimed that it would only run for 30 per cent[10] of the parliamentary seats, it and its coalition partners ended up winning 48 per cent of seats. Similarly, as the elections drew nearer, the MB, claiming an inability to find a suitable non-MB 'patriot' to run for the presidency, announced that it would run Khairat al-Shater, the movement's Deputy Supreme Guide, as its own candidate.

The decision to run Shater was not taken lightly, and when it finally was taken it was due to a narrow vote in the MB's Guidance Council, the top executive authority, and not the FJP itself. That vote had been taken twice before, and both times it had been decided not to run a candidate. Meanwhile, the FJP had its own leadership committee, and it too had consistently voted against running a presidential candidate. But in the end, the party was overruled by the movement, which only confirmed to Egyptians at large that it remained a MB instrument.

Khairat al-Shater was one of the MB's most powerful members, dubbed by many as the 'MB's enforcer'.[11] Described as the 'power behind the throne' and a 'multi-millionaire'[12] with extensive business interests, he was also one of its most conservative and reactionary members, with wide alliances among Salafi groups, and an admirer of Sayyid Qutb. He was part of the core of the internal MB contingent that had outlawed the pluralistic trend of the organisation, and expelled notables like Abu al-Futuh.

However, Shater had been in jail for years in the run-up to the uprising, a victim of Mubarak's regime, and a recent prison record was sure to disqualify him from running as a presidential candidate. As the MB became aware that Shater would be disqualified, it announced a second presidential candidate as a back-up: Muhammad Mursi, the head of the FJP. MB stalwarts argued in the run-up to the presidential election of 2012 and afterwards that they were forced to run Shater and Mursi, in spite of the promises previously made about not running a presidential candidate. Indeed, Shater himself had publicly denied any intention to run when he was interviewed by his friend, Al Jazeera journalist Ahmad Mansur.[13]

But it wasn't true that the MB couldn't have stuck to its original pledge. There was a candidate they could have backed and supported with little difficulty. This was Abd al-Mun'im Abu al-Futuh, one of the most prominent left-leaning and reformist members of the MB's top brass, who had been expelled from the organisation after undertaking to run in the presidential race. In truth, he had been marginalised for quite a while by the conservative wing of the MB, particularly the more Qutbian part of it.

Though there was tremendously bad blood between him and the MB leadership, it was also true that Abu al-Futuh was hardly someone that the MB had to fear in the event of a victory. It was unlikely he would lead a charge against the MB—this was the organisation he had spent most of his life in. Politically, Abu al-Futuh and the MB might have found themselves in different camps. But if the misgivings of the MB were predicated on the notion that a former regime stalwart would win the presidential election if they didn't run a candidate, this could have been dealt with by backing Abu al-Futuh. It was the most basic element of pragmatic party politics, but the MB failed to do it. As it turned out, Abu al-Futuh came in fourth, not even making it to the runoff race, in part due to his lack of organisational muscle. But this result was also perhaps due to the reality that in such a transitional process the 'extremes' usually win—and this is most certainly what happened in the Egyptian case.

In other words, if a rethink was necessary, as the MB argued it was, then surely it would have been better for Egypt, as well as the MB, to simply back an existing presidential candidate whose roots were in Islamism, such as Abu al-Futuh. Just for the sake of argument, one can only imagine what it might have done for politics in Egypt if the MB had backed a candidate with revolutionary credentials like Abu al-Futuh. There could have been a restoration of the alliance between religious and non-religious forces. But instead of building a consensus through an ecumenical coalition to repair Egypt's fractures, the MB opted to go it alone and seek power for itself.[14]

VI

I remember the day of the first round of presidential elections, on 23 May 2012. I was sitting in a cafeteria with friends, including an architect and a businessman. They were in their thirties, and were a motley crew in terms of presidential preferences. All of us had been optimistic about the revolutionary uprising, and we were wondering who would make it into the second round. The businessman was from the economic elite of Egyptian society—yet, unlike many of his peers, had been disgusted by the corruption that surrounded him in his professional world. He had opted to back Abu al-Futuh, not out of any particular sympathies to Islamism (he wasn't even a conservative, to say the least), but because he reckoned the man could be trusted.

I was convinced that Amr Moussa,[15] Mubarak's former foreign minister, and former secretary general of the Arab League, was a shoe-in to get into the next round. I think everyone around the table agreed with me. There was, of course, another former regime stalwart—a *felool* (leftover) candidate, as it were—Ahmad Shafiq, Mubarak's last prime minister, who had been appointed to crush the uprising in 2011. But given the name-recognition of Moussa, who constantly topped Gallup polls in 2011 and 2012 as the front-runner in the presidential race, and who had carefully cultivated a media profile that sought not to anger or attack the military in any significant fashion, I assumed he was the chosen candidate of the SCAF. So, apparently, did he.[16]

A few years later, I spoke with one of Moussa's confidantes. He confirmed that Moussa had, indeed, firmly believed that the military leadership would back his bid for the presidency, even though Field Marshal Tantawi and he had never been on good terms. The insider hadn't been convinced, but Moussa remained resolute. It wasn't until about ten days before the presidential election that the confidante received word that the Coptic Orthodox Church had decided, privately, to back Ahmad Shafiq for the presidency, rather than Moussa, who had been sure about their support. The confidante spoke with contacts within the church, and they confided to him that they had received instructions: the military wanted Ahmad Shafiq to win. Moussa never made it into the second round: he came in fifth, after Abu al-Futuh. The leftist candidate, Hamdeen Sabahi, came in third—a great surprise, and a testament to the grassroots support he managed to cultivate, in spite of being critical of the Egyptian military.

In that café that day, with the out-of-town guest, the architect and the businessman, we started pondering nightmare options. It was said: 'imagine if Mursi and Shafiq make it into the second round'.

It was the doomsday scenario none of us wanted to contemplate, and we nervously scoffed and rejected it as even a possibility. Despite that, one of us pushed the question: 'Okay, it's really unlikely—but if it were to happen, what would you do?'

Someone said: 'Oh, I'd probably shoot myself.'

The choice between a reactionary representative of the right-wing Islamist MB movement, and the most prominent pro-Mubarak candidate, was one that none of us even fathomed was likely. But it is precisely that choice the Egyptian people made. For alongside the post-revolution euphoria, Shafiq's appeal reflected the fears of many Egyptians over what a post-Mubarak era might mean, especially one with the Brotherhood in a prominent position. He craftily cast himself as the experienced political and military insider ready to work with Egypt's generals and put the country back on track, fast. With the old rules seemingly gone, Egypt's extremes—embodied by Mursi and Shafiq—thrived.

VII

What happened in the run-up to and the conclusion of the 2012 presidential election is tremendously important for understanding the faults and flaws of the Egyptian political elite. It also speaks volumes about the revolutionary camp as well—but we will turn to that shortly.

With the second round of presidential elections set for late-June 2012, Mursi and the MB went about looking for additional support in order to offset the support Shafiq had. In round one, Mursi had received 25 per cent of the vote. Shafiq was only 1 per cent behind him. Abu al-Futuh quickly directed his voting block (which came to 17 per cent) to back Mursi in round two.[17] Those who backed Sabahi or Moussa didn't receive any such direction, as calls for boycotts to delegitimise the election grew. 'A return to the old regime is unacceptable, [and] so is exploiting religion in politics', Moussa told reporters after the runoff was announced.[18] But the elections went on.

Mursi's efforts culminated in a famed meeting at the Fairmont Hotel in northern Cairo, where a press conference was held with him flanked by a number of non-Islamist, pro-revolutionary activists. The so-called 'Fairmont Group'[19] included the likes of Wael Ghonim, the administrator of the 'We are all Khalid Sa'id' Facebook group; Ahmad Maher, one of the founders of the April 6 Youth Movement; writer Alaa al-Aswany; and Constitution Party member, Shadi al-Ghazali Harb. Their support for Mursi did not come without conditions, which included guarantees from Mursi to pursue revolutionary goals and to form a national salvation government that included representatives from all political forces, headed by an independent political figure. Mursi agreed, but how much he actually fulfilled these pledges after taking office is questionable, to say the least. Suggestions of a female vice-president and a Coptic vice-president, for example, were never taken up once Mursi entered the presidency. Nevertheless, he had a good proportion of the revolutionary camp's support, though there were those who boycotted the whole process altogether, finding themselves unable to back either Mursi or Shafiq.

There was great irony in this second round, because both candidates were depending on the unpopularity of the other to win. Had Mursi faced off against any other candidate in round two, the other candidate would have likely won; and the same is true of Shafiq. The two candidates contributed to a perfect polarisation: probably around half of each voting block voted for their candidate not because they supported him, but because they so opposed the other candidate.

On 24 June 2012, following the second round, the election commission declared that Mursi had won 51.7 per cent of the vote compared to Shafiq's 48.3 per cent.[20] In the months that followed—indeed, for several years—the outcome was the subject of great controversy. Shafiq supporters insisted that he had really won, but that the military had allowed the MB to win out of fear of the consequences if they didn't, alleging collusion between the military, the Brotherhood, and the election commission. Shafiq filed an appeal in 2012 against the general prosecutor contesting the results, which was dismissed in 2014, the year after Mursi had been removed from office.[21]

The story of the election is complicated. It is true that the MB threatened chaos if Mursi was not declared as president. They had positioned election observers all around the country and were convinced that Mursi had won. Insiders at some of the highest levels of the country's political establishment admitted that there were a number of electoral violations that took place at the hands of both the Mursi campaign and the Shafiq campaign. The question was: did those violations mean Shafiq had actually won—and if so, why wasn't he declared president?

It is unlikely that we will ever know since the relevant official commission never fully investigated all the alleged violations, and the records may not even exist anymore. It is entirely plausible that the final tally, after considering the violations, would have confirmed Mursi as president—but it is also possible that the winner might have turned out to be Shafiq. The Egyptian state wasn't interested in pursuing the enquiry, however. It had other imperatives to consider.

Those imperatives were domestic and international. Domestically, the MB was understandably incensed by the notion that the election could be taken away from it. On the face of the numbers released, it had won. It wouldn't take denial of victory lying down. But there was also an international dimension. According to insiders in Egypt and Western diplomatic establishments, a number of prominent Western governments sent a clear private message to the Egyptian military that Mursi should be in the presidential palace. They would not brook any further investigation into the results. Such an investigation would have had dubious credibility in any case. Accordingly, the military council opted to confirm Mursi as president.

A *Guardian* reporter, Abdel Rahman Hussain, was interviewed just before the results were announced. He captured a great deal of the nuance of what was happening:

> This is the most hotly anticipated press conference in Egyptian history. Any further delay is not good for our hearts and our minds.

> The speculation is intense, every hour it changes. Now it looks like Mursi is winning.

> There have been reports that the MB have been locked in negotiations with the army. The election result hinges on negotiations not voting. I think Mursi is possibly going to be named the president today, and for that to happen they are going to have to give up on [the dissolved] parliament and the constitution.

> If Shafiq wins all hell breaks loose. It is going to be a very visceral, very strong reaction. It's going to be very big, and very negative, and not just by the MB. For all revolutionary forces to see Shafiq assume the presidency a year and half after you've ousted his boss is a bitter pill to swallow.

> Don't be surprise[d] if they say the rerun will have to be redone, or if they annul the results entirely. We would have to start over and start with the

constitution this time and then parliamentary elections and presidential election.[22]

One has to keep in mind that only days before the second round of the presidential election, the SCAF had already issued decrees that would sharply curtail the powers of the president. Tantawi wasn't going to endorse a president who would have full presidential powers. He wanted one who he could share authority with. At least, this is how it appeared he was thinking in late June 2012, particularly in light of the Supreme Constitutional Court's decision to dissolve the recently elected post-2011 parliament in the weeks between the first- and second-round votes, obstructing the route towards a clear separation of powers and delegation of legislative and executive authority. In any case, Muhammad Mursi became Egypt's first democratically elected civilian president on 30 June 2012. And, like Tantawi, Mursi was not destined to last long.

VIII

The MB's political shortsightedness meant they had lost the chance to back a candidate who would have brought much of the country together, rather than polarising it. It wasn't the only one guilty of polarisation. Clearly, the backers of the former regime and the military establishment were unlikely to be concerned with promoting positive change, and these forces undeniably held more cards than the MB, and many of them did what they could to sustain the Mubarak status quo. But the revolutionary camp, distinct from the pro and anti-MB cadres, should have been far more strategically astute.

In 2011 a fledgling movement of activists had accomplished in a few days more than the Egyptian opposition had in decades. Their theoretical perspective, though imprecise, became manifest through popular mobilisation. With that, the revolutionaries were able to fundamentally disrupt the workings of the state, forcing the removal of Mubarak. At the same time, they also missed the opportunity to properly harness and develop their power.

The same year, when the military's transitional roadmap was put to a referendum, the revolutionaries had considerable political capital. That capital, however, was not exploited. This is because the revolutionaries mobilised for a 'no' vote, but as mentioned earlier, did not provide much in the way of a plausible alternative. The result was that they lost the vote. Their failure to properly express a well-developed political vision meant they missed a key opportunity to set the agenda of the post-Mubarak period.

In the meantime, street protests continued to define the revolutionary forces. On 9 October 2011, Egyptian military vehicles, in an act that was broadcast on national television, ran over and struck with live ammunition twenty-nine Coptic Christians, who were among thousands peacefully marching through Cairo's streets in protest against recent attacks on churches. The protestors, a mixture of Copts and Muslims, were also marching together against decades of politicised sectarianism used to keep Egyptians divided.[23] As the gruesome scenes of military vehicles running over citizens unfolded on the nation's screens, one television anchor notoriously called on Egyptians to go out and protect the military.[24]

The Maspero massacre, as it became known, marked a dark turn in the exploitation of religious divides that Tahrir's pluralism had transcended. The revolutionaries struggled to build consensus across confessional divisions, with the military, the Brotherhood, and the wheels of the Egyptian state seemingly aligned against them. Maspero was also followed by a series of violent clashes between Egyptian security forces and various pro-revolutionary protesters: the Muhammad Mahmoud clashes in November and the Port Said massacre of 'Ultras' (organised groups of sports fans) in February, which both left the protesters weakened and increased the public's appetite for promises of stability.

By the spring of 2012, as previously noted, the revolutionaries had another option: that of coalescing around a single candidate for the presidential elections. It is likely that such a candidate would have prevailed. Instead, the revolutionary vote was split between Sabahi and Abu al-Futuh, allowing Mursi and Shafiq to prevail. Some will claim the revolutionaries played a critical role in the subsequent runoff by ensuring that the former regime candidate lost. That is true, but surely the very occurrence of such an abysmal runoff would have been impossible had there been a single, pro-25-January–revolution candidate.

There were those who tried to convince pro-revolutionary presidential candidates to unite under a single banner in order to ensure the revolutionary vote would not be split. But in the cacophony of the post-revolution fervour, neither Sabahi nor Abu al-Futuh—each with their own strong brand as Mubarak-critics and political reformers—united or stepped aside to allow the other to go it alone.[25] Had this happened, one of them would have certainly made it into the second round to face off against Mursi or Shafiq. If that had been the scenario, I do think the pro-revolutionary candidate would have won, and Egypt might have been spared much of the polarisation that followed.

IX

In any sustainable democracy, the institutions of governance ought to be able to take a few knocks. Regardless of who might rule for this presidential period or that, the institutions should be able to persevere, allowing the basic structures to remain in place.

The same fluidity, though, that allowed for a revolutionary uprising in 2011—and could have allowed substantial reform in 2011–12—had a darker side to it. It meant that inside the state and the former Mubarak establishment, there were still immensely powerful forces that were dedicated to ensuring a continuity of another kind—and the flux of political energies allowed them to succeed. Their aim was to maintain as much of the status quo as they could, rather than accede to a changing political framework. If this was at the expense of genuine political pluralism and a just social contract, then so be it.

In the early months of the revolution, the revolutionary camp, the MB and other political forces demanding change had the organisational ability—if acting in concert—to push back against that strikingly counter-revolutionary alliance. The system was weak at the beginning of the revolution. There was a popular mandate for the military to get the country back on track. But it seems that no one who had sufficient political clout, whether from the military or the MB, was that invested in serious transformation.

The military sought to protect their privileged position within the Egyptian state. That is why they so very easily allowed the parliament that had been voted into office in 2011 to be judicially dismissed in 2012. There were genuine legal reasons for that dismissal, but the pace at which it was disbanded indicated that political imperatives were at work as opposed to merely or only legal ones. The MB, on the other hand, simply appeared to much of the Egyptian populace of wanting to replace the Mubarak layer of leadership with their own, and did not give the impression of wanting to change the state beyond that. As for the revolutionaries, they had neither the influence nor the organisa-tional unity (since they were acting in isolation from one another) to develop things any further.

In the absence of those institutions that would hold firmly to values of democracy and rule of law regardless of any particular leadership, there was a need to establish a consensus. The revolutionaries called this process the establishment of 'revolutionary legitimacy'. However, once presidential elections had taken place, revolutionary legitimacy came to an end. The transfer of power from a political leadership that rode into governance on the back of an uprising—the SCAF—took effect, and a democratically elected president, with all the warts and woes this implied, was now in office.

The MB opted to believe that the election of Mursi meant he'd inherited the legacy of revolutionary legitimacy. That belief, in part, led to the overturning of his presidency a year later.

X

The MB was not wrong to continually raise the spectre of a 'deep state' that was working to undo Egypt's post-Mubarak transition. That was a reality, and only the ignorant or the collaborator would have insisted otherwise. But the response of the MB and Mursi was completely counter-productive when it came to dealing with that very threat.

The pro-Mubarak forces that wished to turn back the clock were left in disarray after the uprising. When parliamentary elections took place later in 2011 they generally stayed out of them. There were some excep-tions, but the large networks that underpinned Mubarak's regime decided not to throw their weight behind participating. When it came to the presidential election of 2012, a year or so after the uprising took place, those same networks were not only ready to throw their collective hat into the ring, but they were well prepared and equipped to do so.

In the spring of 2012, I met a well-to-do entrepreneur in the upper-class neighbourhood of Zamalek, just west of the centre of Cairo. Based on the polling numbers that I had seen from Gallup, I knew that the majority of Egyptian voters were undecided about who they would vote for. I also knew that among those who were decided, Moussa topped the ballot—likely due to his name recognition. I still thought at the time he would be the most likely victor in any presidential election. My friend, the entrepreneur, had a different opinion altogether.

'I've been going out of Cairo a lot, and I'm seeing Shafiq posters everywhere. I think the National Democratic Party [of Mubarak] is back. Shafiq is their guy', he said.

My response was that I thought the military wouldn't be so foolish as to support a candidate so clearly connected to Mubarak's regime. How could such a candidate possibly win? Surely, it would be far more sensible for the military to back Moussa, a figure who was sufficiently comfortable with the establishment to not cause alarm?

'Mark my words. Shafiq is going to surprise us', he replied.

He was right. Shafiq did surprise us—but so did the MB. If any other candidate had faced off with Shafiq, that candidate would have won. But, against Mursi in the second round, Shafiq could count on the anti-Islamist vote, which represented a sector of the Egyptian citizenry that had grown fearful of the MB.

The outcome of that election should have taught the MB some lessons about the nature of the post-uprising political arena, and about what was required in this rather extraordinary set of circumstances in order for any reform project to succeed. The election showed that that given the choice in an open election, more than three-quarters of voters would choose non-MB candidates, and that in a showdown between the MB and the former regime, just one year after Mubarak was pushed out of office, nearly half of voters would choose the former regime. That should have shown the MB the modest level of its popularity, and demonstrated the threat that straight counter-revolutionary forces could pose it, not only in the institutions of the state, but in terms of popular appeal.

The MB learned none of these lessons. It blindly accepted that the democratic process had put it into power, and it acted in victory as though Egypt was a fully developed democratic state with institutions that were wholly loyal to the democratic process. That contributed greatly to the MB's downfall. For it to have successfully circumvented anti-democratic forces, it would have had to know how to act in a consensus-based fashion, so as to marginalise those forces. It would have had to recognise that the victory that brought Mursi to power in June 2012 was razor thin, and therefore try to widen its popular base, particularly with the pro-revolutionary forces that had helped to propel him into office. None of that happened. But in retrospect, and perhaps speaking cynically, it was unrealistic to expect it from the MB.

Before the Egyptian revolution began, the MB was a civil-society movement. But then the leadership had to choose whether or not to transform the movement into a political party. Its decision to become a political party had massive repercussions for its future, as well as those of Egypt's political sphere and Muslim communities worldwide.[26]

It was inevitable that MB members would enter into politics in some fashion after Tahrir. But the way they did so in 2011 and early 2012 created tensions within the organisation. Electoral politics means difficult choices, which social movements can avoid. Just the act of forming a political party involved controversy and the subsequent narrowing down of the MB. As noted previously, its leadership insisted that any member who wanted to be involved in politics had to be part of its newly formed FJP—otherwise, they would be expelled. That was a clear message: the MB was no longer a movement, it was a government-in-waiting that demanded loyalty to a small clique—and as such it would frown upon internal dissent.

The decision to transform into a political party came at a price. The MB had been founded on religious grounds decades ago. It had inspired other groups in the Arab world, as well those as within Muslim communities farther afield. The underlying assumption behind its popularity had been its claim to the moral high ground, which was obviously easier to maintain when it was the underdog.

The FJP, on the other hand, was not established as a movement or an opposition force—it was founded to govern. It received the lion's share of seats in both houses of parliament, it dominated the new constitutional assembly, and it took the presidency. It was on its way to power much faster than most had assumed was possible—although no one could have foreseen its eventual reversal in fortunes.

But even in 2012 people wondered what the cost to the MB's reputation would be of its pursuit of political power. Both by breaking its early promise not to contest more than 30 per cent of parliamentary seats, and by summarily expelling Fotouh and other figures, it had not scored many points.

But real discontent was not apparent until the MB entered parliament. It had given assurances that it would not form alliances with the Salafis, a group largely represented by the Noor Party. But expediency overruled those assurances when a collaboration did take place to secure a predominantly Islamist Constitutional Assembly. When the MB then reneged on a further pledge not to field a presidential nominee (by running not one, but two candidates), their credibility took another hit. But those moves, we should remind ourselves, were entirely inkeeping with the impulse of the FJP. It was not created to further the revolution, but primarily to fill the political gap left by Mubarak.

One of the consequences was felt immediately in the form of internal tensions within the MB in 2012. Kamal al-Halbawi[27] a former MB spokesman in Europe, resigned, and other famous Islamists criticised the decision, including Qatar-based Yusuf Al Qaradawi, the movement's most influential living ideologue. There were consequences beyond the Egyptian MB too. The Syrian MB, for example, wanted to play a role in Syria, and found its credibility damaged as a result of events in Egypt from 2012–2013. Tunisia's Ennahdha Party had been far more strategically nimble, but its opponents also began pointing to the mother movement in Egypt to attack its credibility.

Opponents of Islamist movements from all over the world, Muslim or not, tended to view the MB's manoeuvres as a departure point to claim that Islamist projects were, intrinsically, unethical and dangerous. Islamophobes and anti-Muslim writers had already gone to town on the 'double talk' of Muslims generally, and now intensified their criticism when it came to the MB in particular. These kinds of broad-stroke arguments, however, tend to fall apart when faced with the wide range of political projects, parties and programmes that have fallen under the MB banner and its (though, historically, non-mainstream) interpretation of and approach to Islam.

For decades, pro-Islamist movements in North America and Europe had been active in civil society and had engaged in positive ways with society at large. Their activism had aimed to bring good to people on the ground; seeking power had been the furthest thing from their minds. As early as the spring of 2012, due to the MB in Egypt and Hamas in Gaza in 2006, that aim had been fundamentally challenged. Ideologically speaking, the ground had shifted. As for the MB in Egypt, it had made its fateful decision—and so began Mursi's eventful year in power.

PART 2

REAPING THE HARVEST WITHOUT SOWING THE SEED

4

DEMOCRACY, ISLAMISM AND ISLAM

Religion as merchandise? That's an equal opportunity affair in Egypt. Pretty much everyone does it. Not sure it's entirely edifying for religion or believers—but there you go.

Cairene coffee-shop philosopher

I

On 24 April 2012, I arrived at the American University in Cairo's 'new' campus. For some reason, years after the university moved most of its facilities and departments to this 'New Cairo' suburb, to the east of Cairo proper, Cairenes still persist in calling the campus 'new'. Some 20 kilometres to the northwest, the 'new' terminal of Cairo Airport is still described as such, though it has been open for business since 2009.

The 'new' campus of AUC is a bit of a trek for anyone living in Cairo itself, and I've not been there many times. But that day was something of a special occasion: there was a debate scheduled that included Alaa Abd al-Fattah, Sultan Sooud al-Qassemi, Sa'ad al-Zant, Gamal Nassar and Shawki al-Sayyid. The whole event was memorable, but I will always remember it for one particular reaction from a member of the audience.

Rawya Rageh—who, until recently, was the excellent correspondent for Al Jazeera English—moderated the debate.[1] At the time, she was a Cairo-based reporter for that channel—in 2012 Al Jazeera English was truly respected when it came to Egyptian affairs (and was one on which I appeared frequently). It only took a year or so for the reputation of the channel to change tremendously inside the country, and for the Egyptian authorities to treat it with a disdain and fury that led to several Al Jazeera English journalists being imprisoned in the midst of a conflict with Qatar—but I digress. Rawya hosted the debate with poise and grace.

The five panellists were interesting, of course. One of them, Alaa Abd al-Fattah, is an activist icon of the youth of the 25 January revolutionary camp, and is now in jail, serving time for breaking a phenomenally unjust 2013 protest law.[2] At the debate, he was full of energy, passion and commitment to the fulfilment of the 25 January revolution. The last time I saw Alaa was at the 'azza (condolences reception) for his father, Ahmad Seif, a huge figure in the civil rights community. I write these words a few days after the first anniversary of his passing. A book deserves to be written on the struggles of this activist family: Ahmad Seif, Alaa Abd al-Fattah, Mona Seif, Sana Seif (Alaa's younger sister, also in jail at present on absurd charges), and Leila Soueif… the list goes on.[3]

Just before the event, I went to greet Alaa and Sultan al-Qassemi in the green room. Sultan and I are good friends, having first become acquainted through the revolution. In Twitterati terms, Sultan is a basha—an Egyptian aristocratic lord—who shot to prominence through his thousands of tweets and updates during the revolutionary uprisings. Sultan was from the United Arab Emirates (UAE), which was bypassed by the revolutionary wave. More than that, he was an aristocrat. His family, the al-Qassimi family, rules one of the emirates of the UAE, Sharjah. Sultan was an Emirati—Emirati royalty—but while his body might have been in the UAE, his heart was nurtured in Tahrir Square in 2011, even from a distance. I frankly worried that it would eventually get him into trouble. But like so many of this generation—our generation—of Arabs, he saw and recognised a spark in that square—and he let it set him on fire. To have done otherwise would have been a kind of betrayal.

I did not know the other three panellists particularly. One of them, Shawqi al-Sayyid, was the ex-deputy chairman of the Shura Council;

another, Sa'ad al-Zant, was the director of a think-tank. Neither particularly impressed me, to be frank: al-Zant struck a friend of mine as particularly cosy with the military establishment. He was right.

But at some point during the debate, something very poignant happened. Gamal Nassar, a supporter of the Muslim Brotherhood (MB) and one-time director of its public relations arm, was making the case that the Islamist group had not 'hijacked the revolution'. Even as early as April 2012, there had been many who had made that claim—not opponents of the revolution, but rather, its supporters. For them, the MB had jumped on the revolutionary bandwagon when it became clear it could be used for political mobility and the strengthening of its own power base.

After Nassar spoke, a member of the audience, a young man with a trimmed beard sitting next to a woman in a hijab, stood up and began to aggressively cajole Nassar for what he claimed was essentially selling out the revolution for partisan political gain. When he wound up his comments, the man angrily concluded: 'And this is why we call the MB "the merchants of religion" [*tujjar al-din*], and the "Brotherhood of Liars" [*ikhwan al-kazibun*, a play on the name of the Brotherhood in Arabic].'

Nassar was furious—and, to be fair, the young man's comments had been ill-mannered. But I remember that day very well. I didn't speak to Nassar afterwards, but his detractor's comments weren't atypical of those who had historically been antipathetic to the MB, or religion, in any form, in politics. On the contrary, they typified the attitude of many I knew in Egypt who were openly religiously committed, yet who grew to oppose the MB not on a doctrinaire level, but a political one. This important point raises a number of questions.

II

This theme of the role of religion and Islamism in politics has played out in a rather different way beyond Egypt's borders. The man who challenged Nassar was an Egyptian Muslim living in a Muslim-majority society, engaging with Islamism as part of his political reality; those outside Egypt have often approached the issue differently.

In early January 2014, a British journalist, whose work I had greatly respected, decided he wanted to come to Cairo. He'd started writing a few comment pieces on Egypt after Mursi had been removed from power by General Abd al-Fattah al-Sisi, and I met him in London mid-September 2013. I advised him that if he was going to continue writing about Egypt, he probably ought to visit the country. I'd already seen one or two pieces by him that suggested to me that this might be in order.

This journalist was a rather good conversationalist and I enjoyed talking to him. He had the right instincts around notions pertaining to Islamophobia and anti-Muslim sentiment in the UK, although at times I wondered if his beliefs about citizenship and diversity were not more conservative than progressive. Nevertheless, it seemed clear that he harboured remarkably hostile views to neo-conservatives and much of the right-wing in British politics.

But when it came to interpreting the Arab world, it seemed my visitor was bound to frames of reference that worked well in the UK when it came to Islamophobia, but not particularly well in relation to the Arab region. In the West, Islamophobia was fairly simple to define: there was a minority group, 'the Muslims', who received discriminatory treatment on the basis of adhering to a religion, 'Islam', from members of the majority, 'non-Muslims', who disliked or mistrusted what they perceived to be 'Islam'. This is a broad summary of what Islamophobia[4] is commonly perceived to be, without delving into more philosophical discussions around whether the term 'anti-Muslim sentiment' should be used instead of 'Islamophobia'.

However, that kind of referential frame is much less useful when applied to the politics of the Arab world or any Muslim community that exists as a majority. This particular journalist seemed more or less convinced that the MB was being subjected to a crack-down in Egypt due to its being Muslim—that it was being subjected to a broad-based 'Islamophobic' onslaught. In this framework, 'the Muslims' in Egypt were the MB; its persecutors and opponents were 'the non-Muslims' who harboured a distrust of 'Islam'.

Of course, that is a rather odd assumption. While the members of the MB are most certainly Muslims, the vast majority of Muslims in Egypt (around 85–90 per cent of the population) are neither MB members nor supporters. Nearly all of its Egyptian opponents are also Muslims, and are often religiously conservative themselves. The opposition to the MB was political, based on power dynamics—it wasn't necessarily a rejection of 'Islam'.

Now in Cairo, as we walked down the narrow streets in the market of Khan al-Khalili, passing a plethora of Muslim shopkeepers who had backed mostly non- or anti-Islamist political forces in 2011–12, I mentioned something casually to my journalist friend. He was asking me about Salafis, and their own political stances in Egypt, before and after the military removed Mursi.

'They're somewhat split,' I told him: 'some of them—indeed, likely most of the rank and file—supported the pro-Mursi sit-ins after the coup; others decided to go with the military. It's not a foregone conclusion that religious conservative Muslims in Egypt will automatically be pro-MB or, indeed, pro-Islamist in general.' When I added that nearly all the opposition to the MB in Egypt came from Muslims, my guest stopped in his tracks and turned to me. 'That's a really good point, you know. A really good point!'

He seemed a bit stunned by what I had said, as though no one had quite had that idea before. From my vantage point, I was stunned that he had thought otherwise; but that kind of confusion about the differences between Islam and support for specific forms of Islamism is not at all rare in contemporary discourse. My journalist acquaintance from London had expressed that confusion in one way—and the young revolutionary activist in the American University in Cairo had exposed it for the confusion that it was.

III

There will be those who dislike the use of the words 'Islamism' and 'Islamist' for a number of reasons—mostly because they suspect it is a code word for 'Islam', and a way to express Islamophobia without being criticised for bigotry. There is, however, a conundrum, and that is that Islamists themselves regularly use the term 'Islamist', especially in Arabic. For my British journalist friend, as he strode through Cairo, it was almost instinctive for him to see Islamism as simply 'Islam in politics'. There are a number of problematic issues to unpack contained in that assertion.

Islam does not have a church-like structure. There is no ecclesiastical, hierarchical authoritative structure in Islam; the religion has no institution corresponding to the Catholic Church and the papacy, for example. There will be many who mistakenly consider Shaykh al-Azhar, the head of the Azhar establishment in Egypt, to be analogous to the pope. But his position is far more similar to the chair of the theology faculty at Oxford University—his is an academic position. Religious authority in Islam is often compared to the academic peer review system because, indeed, that's historically how it has worked out, and Islam contributed to the development of the modern academic system. Modern scholars, such as George Makdisi, have written a number of works deliberating over the origins of the Western 'college' and its relationship to Islamic educational modes.[5]

Islam has a number of different fields of study, and traditionally Muslim *'ulama* (religious scholars) have categorised those fields into three parts. These are based on a *hadith* (prophetic account) where the Archangel Gabriel encounters the Prophet, and asks him to 'tell me about Islam'; 'tell me about Iman'; and 'tell me about Ihsan'. Islam here refers to proper practice, and covers those Islamic disciplines related to correct action. *Iman* relates to theology and belief, and *Ihsan* refers to spirituality and the refinement of the soul.

For each of these fields, religious authority for Muslims has historically been constructed via sophisticated systems of knowledge transmission, referred to as the *sanad* by *'ulama*. The *sanad*, which is the actual transmission, contains within it a *silsila*—a chain of individuals that go from one generation to the next, back, as the system claims, to the Prophet himself. One who is deemed worthy of being included in the *sanad* is often presented with an *'ijaza* (license), which imbues such an individual with the authority to teach, with the full confidence he is transmitting his teachings not simply on the basis of his own understanding, but that of all those contained within the chain.

So Muslims have traditionally considered religious authority to be transmitted as the result of studying with an authorised, 'peer-reviewed' expert. The great educational institutions of Islam, such as al-Azhar in Egypt, the Qarawiyyin in Morocco, and the Qayrawan in Tunisia, were historically less like institutions than gathering places for individuals noted for their academic excellence. If a student came to those institutions, and was successful in his (or her) studies, they would receive a licence to teach; but that licence wouldn't represent the institution. It would represent the teacher, and therefore reflected a far more personalised pedagogy than modern university structures are wont to do.

That, then, is the system of education that underpins Islam. If there is a 'normative Islam', its source is, historically, the system of *sanad*.[6] But, as with most religions, Islam has also been subjected to a number of reformation exercises. They weren't terribly successful, since the system of *sanad* was difficult to dislodge, but they made their marks, albeit in different fashions.

The first 'reformation exercise' was carried out by Muhammad bin Abdul Wahhab and his students in the eighteenth century within the Najd region of the Arabian Peninsula.[7] The movement, which was aggressively opposed to much of what was considered to be permitted by mainstream Islamic thought, became known, usually pejoratively, as 'Wahhabism'. However, its followers ascribed themselves another label: 'Salafism'. The word 'Salafi', hitherto, had generally described an historical epoch—the early pious generations immediately after the Prophet. The Wahhabi or purist Salafi ('purist' to distinguish from other types of Salafis mentioned below) premise was simple: the vast majority of Muslims had gone astray, and needed to be theologically corrected by going back to 'basics'. 'Basics' here meaning a reduced and selective version of early Islam that sometimes spurned centuries of academic tradition. Needless to say, the vast majority of Muslims and *'ulama* took exception to that idea—an idea that sometimes resulted in grievous and violent repercussions. The first purist Salafis viewed themselves, and continue to view themselves, not as a conservative or especially pious tradition within a broader Muslim vanguard, but rather as the 'true Muslims' among a community that has strayed.

The ramifications of this have been tremendous, and certain developments in purist Salafi thought have found themselves as part of the ideological underpinnings of a number of radical groups in the twentieth and twenty-first centuries. That said, it is important to note that the majority of purist Salafis in the present era do not adhere to violent activity as a tool of political change—even though bin Abdul Wahhab and his followers did not seem to be particularly averse to that.

Among purist Salafis, there are a number of different groupings: quietist Madkhalis, more activist Sahawis, and others. In Egypt, the purist Salafi community formed a number of political parties after the

2011 revolutionary uprising, first and foremost among them being the Noor Party.

These so-called 'purist Salafis' are different from a more contemporary evolved Salafi movement, which is often described as 'modernist Salafism'. While the purists have their roots in eighteenth-century Najd, the 'modernist Salafis' have coalesced from more cosmopolitan milieus. Muhammad Abduh, an Egyptian scholar at al-Azhar at a time when al-Azhar was still reeling from the colonial era's effects on Egyptian education, was deeply influenced by the pan-Islamism of an Afghan figure, Jamal al-Din al-Afghani. Abduh had a particularly modernistic approach to the religious sciences, and relied heavily on nineteenth-century notions of rationalism.[9] Unlike the purist Salafi movement of nearby Arabia 100 years before, he wasn't particularly radical about the faith of his opponents in more mainstream and historically normative Sunni Muslim traditions. Abduh had a tremendous influence on a Syrian figure, Rashid Rida, who carried Abduh's project through publications after the latter's death.

The intellectual tradition of Abduh was met with great opposition from within the religious establishments in Egypt and Syria at the time. To use a clumsy comparison, the bulk of the *'ulama* often viewed modernist Salafism as a kind of Protestantism, feeling that it watered down the tradition of Islamic scholarship, and created epistemological problems in terms of the basis of Islamic thought rather than addressing issues of educational reform. The *ulama* would typically follow classical Sunnism, which was at the bedrock of the Azhari establishment in Egypt and the circles of learning in Syria, as well as the broad majority of the Muslim world at the beginning of the twentieth century.[10]

This type of modernistic approach to the Islamic tradition found its most prominent expression, however, in the politics of a schoolteacher by the name of Hasan al-Banna in Ismail'iyya in Egypt. His type of 'reformism' or 'modernist Salafism' was the origin of the religious thought of a famous religious movement in the twentieth century: the Muslim Brotherhood.

Al-Banna, the founder of the MB, came from a far more traditional Muslim background than one might assume, given his attraction to the works of Abduh and Rida, and the MB has certainly contained within it a number of different trends throughout its history. But one can also point to a number of different trends that flowed from Abduh himself: he inspired, for example, the early Egyptian nationalist figure, Sa'ad Zaghloul, as well as al-Banna. The latter himself inspired the likes of Sayyid Qutb, who wrote significant inflammatory treatises; but he also inspired far more liberal figures such as Hasan and Maher Hathout, the Muslim intellectuals who later migrated to the West. In that, perhaps, is a lesson about ideological formations: they are often difficult to essentialise.

IV

Thus when we discuss 'Islamism' and 'political Islam', the distinctions become critical. The phrase 'political Islam' seems to describe the application of the historically mainstream interpretation of Islam to political life in public. That has obviously taken place a number of times. The Libyan resistance leader, Umar al-Mukhtar,[11] was a Muslim scholar in a traditional Sunni mode, who nonetheless engaged in a political and military struggle against Italian fascism for almost twenty years in the early twentieth century. Abd al-Qadir al-Jaza'iri,[12] the Algerian sage, fought the French colonial invasion of his country in the mid-nineteenth century. There are many examples of Muslims who adhered to a historically mainstream interpretation of their faith, but who engaged politically according to what they understood to be religious imperatives.

But while some faithful Muslims attached to classical or historically mainstream interpretations of Islam argue that Jaza'iri and Mukhtar are models for religious engagement in politics, modern Islamist claims may not be quite so rooted in that mainstream tradition. Contemporary centrist Islamism finds political expression in the MB, and, as noted above, that movement sprang from a reformationist movement established in the late nineteenth and early twentieth centuries. Other, less modernist, forms of Islamism are Salafi in essence, and the vast majority of Muslim religious authorities view their roots as being even more distant from the historical trajectory of Islamic scholarship.

That raises the question: is there much utility in the term 'Islamism'? Labels are meant to distinguish on the one hand, and elaborate on the other. The word 'Islamism' does distinguish between Islam as a world religion, and religiously inspired political ideologies. And we saw earlier that Islamists themselves use the word 'Islamist'. But when Muslim figures in previous eras engaged in political life, even owing to religious precepts, they didn't generally use the terms 'political Islam' (*islam al-siyasi*) or 'Islamists' (*islamiyyun*)—indeed, such distinctions and terms would have seemed out of place. Did the Ottoman Caliphate, for example, use such terms? In the more recent struggle against Bashar al-Assad in Syria, many Sufis have engaged in military resistance but they have not tended to ascribe these terms to themselves or their approach.

Therefore, if the word 'Islamism' is used it ought to be used primarily to describe groups that themselves use it—mainly the MB and its offshoots. But, perhaps more importantly, when one writes about Islam and Muslim political movements of all sorts, identifying their origins and sources is crucial. Otherwise, confusion sets in and we are unable to properly situate groups in their correct context.

V

Returning to our young revolutionary activist in Egypt in 2012, the appellation he deployed ('*tujjar al-din*') might have been particularly—perhaps uniquely—applicable to the MB and its supporters. But only in 2012 would one have made that argument, and even then the burgeoning movement of Egyptian political Salafism was fully and openly engaged in the political arena. For, in 2013 and thereafter, it was not only the MB and Salafis who were instrumentalising religion for partisan political gain.

On the contrary, some hard-core supporters of the Egyptian state, and opponents of the MB, were involved in precisely the same kind of endeavour. There was a key difference—they were anti-MB and often anti-Salafi—but they certainly engaged in much of the same play, and it did not appear any more edifying for religion.

In the aftermath of the military's removal of Mursi in July 2013, there were a number of religious arguments deployed in support of the army's moves. When General Abd al-Fattah al-Sisi announced the detention of Mursi, he ensured the head of al-Azhar, Ahmad al-Tayyib, was present to validate the decision. In the weeks and months that followed, many different scholars from the Azhar establishment, Salafi preachers, and even some Islamists who had fallen out with the MB, gave their own religious arguments supporting the coup.

Religious scholars might have been expected to argue that the transfer of power had taken place, and 'so, like it or not, we must accept it, and work within the new political reality, for to do otherwise would invite civil strife'. There are many precedents in Muslim history for such a stance; the avoidance of internecine discord and conflict is an important imperative within Sunni Islam. Such arguments are often accompanied by silence. In other words, in the interests of what they perceived as the greater good, scholars would not speak out against injustices around them—even though they recognised them as injustices.

But while a number of *ulama* in Egypt took this course for years after the revolutionary uprising in 2011, other religious scholars instrumentalised religion, using it against Islamism in support of abusive state institutions.

Unlike Mubarak, Sisi was well known as an observant Muslim. He practiced the rituals of Islam rigorously and frequently mentioned religion and God in his speeches. There were thus those in the MB who thought this career military officer, who served as head of the military's intelligence section, might be sympathetic to the MB's Islamism. Of course, they simply confused a common Egyptian religious conservatism with a susceptibility to MB Islamism.

They were not the only ones. Many in Egypt's non-Islamist and anti-MB political elite in mid-2012 thought that Mursi had successfully removed his main political rival, Field Marshal Muhammad Hussain Tantawi, and replaced him with an MB-friendly officer. Even some academics thought the same.

My own perspective was that Sisi was not MB-friendly at all: he was a conservative, ritually observant Muslim, who was fiercely loyal to the military and the Egyptian state. In that regard, he was an Egyptian 'statist' first and foremost, rather than an Islamist of any kind, and his own brand of religious conservatism did not change that. If it had done, then much of the Egyptian bureaucracy, as well as much of the population at large, would have been Islamist—and it patently wasn't, as later events would show.

VI

There were other religious Muslims who opposed Mursi's government, as well as Islamism more generally. They were not state figures per se, but in a way they were state functionaries—and often they came right out of the religious establishment. In February 2014, some six months after Mursi's removal, Sa'ad al-Din al-Hilali, a noted Azhari *alim* (religious scholar) of reputable standing by all accounts, hyperbolically compared Sisi (then still the defence minister) and Muhammad Ibrahim (then the interior minister) to two of Islam's most revered prophets,[13] the Prophet Moses and the Prophet Aaron. He wasn't the only religious leader to engage in that sort of pro-military discourse—he was just one of the more prominent ones. Similarly, the former mufti of Egypt, Ali Gomaa', openly supported the military-backed government in a consistent way that caused a great deal of consternation in Muslim communities far beyond Egypt.

On both sides of the pro- and anti-Mursi divide, partisans instrumentalised religion for their own purposes. This was far more endemic in and emblematic of the pro-Mursi side but, particularly post-2013, many of those who opposed Mursi had few inhibitions in instrumentalising religion for political purposes.

VII

The MB is as much a product of its era, which was defined by anti-colonialism, as of the ideological tradition of Abduh-Rida-al-Banna. The core of the MB is ideological in terms of its religious approach; but it is also politically defined, and the influences of other twentieth-century political movements remain profoundly present. The notion of the vanguard, for example, a typically European idea of the nineteenth and twentieth centuries, is prominent in the MB, as well as in other Islamist movements. It is probably most blatant in a radical group like Hizb ut-Tahrir: if you go through that group's quasi-constitutional document for the future 'Islamic State',[14] and just change the vocabulary around, you wonder how much its writers took from Marxist-Leninist ideas, unconsciously or otherwise.

The experience of the mid-twentieth century, both through the anti-colonialist era and the repressive regime of Gamal Abd al-Nasser (who the MB ironically aligned itself with at one point), imprinted itself forever on the MB, manifesting in its focus on the 'group'. That has been both a strength and a weakness for the MB: a strength because it has been able to survive for so long by prioritising the long-term existence of the group over even ideological goals; a weakness because it has become more and more insular. As one of the Hathout brothers, who were direct disciples of al-Banna, reportedly said to a student: 'The MB died with Hasan al-Banna'. A non-member of the MB is obviously not remotely qualified to judge the veracity of that statement—but it is an interesting perspective.

It is, though, true that historically, given the above, the MB has indeed been a 'broad church'. Ibrahim el-Houdaiby, an exceedingly perceptive observer of the MB, and a former youth member who comes from a long pedigree of senior MB leaders (including two 'supreme guides'), usefully identified four trends that existed within the group at least until 2011.[15]

The first trend, which was dominant from the MB's inception until the 1960s, was the modernist trend exemplified by al-Banna and his intellectual grandfather, Muhammad Abduh. The second trend was far more sympathetic to the traditional Azhari, or classical Sunni, intellectual tradition, which is historically standard for Muslim religious scholars. This trend was particularly well represented in the Syrian MB early on, through figures like Abd al-Fattah Abu Ghudda. Houdaiby's sensible assessment, nevertheless, was that both of these trends have been in decline since the 1960s, and have been strongly influenced, if not at least partially replaced, by two other trends: 'Qutbism' and 'purist Salafism'.

Qutbism has been blamed for pretty much everything radical under the Muslim sun in modern parlance. Sayyid Qutb, an early MB ideologue, was hardly a progressive figure. It is rather misleading to characterise him as some kind of 'Muslim Che Guevera', even if some (particularly in the West) would like to ascribe radical ideas of leftwing social justice to him. It is true that extremist & violent Islamist ideologues often claim to follow him. And his highly politicised reading of the Qur'an—which divides the world simplistically into those who support the Islamist vanguard and those who don't—does bear the hallmarks of extremism.

Having said that, the mainstream interpretation of Qutb and his legacy within the MB is keen—even while it might incorporate much of his radical worldview—to eschew the notion of a military vanguard. There was a military wing of the MB at one time, but it was dismantled in 1954. The second *murshid* (supreme guide) of the MB, Hasan al-Hudaibi, who succeeded al-Banna after his assassination, wrote a book that was essentially a retort to Qutb's ideas.[16] At the same time, it is also true that the MB has become increasingly influenced by Qutb, at the expense of less polarised worldviews, and has remained as such, particularly after 2011.

Finally, the fourth trend that characterised the MB prior to the revolutionary uprising of 2011 was the purist Salafism that came into Egypt more widely from the 1970s onwards.

VIII

All of these trends are important to understand as we look at the MB in 2011. The Tunisian MB-influenced Ennahdha Movement has the same trends, but in different proportions. The supremely dominant trend in Ennahdha, represented first and foremost by Rashid al-Ghannushi, is closest to the Banna-Rida-Abduh modernist tendency, which, as Houdaiby and others have noted, began to diminish tremendously in importance in the Egyptian MB from the 1960s onwards. This fact is important when it comes to trying to understand the state of the Egyptian MB on the dawn of Egypt's revolutionary uprising. There was a trend within it, labelled 'reformist', that remained connected to the modernist Salafism mentioned before. Its foremost figure, at least in terms of fame, was Abu al-Futuh, who, as we have seen, ran for president and was expelled from the party. That 'reformist' trend, then, was greatly marginalised. The dominant trends were the MB's version of Qutbism and its incorporation of purist Salafism.

For a time, analysts have been content to describe the MB as the Muslim version of the Christian Democrats of Germany; this idea suggests that the mainstream of the Islamist movement is essentially the partner of mainstream centre-right politics. Even if we argue that al-Banna's style of Islamism is, indeed, simply centre-right politics (and that ought to remain to be a contested point), there is a problem in that the MB, at least in Egypt, has not been led by that trend for the past few decades. Those in the MB who did lean in that direction were, nevertheless, the ones who generally engaged with academics, analysts and foreign governments. When one looks at much of the primary material that has been collected on the MB and published in the West, one can clearly see names like Abu al-Futuh, Ibrahim el-Houdaiby (before he left the MB in 2008), Kamal al-Halbawi (the international spokesperson of the MB, based for a long while in London, before leaving the MB after the 2011 uprising) and others who all partook in that more reformist and modernist Salafi mode of al-Banna-style Islamism. And, as mentioned, this approach dominated the Tunisian MB discourse. But in Egypt, the same approach was sidelined long before the 2011 revolutionary uprising.

IX

Islamism in the early twenty-first century has incorporated a wide range of viewpoints; and outsiders' conceptions of Islamism have been similarly varied since 2011. One extreme viewed all Islamist groups as more or less the same as al-Qa'ida in terms of their beliefs, seeing only differences in tactics. A substantial number of political figures in the Arab world shared this view. The other extreme viewed Islamism as generally progressive and pluralist, assuming that the likes of the Tunisian Ennahdha Movement were representative of the Islamist universe. Both of these approaches were shortsighted and too generalising. Islamists are neither automatically equivalent to al-Qa'ida nor automatically natural allies for progressive, democratic politics. Just as there were a variety of strands of communism and socialism, which produced peaceful as well as violent outcomes, so there is a complex set of political ideologies within Islamism.

From 2011 to 2013, Western governments found themselves engaging with a reactionary political force in the shape of the Egyptian MB, which was given to severely reactionary rhetoric. Meanwhile, the MB branch in Libya refused to recognise the results of Libya's 2014 election, and remained in a broad coalition that included extremely radical groups. In contrast, over a similar period the Tunisian Islamist party, Ennahdha, showed itself to be profoundly committed to that country's democratic experiment, even if some argue that it was substantially motivated by trying to avoid a repetition of what happened in Egypt. Many hoped the MB and other Islamists elsewhere would follow the lead of relatively open-minded figures such as Ghannushi in Tunisia. But that did not happen, and in any case it was naïve to believe that movements based on reactionary ideas, raised in environments of oppression, would automatically be genuinely reformist or progressive once in power.

Consistency demands a recognition that challenges to a more progressive, democratic future in the Middle East are not solely born of Islamist movements. Indeed, in Syria the forces of Bashar al-Assad have taken far more lives than Islamists everywhere. Different types of authoritarianism continue to exist across the region—some, if not many, in hardline opposition to Islamism.

Consistency is not easy, but it is possible. In my Prologue I gave the example of how, in 2002, Edward Said and others formed the Palestinian National Initiative, an effort to carve out a third way that rejected both the radical reactionaries of Hamas and the corrupt Fatah movement. Likewise, although political upheaval in Egypt produced many faux liberals, it also gave rise to principled voices, some of whom were at the heart of the 25 January revolutionary moment. Before the widespread brutal crackdown on the MB, public intellectuals such as Ibrahim el-Houdaiby and human rights defenders including Heba Morayef simultaneously engaged productively with, and criticised constructively, the MB. Groups that tended towards sectarianism and flirted with vigilantism needed to be critiqued, but with nuance, without automatically equating them with al-Qa'ida.

X

The ousting of President Muhammad Mursi by the military, and the interim government's resolve to rewrite the 2012 constitution, almost immediately raised general questions about the use of religion in public life.[17] The head of the Coptic Church, Pope Tawadros II, asked for a change to the wording of an article relating to religious rules, while Grand Mufti Shawqi Allam announced his rejection of the idea of a theocratic state. Muhammad Abu al-Ghar, a Constituent Assembly member from the Social Democrats, separately advocated that Islamic law have a role in legislation, which appeared to be a matter of consensus.

These words held very deep implications. As the Maspero massacre showed, while the state has long championed the idea that Muslims and Christians are officially 'one hand', in practice many forces have instrumentalised religion and sowed sectarian discontent to keep Egyptians divided and disempowered. Various political leaders justified curtailments of political freedoms in part as a necessary tradeoff to stop the threat of extremist Islamist terrorism, while at the same time Christians have often criticised the state for not adequately protecting them against sectarianism. So, did Egyptians want religion to have a role in the public arena? If so, what sort of role?

Polling data has appeared to demonstrate conservative religious attitudes among the Egyptian population, but also scepticism towards political parties declaring a monopoly on religion. In general, Egyptians have always been considered a conservative people, with religion being a fundamental part of their identity—whether they are Muslim or Christian. Surveys done by Gallup and TahrirTrends (which, like Gallup, I was involved with) over several years indicate that Egyptians are clear about their identification with religion. 98 per cent of those surveyed by TahrirTrends considered religion to be 'very important' on a day-to-day level. The remainder said 'somewhat important'.[18]

This suggests that religion is an identity marker, but it does not necessarily indicate support for a specific political role for religion, or support for specific Islamist political parties. Other data would be required to support such suppositions. Otherwise we risk conflating religious conservatism with support for the MB or other similar political parties, which would be misleading in the Egyptian context.

When Gallup surveyed Egyptians in December 2011, it found that 95 per cent of Egyptians had confidence in al-Azhar. When TahrirTrends asked a similar question in May–June 2013, the results indicated that 91 per cent of Egyptians had either a great deal of confidence (79 per cent) or some confidence (12 per cent) in religious institutions in general.[19] This response begs the question: what type of secularism would suit Egyptian sensibilities? Would it involve a sharp separation between the *state* and religion, or *politics* and religion? And would there be a clear distinction between political *parties* and religion?

The clearest answer to these questions may have come from then-Vice President al-Baradei during an interview on the HayahTV channel during the summer of 2013. At the time, he explicitly expressed no opposition to the involvement in politics of the MB's Freedom and Justice Party (something that the Egyptian authorities later recanted when the party was forcibly closed by a judicial order in August of 2014) or the Salafi Noor Party, but he did reject parties established 'on the basis' of religion.[20]

Therefore, at least in this narrative, a party with a 'religious reference' (that is, a party that referred to religion or religious ideas in its policies) may not be particularly controversial: but, as far as al-Baradei was concerned (and this is the crux of the issue), no politician should speak in the 'name of God' or the 'name of Islam'. Political speech, the argument goes, cannot be considered 'holy' since it merely reflects a worldly political argument. That distinction may be lost outside of Egypt, but it does represent a view that has been expressed via various media within Egypt.

How does this relate, then, to Egyptian sensitivities about religiously-based parties more generally? And, further, how does it relate to sensitivities about religious leaders engaging in legislative matters?

Between late May and early June 2013 Egyptians were asked: 'regardless of whether or not you would support them, do you think parties based primarily on religious identity, regardless of the religion involved, are a good idea?' 65 per cent of Egyptians said they are a bad idea and only 31 per cent said they are a good idea.[21] A broad majority of Egyptians appeared to prefer not to have such parties, then. However, this does not necessarily mean that they supported legislation that *banned* such parties.

TahrirTrends also asked what role Egyptians thought religious leaders should have in writing national legislation. The answers seem to confirm that while Egyptians may indeed think very highly of religion as an identity marker, and respect religious institutions overwhelmingly, this does not necessarily translate into their supporting religious leaders having a direct role in writ national laws to which they would all be subjected. When Gallup asked a similar question in 2011, shortly after the 25 January uprising, 69 per cent of Egyptians said that religious leaders should advise those in authority over the writing of national legislation;

14 per cent said they should have full authority in writing national legis-lation; 9 per cent said no authority at all; and 8 per cent either refused to answer the question or said they did not know.

Two years later, Tahrir Trends' results indicated a shift. A majority of Egyptians did want religious leaders to advise those in authority with writing legislation, although, at 60 per cent, the number was slightly less than when Gallup conducted its poll in 2011. The number of people who said that they should have *no* role at all increased signifi-cantly from 9 per cent to 23 per cent. It is difficult to relate this change directly to Islamist rule *per se*, as the actual role of religious leaders in writing legislation has not changed at all in the past few years. Nevertheless, it is clear that between 2011 and 2013, Egyptians began to reassess their feelings around the theoretical engagement of religious leaders in the legislative process.[22]

The overall picture, therefore, around Egyptian attitudes vis-à-vis religion and the public arena is a rather complex one. It seems that theocratic rule would never be popular in Egypt, whether of the Iranian 'republican' style, or in any other form. That the citizenry has such respect for religious institutions unsurprisingly means that an advisory role for religious leaders (that is, a non-binding one) would be desirable for a majority, but there would still be significant resis-tance to this. Arguably, it already exists in the Egyptian context anyway. The significance of religion in terms of Egyptian identity notwithstand-ing, most Egyptians would not favour parties based primarily on reli-gious identity.

None of this ought to imply that Egyptians would necessarily back a ban on any particular group: citizens can think something is not a good idea without wanting a legal or constitutional stipulation reflecting their preferences. Nevertheless, it does suggest that parties and politi-cians in Egypt, of any stripe or disposition, that seek to instrumentalise religion in any way, might be well advised to think twice.

The question of the correct relationship between religious figures and political power, however, is far more difficult to answer.

Historically speaking, classical Islamic tradition identifies two acceptable approaches for religious figures engaging with political power. The first, typified by Imam Hasan (a nephew of the Prophet Muhammad) is a forbearing position, designed to avoid making an already bad situation worse for the community at large. It involves engaging in prudent silence in the face of an unjust ruler. In contemporary times, we have seen this approach applied by Indonesian *ulama* for thirty-one years, even during the uprising against President Suharto in 1998. This approach was also the one that many Syrian *ulama* believed they were taking with regards to President Bashar al-Assad for quite some time after the unrest in Syria began.

But there is also the model of Imam Husain (the younger brother of Hasan), which many Syrian *'ulama* switched to as the conflict raged on. This approach sees that, at times, being silent and allowing injustice to fester will actually create far more injustice. This position is an exceptional one, taken by Imam Husain in a very profound manner as history recounts. It is characterised by vocal opposition to power when that power is tyrannical.

Beyond these two approaches, there are harsh warnings in classical Islamic texts about the *'ulama al-sultan'* (scholars of the ruler). These are *ulama* who are ingratiated with and reliant upon the circles of political power, even when the powerful do wrong—such *ulama* are described in those texts as having 'insincere motives'.

The modern expression *'tujjar al-din'* may not be the contemporary equivalent of *'ulama al-sultan'*, for sincerity may yet be present among those given the former label. However, the instrumentalisation of religion for partisan purposes, regardless of which party it is meant to empower, is fundamental to both expressions.

From 2011 to 2015, few people exemplified the Husaini model of speaking truth to power in the midst of the Egyptian revolution. One prominent example was Emad Effat, a jurist from the Dar al-Ifta (Abode of Verdicts), which is the official state body for issuing advisory religious verdicts (*fatawa*). Ironically, he served at a time when Ali Gomaa, who later backed the military after the removal of Mursi, was head of that institution. Effat disagreed with Gomaa's politics—but, according to numerous accounts from his students and peers, he loved and respected him dearly. As mentioned in Chapter 1, media reports indicate that security forces killed Effat during clashes with protesters in December 2011. Effat was opposed to the return of the Mubarak regime, deeply critical of the military council of the day, and simultaneously had antipathy towards the MB. When he died, he earned two titles: '*shaheed al-Azhar*' (the martyr of al-Azhar) and '*shaykh al-thawra*' (the shaykh of the revolution). Since his passing, no one else has been bestowed with that banner.

No one could. In the years running up to the 2011 revolutionary uprising, Effat wrote to his student, the revolutionary figure Ibrahim el-Houdaiby. The contents of that message show clearly how rare the likes of Effat were:

> There are all these good words about respect for shaykhs, giving them leeway and excuses, but where is God's right to His own religion? Where is the right of the public who are confused about the truth because shaykhs are silent, and your own silence out of respect for senior shaykhs? What is this new idol that you call pressure; how does this measure to Ahmad ibn Hanbal's tolerance of jail and refusing to bend and say what would comfort the unjust rulers?

> What is this new idol you invented? The idol of pressure! If we submit to these new rituals, to this new idol, we would then tolerate everyone who lies, commits sins and great evils under the pretext of easing pressure and escaping it. O people, these pressures are only in your head and not in reality. Is there a new opinion in jurisprudence that coercion can be by illusion? Have we come to use religious terms to circumvent religion and justify the greater sins we commit? So we use legitimate phrases such as pros and cons, the lesser of two evils, and pressure to make excuses for not speaking up for what is right and surrendering to what is wrong![23]

XI

Both the Hasani and the Husaini approaches are persistent refusals to apologise for those in power. There may be times when silence is prudent and other times when a call for activism against injustice is required. In both cases, actively and vocally supporting the unjust ruler is, at least against the backdrop of historically mainstream Islamic precedent, a priori—and definitively—rejected.

Egypt remains a deeply controversial issue within Muslim communities worldwide. The broader Middle Eastern proxy war between Qatar, Turkey, Egypt and the UAE is likely to continue for years to come. While Saudi Arabia was the country that used to fund Muslim communities in various fashions globally, its support of institutions and leaders outside of its borders has diminished tremendously. New infusions of financial support, though, are coming—particularly from Turkey, Qatar and the UAE—and so the effects of the proxy war continue.

One wonders, how will Muslim communities outside of Egypt engage on Egypt? Might they provide what the democratic-socialist philosopher Cornel West describes as a 'prophetic voice'—a voice ensuring a sense of 'prophetic pragmatism' whose praxis is 'tragic action with revolutionary intent, usually reformist consequences, and always visionary [in] outlook'?[24] Would that restore the classical choice between Imam Hasan's approach and Imam Husain's, and, irrespective of consequences, maintain consistency in critique and consistency in speaking truth to power, as well as absence of partisanship?

In Egypt itself, simply calling power to account—regardless of who is in power—has been limited to an occasional minority. There were few who stood against the excesses of military rule in 2011–12, then criticised the rule of the MB in 2012–13, and then attempted to hold the post-Mursi authorities to account.

But there is an argument to be made that such an exceptional minority can provide a healthier model for Egyptian politics than the majority have provided. Arguably, it is their model that comes closest to the position of speaking truth to power always, regardless of whose power-politics it interrupts. What remains abundantly clear is that good examples are rare indeed. Effat, *shaykh al-thawra*, expressed this sentiment best when he wrote, '[The] Shaykhs of Al-Azhar used to leave their resignations in the drawers of their secretaries, and told them: "if you see us submitting to pressure hand over the resignation to the press." For indeed, when they are honest to God, He makes them victorious and cherishes them.'[25]

5

THE RISE AND FALL OF THE FIRST
DEMOCRATICALLY ELECTED PRESIDENT

It isn't that Mursi is wrong. Of course they're out to get him. The question is, why is he making it so easy for them, by ticking off everyone else who might support him to save the revolution?

Conversation with an activist, late 2012

I

Some time around late 2012, I found myself having discussions with a pro-MB activist in the UK. He wasn't Egyptian, but was a second-generation Muslim Briton of South Asian descent. He had not spent a particularly long time in Egypt, but had been heavily influenced by the Muslim Brotherhood (MB) in their international dimension—particularly by those on the more liberal or left-wing side of the organisation. He understood the MB through the lens of people like Ghannushi, the Tunisian Islamist leader; Kamal al-Halbawi, the Egyptian who represented the MB in Europe for a time; and, to some extent (as he didn't understand Arabic particularly well), Abu al-Futuh. For him, the MB was a pious Muslim organisation that could be a 'progressive' and 'left-wing' political force—marrying his British leftist politics with his sympathies for MB-Islamism.

Our discussions went round in circles. I put it to him that if the MB were genuinely interested in pursuing a revolutionary agenda that was rooted in the eighteen days of uprising, they wouldn't have pushed Mursi as their presidential candidate. Rather, they would have kept to their pledge of not running a candidate, and supported Abu al-Futuh, who was by then not a member of the MB.

My British pro-Islamist interlocutor then said something that surprised me tremendously. He argued that the MB had intended to back Abu al-Futuh for the presidency, but that the 'deep state' had blocked the move. It was a claim that not even MB members in Egypt made. But this claim did illustrate the concern about the 'deep state' within the MB, both domestically and internationally. In fact, the perception was that the 'deep state' had been responsible for all the MB's ills.

In reality, Joseph Heller was right when he said: 'just because you're paranoid doesn't mean they're not out to get you'. The MB was indeed paranoid, but that didn't mean its opponents weren't out to get it. Indeed, the MB was right to be concerned that elements of the former Mubarak regime would do whatever they could to put Egypt's democratic experiment out of commission. In June, the Supreme Constitutional Court dissolved the MB-dominated parliament and SCAF made a last-minute power grab just two weeks before Mursi was announced the winner of presidential elections. Two months before that, in April, another ruling dissolved the first Constituent Assembly, which Islamists had also dominated. Where the Brotherhood went terribly wrong, though, is in how they responded to these challenges, making the job of their opponents that much easier as a result.

II

As noted earlier, of the several trends within the MB (which were discussed in Chapter 4), the one that dominated among the leadership in 2012, when Mursi took over, was easily identifiable. It was the most conservative and reactionary trend. The narrow margin of their victory against a member of the Mubarak regime in the presidential election should have taught the MB that there were a substantial number of Egyptians who did not want it in power. But the MB adopted the more convenient approach. There were, it felt, a substantial number of people who did want it in power and, thus, preferred it to the former regime. As such, the MB didn't need to worry about those who didn't want it in power; certainly not in terms of winning them over.

That kind of triumphalism led the MB to embrace what was essentially a majoritarian form of democratic politics. In that regard, the MB was not unique. Most liberal democracies around the world practice a form of majoritarianism, in that whoever wins 50-plus-1 per cent of the vote gets the ability to form the ruling administration. But sustainable democracies have institutions that ensure that such a democratic vote will not only be respected, but safeguarded. European history in the twentieth century is full of regrettable examples of leaders who came to power via a democratic vote, but whose rule was punctuated by flagrant abuses.

The MB certainly wasn't the same as some of those extreme European leaders (such as Mussolini and Milosevic), and obviously any suggestion that they were is absolutely preposterous. But the MB did err exceedingly in identifying the lay of the land. Egypt had a democratic vote, which the MB won, but Egypt was not a democracy. It was going through a democratic experiment, and as part of the experiment, Mursi had become president. Egypt couldn't be a democracy, after decades of dictatorship and autocracy, by simply having a single democratic presidential election. There had to be institutional checks and balances put into place, with accompanying agreement over the rules of the political 'game'. That hadn't happened yet. Egypt's democratic experiment was still fragile—and while Mursi had the mandate to be president, it was all predicated on the success of the democratic experiment itself.

Rather than treat Egypt's political frame in that fashion, where democracy was an experiment, Mursi and the MB opted to see the political arena with two lenses. The first was that of victory. The MB had won the election and deserved to refashion the political landscape in the manner it saw fit. The MB was, it was argued, under no obligation to form a consensus government, or generally to seek consensus. It only needed a majority, and it had one. The second lens focused on existential threats: forces opposed to the MB—those looking for a counter-revolutionary return to a pre-revolutionary status quo—were trying to mischievously close in on it.

The two lenses combined made for a testing scenario. The MB was in a precarious position. That was precisely why it needed to think beyond simply governing by way of a majority. It needed to look for a consensus-based approach to ensure that the democratic experiment would endure and win out. In late November of 2012, I argued that Mursi—in consideration of the special needs that a post-uprising Egypt had and the importance of continuing to pursue revolutionary trans-formation—should put together a presidential council composed of three other key former presidential candidates: Hamdeen Sabahi Abu al-Futuh and Amr Moussa.[1] With those figures in tow, Mursi would have accounted for the overwhelming majority of votes in the presi-dential election, and provided for a decent alternative to a legislature until one was elected.

Ironically, their ideological cousins, the Ennahdha Movement in Tunisia, had understood this extremely well, and had compromised sev-eral times in the aftermath of their uprising. But it was led by Ghannushi, who corresponded most closely to Egypt's Abu al-Futuh. Mursi was no Ghannushi, and neither was anyone in the Egyptian MB leadership.

III

The MB won the presidential election in June 2012, and had its next big public relations success about six weeks later. On 5 August sixteen Egyptian soldiers were killed in a militant attack on Egypt's eastern border in Sinai, something that many Egyptians believed could have been averted had the SCAF been solely concerned with national secu-rity issues, as opposed to affairs of governance.[2] Though Mursi had won the presidential election in June, the SCAF had still maintained a num-ber of powers that would normally have been reserved for the presi-dency. These included the ability to appoint senior military officers, dismiss parliament and appoint a new committee to write a fresh con-stitution for a public referendum.

With the killings in Sinai, there was likely a burgeoning pressure from within the Egyptian military itself to take a step back. There had been reports of discontent among younger officers,[3] who felt Tantawi was overstepping his bounds and placing the military establishment into jeopardy by being so directly and openly involved with governance. It was one thing for the military to have substantial powers and economic interests—effectively running a state within a state in the background—but it was quite another for Tantawi to be effectively a co-president with Mursi.

All of that changed on 12 August. In an unexpected twist, with few aware of the plans outside of a small clique of senior military officers and the presidency, Tantawi was removed from office as defence minister and appointed as presidential advisor. The military's chief of staff, Sami Annan, received a similar treatment. In their places were appointed younger members of the SCAF—two generals who had hitherto been relatively unknown to the outside world.

General Abd al-Fattah al-Sisi's name had only come up previously in international circles as part of attention given to the infamous 'virginity tests', which the Egyptian military were accused of carrying out in 2011. But he was now defence minister.[4] Over the next few days, a major reshuffle of the SCAF took place. In the same move that saw Sisi become defence minister, Mursi also delegated himself the authority to create a constitutional committee, which had previously been with the SCAF, and granted himself legislative authority. If Mursi entered the presidential palace on 30 June, he effectively became president on 12 August.

IV

In March 2013 I attended a lunch in Cairo with a number of European diplomats, and a senior MB leader, to discuss the country's political situation. It was a small, intimate affair, and the MB leader felt confident in the fortunes of his party. At one point, the subject of Sisi cropped up, and we discussed the circumstances of his becoming defence minister. I cannot recall if we discussed the subject of Sisi's religiosity, which had by now convinced huge swathes of Egypt's non-Islamist political elite that he was a closet MB supporter. We might have, particularly since MB supporters had revealed that Sisi's wife had read the Qur'an together with Mursi's wife—and, thus, could be trusted. The naïvety of both the anti-MB political elite and the MB establishment was staggering.

What I do remember very clearly was that when the subject of Sisi's appointment as defence minister came up, the MB leader took great pride. He revealed that he had been very surprised that Mursi had been able to remove Tantawi from office, but believed that Mursi had received divine assistance to do so. From his perspective, Mursi had removed Tantawi in a spectacular strategic move. He had managed to place a loyal stalwart—Sisi—at the head of the military establishment. The MB leader's esteem for Mursi could only be matched by the anti-MB political elite's dismay that the most significant bulwark to the elected president had been removed—and ostensibly replaced by an MB-friendly officer, if not an Islamist himself.

This bullish confidence of the MB would later prove to be the key to its downfall at the hands of enemies who had never wanted to give it an opportunity to rule. But neither the MB leader nor the upper-class elite of Zamalek and Heliopolis, Cairo's most affluent suburbs, got it right. After lunch the MB leader left, seemingly satisfied that he had got his point across to the Western diplomats and political commentators like me. I stayed behind, and had a further conversation with the diplomats. It was unclear to me how Mursi could take credit for a change in the top military brass. The military was a ferociously independent institution, and had been for decades. Mursi was a complete outsider to it. Even though as the elected president he might have had the right to sack Tantawi, it was unlikely that he would have had the effective authority on his own to pull it off. What seemed obvious to me at the time—but somewhat counter-intuitive—was that the main driver for the change had been not the presidency but the SCAF itself. What I suggested was that Tantawi had been sacked, to be sure, but primarily by his own brothers in arms rather than the MB.

The question that remains shrouded in doubt is simply this: who initiated the process? A confidante of Mursi indicated privately to me that the decision came about as a result of an intense disagreement within the president's team in the aftermath of the Sinai attacks about the competence and subordination of Tantawi.[5] Did the SCAF-in-waiting, led by Sisi and others, send a message to Mursi, informing him that they were about to carry out this internal reshuffle so that he could come on board? Or did Mursi, in an incredibly gutsy move, having heard about grumblings within the younger officer corps of the military, first reach out to Sisi? No one on the outside quite seems to know—and those on the inside are obviously incredibly partisan about the events in question.

V

Irrespective of how Tantawi was removed from office, he was removed. Mursi went from being a 'spare-tyre' presidential candidate, who was only proposed due to the legal inability of Khairat al-Shater to run, to a daring president who had restored power to the presidency after clipping the SCAF's wings.

But the military didn't suddenly fade away from all power nodes within the country. For decades it had maintained a great deal of power. It was an economic powerhouse, estimated to control between 25 and 40 per cent of the Egyptian economy by some reports.[6] It had the ability to shroud in mystery the extent of its power. The military also had a great deal of public support. Its decision to leave the public political arena was not the result of it being forced out by popular demand, or even because Mursi wanted to assume the powers that he rightfully deserved as the elected president. Rather, the SCAF had decided it was time to return to the space it felt most comfortable in: the background.

The Mursi presidency enjoyed yet another successful moment some weeks later. Israel launched a round of attacks against the occupied Palestinian territory of the Gaza Strip in November. In the mediation that led to the end of the conflict, Mursi proved to be a 'pivotal' figure.[7] He had clout with Hamas, the Palestinian version of the MB, which few Egyptian politicians could have historically matched. And, added to this, the existing intelligence services, which generally remained intact in the state they had been under Mubarak, had good relations with the Israelis. When the ceasefire was finally agreed in Cairo on 22 November, Mursi's international standing became even more prestigious. The MB had shown the international community that it could be relied upon to play the same role as Mubarak when it came to mediation between the Palestinians and the Israelis, and significantly, to not negate or call into question the 1978 Begin-Sadat treaty between Israel and Egypt. Mursi had faced his first international crisis test, and on all counts he had managed it effectively.

There was no party in the crisis that wasn't satisfied, in the end, by Mursi's mediation, save perhaps the Palestinian Authority of Mahmud Abbas, which saw the political capital of Hamas increase at its expense. Mursi didn't engage directly with Israeli officials, but gave free rein to a variety of elements within the Egyptian security sector to do so. Hamas had an easier time with Mursi than they would have had with Mubarak in some respects—but in others, not. Mursi's administration made it clear to Hamas that trouble on the border wouldn't be tolerated. The steps that Egyptian civil society took to express solidarity and support—a number of groups of high profile Egyptians crossed the border into Gaza—gratified the Palestinian public. Mursi dispatched his own prime minister, Hisham Kandil, to Gaza—something Mubarak never would have done. The international community saw a Cairene administration that managed to be in solidarity with the Palestinian people of Gaza on the one hand, but play an effective role in de-escalation on the other with the Israelis. It was a success for the Mursi government.

VI

The downside of that success was the emboldening of certain elements within Mursi's own camp, which had been somewhat demoralised with their domestic situation a month earlier. In the aftermath of a high-profile trial over killings in Tahrir Square during the eighteen days of uprising, which saw a slew of acquittals, Mursi had attempted to remove the prosecutor general, Abd al-Majid Mahmud.[8] The latter was one of the most high-profile Mubarak 'left-overs' (felool)—and his removal was certainly something that would have been tremendously popular with revolutionaries and MB supporters alike. There was just one problem. According to Egyptian law, the president was not entitled to dismiss the prosecutor general. The powerful judges' association was very clear in declaring that such a move would infringe on the judiciary's independence. Mursi's political capital and popular standing at the time wasn't nearly strong enough to go over their heads, and so he found himself at loggerheads with the Egyptian judiciary—even though many pro-revolutionary forces would have supported the departure of the prosecutor general.

In his attempt to remove Mahmud, Mursi made two errors. First, he neglected the lack of internal support among the judiciary itself for such a move—which differed from the situation inside the SCAF, where powerful internal dynamics supported the replacement of Tantawi with Sisi. Mursi wasn't just going to war against Mahmud in trying to remove him from his post: he was declaring war on the judicial establishment, and they weren't about to stand for that.

Secondly, Mursi overestimated the popular mandate he'd been given—a mistake he would constantly make during his year in power. If Field Marshal Tantawi, in his capacity as the head of the SCAF after the departure of Husni Mubarak, had tried the same move by issuing an executive decree in early 2011, he probably would have managed to pull it off. However, the SCAF had the overwhelming confidence of the Egyptian population. It is doubtful the judiciary would have opposed it. When it came to Mursi, the situation was different. The judges knew Mursi was not remotely as popular as the military, and the law was on their side anyway. A few days after Mursi tried to force Mahmud out of office, a deal was struck that allowed him to remain on the bench until the age of retirement.[9]

There was no way to describe the outcome except as an embarrassing defeat—a defeat that even some pro-revolutionary forces were pleased about. Why? And what does this say about the state of play in Egyptian politics, the rule of law, and revolutionary governance?[10]

Over the eighteen months following Tahrir, a great deal had taken place. The head of the regime, Mubarak, had been forced to resign by the very military establishment from which he'd emerged. Under the aegis of a junta, presided over by a field marshal, there had been relatively free parliamentary and presidential elections. Not too long after the newly elected president had taken office, the junta had opted to depart from the governing arena, and had indicated to the presidency that it would return to the position it had prior to the revolution. That meant the end of the governing junta (which had hitherto shared the function of the presidency with the elected president), and its return to the privileged, quasi-state-within-a-state position it had previously held. At least in terms of affairs not governed by foreign policy, defence and the military budget, the elected president had free rein to engage with state institutions to implement his manifesto.

At this juncture, it is important to again recall precisely what sort of victory the newly elected president had won. The first round of the presidential elections saw a turn-out of 43 per cent of the electorate—not particularly high. Mursi came in first with about 25 per cent of the vote—in other words, about 75 per cent of the voting electorate (not to mention those who did not vote) chose to vote for other candidates. Mursi then beat Shafiq, Mubarak's last prime minister, in the second round, acquiring 52 per cent of the vote. The turn out was slightly better in the second round, but more than half of the electorate chose not to vote. It is crucial to remember this: Mursi won the election, but he couldn't claim to represent even a majority of Egyptians, let alone the overwhelming majority, since many had simply made a tactical choice to vote for him, when faced with the alternative of a representative of the former regime.

Many countries experience low turn outs in elections. Where there is a presidential system combined with a 'winner takes all' approach, invariably the winner does not possess a massive mandate. Nevertheless, the person would still be president without further discussion. In Egypt, after the 25 January revolution, there were two major differences. The first was that Mursi came to power at a time when there was no standing parliament—in other words, executive and legislative authority existed as one within the presidential office. The normal checks and balances on Mursi did not exist, and continued to be absent (except, as previously implied, in the domains of defence and foreign policies, where the Supreme Council of the Armed Forces was still overwhelmingly influential).

There was one more unique aspect to this period of Egyptian history: namely, the revolution itself. The revolution was supported by an overwhelming majority of the Egyptian people. It was, as the perhaps tired but nevertheless accurate cliché goes, 'a people's revolution'. As noted previously, Gallup polls taken multiple times during 2011 showed that eight out of ten Egyptians supported Tahrir. It was that wide acceptance of, and support for, the revolution that laid down the justification and authority to enact change to fulfil the revolution's demands. However, revolutionary change must be enacted through an authority that has similar levels of widespread support in order to be effective. Otherwise, that authority would simply be acting on the basis of normal politics—not revolutionary politics. The rules of the game are different, depending on the sort of politics one is engaging in.

That, perhaps, is the crux of the matter when it comes to understanding the state of play within Egypt during Mursi's period in power. If it was, indeed, a revolutionary political period, then special extraordinary measures could indeed have been taken, bypassing the normal system. Such measures would have been inkeeping with the moral and ethical authority lent to the new ruling authority by the revolution—demonstrated, for example, by the armed forces being able to legitimately force the resignation of Mubarak because of the overwhelming support for their action among the population. Nevertheless, the fact that the revolution was based on mass, popular support meant that any authority that sought to implement revolutionary changes by bypassing normal procedures had to likewise have overwhelming popular support.

An authority without such overwhelming support couldn't be described as being endowed with revolutionary authority to go beyond established normal procedures enshrined in existing law. It was still the legitimate authority, of course, but it could only act through legally legitimate means—not revolutionary, extra-legal means.

Herein lay the rub. When Mursi attempted, unsuccessfully, to dismiss the prosecutor general many defended his action as an attempt to achieve a demand of the revolution. But, as the president of the republic, he had no legal authority to dismiss or 'persuade' the prosecutor general to resign. His move was simply perceived as the president attempting to enforce his own vision upon the judiciary. With this, Mursi failed. The judiciary responded and resisted in a united fashion, and no other political player supported him.

Mursi governed Egypt as a legitimate president curtailed by an admixture of the law and the existing system. He suffered from the absence of a parliamentary check. Indeed, this was actually a handicap, as it made him vulnerable to the accusation of heavy-handed authoritarianism—whether guilty of it or not. Finally, he emanated from a movement that was deemed to be deeply suspect by different sections of Egyptian society.

He did not, therefore, govern Egypt as a revolutionary president—one that might go above and beyond established procedures to institute a truly non-corrupt and independent judiciary, for example. His presidency was not endowed with that authority. Rather, it was 'political business as usual'.

Taking all of this into account, Mursi and the MB had a choice as the largest power brokers on Egypt's political landscape. Either the revolution would continue, or it wouldn't. Many in Egypt at the time believed that the revolution had ended on 11 February when Mubarak had been forced to step down. Others believed it had ended when Mursi took office. Still others believed it had ended at other points; but they all believed it had ended. So, if it had ended, then revolutionary political governance would no longer be applicable, and Mursi had to go through the established systems—without circumventing them as he had tried to do with the prosecutor general.

If the revolution, however, had to 'continue', then to achieve its revolutionary aims it would have required Mursi to act in concert with other political forces, so that he could speak on behalf of the overwhelming majority of Egyptian citizens. In other words, he would have had to have engaged in a government of national consensus, and genuinely draw in different sectors of the opposition that had supported the revolution.

That never happened. That it did not happen should not have resulted in his demise—he was the elected president, after all—but it was entirely foreseeable that it would.

VII

The Mursi government and the MB more generally were running into another problem when it came to the judiciary. This related to the prize of the Egyptian constitution. After the parliamentary elections of 2011, and before Mursi's election, Egypt's parliament elected its first Constituent Assembly to draft a new constitution. The assembly was meant to represent the broad diversity of Egypt's population but, instead, two-thirds of it was from the MB or Salafi groups. Out of 100 members, there were only six women and five Coptic Christians. Crucially, the parliament had voted for many of its own pro-MB and pro-Salafi constituencies to be on the assembly, something which many argued was in violation of the constitutional decree issued by the SCAF in March 2011.[11]

The Egyptian judiciary was none too sympathetic to such an assembly. Neither were a plethora of non-Islamist political parties, who saw the assembly as a way for groups like the MB to impose a narrow ultra-conservative agenda. Many of those non-Islamist parties had boycotted the selection process to constitute the assembly in protest; some had been appointed to the assembly and then withdrawn. The matter of the assembly went to court, and on April 10 of 2012, the Supreme Administrative Court suspended the assembly for being too unrepresentative of Egyptian society.[12] The presence of parliamentarians within the assembly was also problematic, although it wasn't clear if this directly contradicted the existing legal framework. The SCAF announced that a new executive decree would be issued specifying precisely how the Constituent Assembly ought to be formed, out of concerns that the existing assembly had been in the 'hands of one force'.[13]

In June of 2012, a new framework for deciding on a Constitutional Assembly was agreed upon.[14] The new assembly would include politicians, members of various state institutions, unions and religious leaders from both the Christian and Muslim establishments. Nonetheless, thirty-nine out of 100 seats were still allocated to members of parliament, leaving the assembly open, fairly or not, to a similar accusation: that it violated the notion that parliamentarians should not vote themselves onto it. Another court case was heard on that basis after non-Islamists in the assembly argued that the MB was trying to dominate it.[15]

The issue of parliamentarians being included in the membership of the assembly became something of a moot point, however, because amid all the back-and-forth a court ruling on 14 June in 2012 dissolved the parliament. The Supreme Constitutional Court ruled that the election had been unconstitutional, and that a third of the winners were illegitimate in view of electoral law.[16] Following the presidential election a few weeks later, Mursi issued an executive decree that tried to return the parliament to session, but the Supreme Constitutional Court, along with the SCAF, rejected the decree.[17] In the showdown, Mursi acquiesced and the parliament was never reinstated.[18]

Yet again, the issue of revolutionary popular legitimacy and presidential legitimacy arose. Mursi was trying to assert revolutionary popular legitimacy, as had the SCAF before him, but he was paradoxically doing so through a political legitimacy that was the result of a democratic presidential election. The SCAF had enjoyed mass popular support in the aftermath of the uprising and could claim revolutionary legitimacy. Mursi had legitimately become president but he couldn't claim to have come to power as an immediate result of Mubarak's departure, nor could he claim the same mass mandate that the SCAF had on 11 February

2011. He had, for better or worse, become Egypt's first democratically elected president. This came with benefits, but also limitations.

The Egyptian state's institutions had been rotten in a variety of ways, and required deep and widespread reform. But the only way to accomplish such a task, just like in any democratic state, would have been to go through the system or, alternatively, deliver such a wide and mass popular revolutionary consensus that the system would have been unable to withstand it. Mursi didn't have the latter, but he was acting as though he did. The judiciary wasn't interested in reform of any kind, let alone revolutionary reform. But if Mursi wanted to outmanoeuvre it, this tack wasn't going to work.

VIII

By the time the Gaza crisis had de-escalated via Cairo's mediation, the Constitutional Assembly was already in an awkward state. Before the Gaza mediation had succeeded, I met with a visiting European foreign minister and a number of Egyptian civil society representatives—including one of the pro-revolution members of the Constituent Assembly, Ahmad Maher. The latter, one of the founding members of the April 6 Youth Movement, expressed deep exasperation at the way in which the assembly was conducting its business, and was convinced that his presence, along with that of those who were not on the same page as the MB and their allies, was simply window dressing. The assembly was conducting its business according to apparent directives from the MB, and non-Islamist members were incensed. Less than a week after our meeting, Maher had withdrawn from the assembly, as had Muhammad Anwar al-Sadat (son of the former president of Egypt, Anwar al-Sadat), Amr Moussa, the former secretary general of the Arab League, several Church figures, the New Wafd Party, and others. Not long thereafter, representatives of the journalists' syndicate and the farmers' syndicate did the same, causing the assembly to lose the quorum it required in order to vote on any constitutional articles.[19]

Given the polarisation that the country was experiencing on an increasing basis, it would have been wise for the MB and the presidency, as the most powerful political force in the country, to attempt some sort of reconciliation. The MB, as mentioned previously, saw their situation as one where the forces of the 'deep state' were constantly trying to tie their hands and undo the democratic experiment. They were not wrong about that, but the tactical decisions of the MB in response to this were a gift to its detractors. As the 'deep state' engaged in coalition building against the MB, the MB withdrew into its closed circles and proceeded to make the worst mistake of Mursi's tenure.

When Mursi came into office, there were already indicators that powerful forces in Egypt were unwilling to let him make headway. Nevertheless, there were a number of non-MB and non-Salafi group-ings who were willing to engage with him. In the months after Mursi's removal from office in 2013 MB sympathisers put into play a revisionist history. In their seemingly parallel universe, Mursi had never enjoyed any real power within the Egyptian state or in the country, and had been merely a figurehead. The real power had been diffused amongst structures connected to the 'deep state'.

That was partly true—but only partly. As we go through Mursi's year in power, it's clear he did have effective control over certain parts of the state, even while others like the judiciary resisted him. Critically, though, he also had the conditional cooperation of a number of non-Islamist elements outside the pro-Mubarak portions of the business elite and the upper echelons of the professional classes who were will-ing to accommodate the seemingly new political dispensation. Many of them publicly voiced their vexation at trying to engage with the new authorities, citing a deaf ear as the administration's typical response. Mursi preferred to work with stalwarts of the MB or close allies, which might have been fine in a country that had long-established democratic institutions, but he was the first president of a post-uprising Egypt in the midst of an as yet incomplete democratic experiment.

As the Middling Muslim Brothers blog noted in the aftermath of his fall:

> This isn't an issue of the former president's stubbornness or blindness or whatever. It's his embodiment of a mode of leadership that's common in the world of politics but very inadequate for the treacherous terrain of post-revolutionary politics. Dr Morsi's fatal weakness is that he's a proto-typical party oligarch, and this [has] made him distinctly unsuited for the extraordinary responsibility he took on.[20]

There were some MB figures who might have been able to engage more effectively with non-Islamist allies: not just more reformist types like Abu al-Futuh, but even more conservative characters like Muhammad al-Baltagi. Mursi, on the other hand, was an apparatchik par excellence. He was an enforcer of the movement and deferential to its leadership, and this image of him was set in the popular imagination even after he became president.

It was unsurprising, therefore, that when there were mass resignations from the non-Islamist members of the Constituent Assembly, the MB's response wasn't to engage with them and bring them back. On the contrary, they were simply replaced by alternate reserve members—mostly pro-Mursi figures. There followed a catastrophic move by Mursi.

IX

It was gutsy, to be sure. That's probably the most complimentary thing that can be said about it.

In comparison to many of the subsequent events in Egypt's post-uprising history, 22 November 2012 was not the most dreadful or destructive. But in the context of 2012, and the democratic experiment, it was one of the most crucial milestones. For Mursi issued a constitutional declaration that simultaneously did several things.[21] It first, again, forced the dismissal of Abd al-Majid Mahmud, the public prosecutor, replacing him with Tala'at Ibrahim Abdallah, who later turned out to be to Mursi what Mahmud was to Mubarak. But it did far more than that. The decree ensured that: investigations into the killing of protesters would be re-conducted; all decrees made by Mursi could not be appealed by any body; the public prosecutor would be appointed by the president for a fixed term of four years; no judicial authority could dissolve the Constituent Assembly and Shura Council; and the presidency would be authorised to take any other measures that it saw fit to 'preserve the revolution', 'nationality unity' or 'national security'. With parliament gone, this made the MB-dominated Shura Council, Egypt's usually consultative upper house, an even more important legislative power. Later (in June 2013), a court would invalidate the Shura Council on the basis that, like the parliament, elections to it were based on an unconstitutional law. But for now the Shura Council, and Mursi's hold, were strengthened to an unprecedented degree.[22]

Wholly expectedly, protests erupted all around Egypt. With that decree, Mursi had given himself immunity from any check or balance in the most brazen of fashions. Even the SCAF had not dared to indulge in such a symbolically aggressive gesture, though they wielded much, if not more, of the same power, while Mursi was markedly less popular. Opposition leaders accused Mursi of acting like a 'new pharaoh'. Mursi supporters would use the same epithet less than a year later for Sisi, but in November 2012 it was Mursi and his administration that were accused of a 'coup' against 'legitimacy'.[23] Even noted human rights activists such as Heba Morayef, the Egyptian director for Human Rights Watch, argued that while the country needed judicial reform, 'granting the president absolute power and immunity is not the way to do it'.[24] Most of Mursi's non-Islamist presidential advisors, who had had little impact on his policies in any case, resigned.

Protests continued nationwide, and some ended with the burning down of offices of the MB's Freedom and Justice Party (FJP).[25] Strikes by judges and prosecutors took place; human rights groups lodged lawsuits at the Court of Administrative Justice; and protesters clashed with security forces, as well as with supporters of Mursi's government. Several hundred people were injured in clashes with the Egyptian police.[26]

Negotiations began—but it was striking how few people had been in the know about Mursi's decision beforehand.[27] His own justice minister, Ahmad Makki, publicly acknowledged that he had not been informed about the decree, that he would have advised against it, and that he could never have signed it himself because it violated his 'core convictions'. Makki even publicly declared that Mursi should amend the decree.[28]

In the aftermath of the decree, most of the political parties opposed to Mursi banded together in a short-lived coalition named the National Salvation Front, as mentioned in Chapter 2. It was a motley crew. There were, by some counts, more than thirty different parties represented: Nasserites, liberals, leftists, and others—including those who had enjoyed an uncomfortably friendly relationship with Mubarak's regime. As a result of the latter, student members of the Constitution Party, the Socialist Popular Alliance, the Egyptian Popular Current, and others, pushed their parties to leave the coalition (to no avail).[29] Abu al-Futuh, who had established himself as a harsh but constructive critic of Mursi's administration, refused to join the Front, insisting that it 'purge' itself of figures connected to Mubarak's regime. Many suspected he was referring to the likes of Amr Moussa, who had been Mubarak's foreign minister.

In an interview a year later, in 2013, Abu al-Futuh argued that the opposition to the MB had turned the political conflict 'into an ideological conflict, which we are against'.[30] There was some truth in that: many of those who had before sought to avoid engaging in a dogmatic, essentialist struggle against the MB, started doing just that in the aftermath of the decree. Of course, the MB camp was also deeply entrenched in a dogmatic, ideological worldview of its own: for many of its members, this was a struggle between the forces of Islam, and the forces of darkness and disbelief. But that did not remove the fact that the organised political opposition, by and large, was rooted in simply opposing Mursi: it had little in terms of a positive alternative of its own.

In April 2013, I participated in a debate on the subject of the opposition.[31] My rule had generally been to leave the opposition alone in terms of criticism. It was not in power and had no realistic mandate to run a government. As an analyst, I believed in primarily critiquing those who could actually effect change, and that meant the MB at the time. Primarily didn't mean always, however, and the opposition, in my opinion, was shirking its responsibilities tremendously. It was in Egypt's interests to have a strong and organised opposition that could hold the executive to account, and this opposition, as represented by the National Salvation Front, was anything but strong and organised.

In response to Mursi's decree, which insisted on the constitutional referendum going forward on 15 December of 2012, the opposition was unable to speak with one voice, let alone make a decision. For days it had sent mixed (if any) signals about whether or not it would boycott it (not exactly a proven tool of effective politics in Egypt) or push for a 'no' vote. It was hardly the kind of decisive leadership needed for the crisis. When the streets of Egypt arose in anger, the opposition could do, or did, nothing to stop the attacks on the FJP's offices, let alone provide a genuine alternative. It wasn't that they didn't try, but their failure was clear evidence of their lack of leadership and their inability to provide direction.[32]

Amidst the protests, the Constituent Assembly rushed to complete its work. A case that might lead to the dissolving of the assembly was due to be heard by the Supreme Constitutional Court on 2 December. The MB hoped to pre-empt that by having a constitutional draft ready. Composed nearly completely of pro-Mursi members, the assembly rushed ahead by working non-stop and literally overnight on a new constitutional draft.

X

The content of the constitutional draft was hardly inspiring. It contained many problematic articles and ambiguities that were hardly going to be the pride of a country that had gone through a revolutionary uprising on the one hand, and had long been renowned across the Arab world for its constitutional legal tradition on the other. But the core problem with the constitutional draft was the process that brought it into existence. When Mursi abruptly changed course in November 2012 and announced that the draft would be put to a referendum in December, he set the country's polarisation into overdrive. From the perspective of the MB, the dizzying speed at which these measures were taking place would allow it to overcome the civil unrest. From the perspective of almost everyone else, it would mean the exact opposite—the prospect of more unrest. Indeed, on 5 December large-scale protests erupted in Tahrir Square and at the presidential palace, leading to a further escalation of tension.[33]

A day later, I wrote the following essay for the American periodical *Foreign Policy*, which I feel gave a taste of the time:

> With the violence that broke out in front of the presidential palace in Egypt yesterday, one can no longer describe the constitutional draft produced under the Muhammad Mursi government as just 'flawed'. In process, the draft is abysmal. In context, it revises history. In content, it is silent, vague, and problematic. In consequence, it is bloody. It isn't just that Egypt can do better. Ratifying this constitution would reward, and deepen, polarization—and the goals of the January 25 revolution would be that much further away from being achieved.
>
> The most obvious problems with the constitutional draft are procedural. The process was supposed to deliver a representative Constituent Assembly, which would produce a consensus-based document that the overwhelming majority of Egyptians would sign up to, and feel invested in. The first assembly was dismissed in April, after the supreme administra-

tive court pointed out members of parliament could not elect themselves onto the assembly, and that the assembly involved too few women, young people, and representatives of minority groups.

Most hoped that the next assembly would be more representative. It was, initially, but it was still overwhelmingly Islamist, and still included members of parliament. With the dismissal of parliament shortly thereafter, President Mursi had the legislative ability to reappoint a new assembly altogether, which he could have done in conjunction with other political forces, ensuring a popular consensus. Instead, the president protected the Islamist-dominated assembly for months despite widespread criticism and the resignations of the majority of non-Islamist political forces.

In his recent decree allocating himself freedom from judicial oversight, Mursi declared [that] the assembly had three more months to complete its work. A few days later, he ignored his own decree. Instead of three months, the assembly was directed to complete its work in a matter of hours, in a process even more dominated by Islamists after the overwhelming majority of non-Islamists withdrew in protest. If the first assembly was unrepresentative, this one was even more so.

That procedural disaster extends to the referendum, which is scheduled at the end of next week. It's likely a majority of Egyptians will not even understand the draft, considering the time frame: and rather than being a force for consensus building, the draft, by virtue of the process that produced it, is a force for deepening polarization in Egypt.

Beyond the process, the context of the draft makes things more bizarre. It is clear in the past two years the transition had been, to put it politely, less than smooth owing to the decisions of the Egyptian military leadership. Yet, the draft implies that they protected and upheld the revolution. That will be news to the protest movement that directed its ire against the military for the past two years. Then again, the constitution also protects the right of the military to try civilians in military courts—so perhaps there is more than enough strange news to go around.

The content of the constitution does not make for absolutely awful reading, it should be said. It is not totalitarian, although it provides an incredible amount of power to the executive, without according a sufficient check from the legislative. Nor does it create a conservative Islamist theocracy, even though it does vest the state with powers to enforce and preserve 'morality'.

But the people of Egypt did not engage in a popular revolution for a constitution that was not 'awful'. No constitution was ever going to be perfect: but this constitutional draft is mediocre at best. At worst, it is open to incredible abuse—a problem in a society increasingly riven by mistrust and damaging splits. It privileges the state above and beyond civil society in so many ways, giving the state powers to intervene in areas where it should have no competency.

Moreover, it provides the executive with such power that autocracy is incredibly tempting, if not mandatory. Considering that the revolution owes its very existence to civil society, and Egyptians revolted largely against the dictatorship of former President Hosni Mubarak, that is hardly an encouraging affirmation of the revolt. Protection and encouragement of civil society should have been at the core of this constitution—it almost seems barely tolerated, instead.

And finally, in consequence: it is bloody. The draft, as far as the supporters of Mursi are concerned, must go through. It must be put to a referendum. Opposition to him, his decree, and his draft, is no longer simply a political disagreement that can be rationally disputed. Rather, it is a sign of a more existential battle against the MB. It is that worldview that unfortunately led to some of Mursi's supporters descending upon a peaceful protest in front of the presidential palace yesterday, resulting in a predictable conflict that led to [at the time of writing] 6 people dying. Their blood stains this constitutional draft.[34]

When the referendum took place, it was not seen as being about the articles of the constitution. It was never going to be treated as such in the aftermath of the violence outside the presidential palace.[35] Rather, it was seen as a referendum on Mursi and his leadership. Its passing was therefore seen by the MB as a validation of Mursi's decree in November and the MB at large. If it had failed, the opposition would undeniably have insisted it was a clear rejection of Mursi. Of course, none of this is what Egyptians should have been focusing on in their first free constitutional vote.

With the passing of the draft, it was clear that the dynamism of the revolution would be reduced, and schisms would be deepened even further. The MB's insistence on trying to approve a new constitution in the middle of a political crisis would weaken the constitution's credibility during its short life span, as well as the MB's moral standing. Revolutionary activism was not about to end—but it was to be dealt a blow. That was never going to be good for Egypt, and perhaps should have been one thing that gave both the MB and its opposition food for thought.

There were forces within the 'deep state' that had wanted to derail Egypt's nascent democratic transition; and the MB, as well as the opposition, knew it. But the MB's best partner in tackling them at the time of the constitutional referendum was, in fact, the opposition—something it needed to realise, but tragically did not.

If Mursi had made the argument that in order to not only tackle Egypt's 'deep state', but also to uphold Egypt's societal unity, he needed to take drastic steps, he could still have turned this crisis into an opportunity. A new decree that rescinded his supra-legal power, revoking any effects of his decisions of those weeks, the cancelling of the referendum and the building of a revolutionary legislative council made up of Egypt's key political forces was still an option in those days. It would have been no more extraordinary than the decree that he had issued giving himself freedom from judicial oversight.

The opposition also faced a choice. The MB would never have advocated the idea of a supra-legal president had it been Shafiq, Sabahi, Abu al-Futuh or Moussa in power. With Mursi at the helm the opposition should have reaffirmed that its goal was not to force him out of office, but just for him to do his job properly. Moreover, they needed to do their job as a loyal opposition as well, which was to constructively and effectively hold the government to account.

Regardless of how one might have felt about elements of the opposition's patriotism and passion, one could not deny its collective lack of strategic thinking. The opposition ran the risk, even then, of just running out of steam: continuous protests without a strategic vision were always going to be unsustainable. They were not only in danger of failing themselves, but Egypt too.

No legal historian can consider modern Arab law without acknowledging the role of Egyptian jurists: contemporary Arab law almost owes its existence to them. Egypt could have produced a constitution worthy of that heritage. It could have earned the admiration of many, regionally and internationally. A revolt of eighteen days was a transient experience: a constitution would have left a lasting legacy.

But, bizarrely, the crisis intensified. Mursi's newly installed prosecutor general filed a complaint charging former presidential candidates Moussa and Sabahi, along with opposition politicians Muhammad al-Baradei and the Wafd party leader, al-Sayyid al-Badawi, with espionage and incitement to overthrow the government via a 'Zionist plot'.[36] On 5 December large-scale protests erupted in Tahrir Square and at the presidential palace in Ittahidiya, leading to a further escalation of tension.

In the midst of those protests, particularly in front of Ittahidiya, the polarisation of Egyptian politics was set, and political vigilante violence, mixed in with a nasty sectarianism, tended to be the norm. Human Rights Watch recommended the following in the aftermath:

> Egypt's public prosecutor should investigate the detention and abuse of several dozen anti-government protesters in Cairo by MB members on December 5 and 6, 2012. At least forty-nine protesters opposed to President Muhammad Morsi were unlawfully held outside the Ettihadiya presidential palace gate, an area then occupied by the MB and overseen by riot police, detainees and witnesses told Human Rights Watch. The detentions followed armed clashes that resulted in the deaths of ten people, mostly MB members, and injuries to 748 more, according to the Health Ministry.[37]

It was an ugly episode. Senior MB leaders such as Essam al-Erian and Muhammad al-Baltagi publicly engaged in incitement, with al-Baltagi claiming on national television that most of the protesters were Christians,[38] and al-Erian calling on MB supporters to fall upon them. The spectacle of senior members of the ruling party—and former parliamentarians—involving themselves in vigilantism was strikingly unedifying. Joe Stork of Human Rights Watch also noted that, 'Instead of condemning illegal detentions and abuse right outside the presidential palace, President Morsy spoke out against the victims'.[39]

Mursi's supporters were not the only ones who attacked the anti-government protesters: police officers participated as well, which also showed that at least in December 2012, the police force was still paying attention to the presidency's orders. But the question remained: how long would it?

The ugliness continued, even in the midst of death. When the funerals took place for MB members, the chants that accompanied their processions turned the political conflict into something else, for MB supporters declared that its fallen were in heaven while the opposition's fatalities were in hell.[40] This was not a random set of chants: it was a repetition of what the prophetic companions had said after a battle against the pagans of Makkah. The political dispute between the MB and their opponents had become something far more 'fundamental'. By conveniently evoking a historical parallel, the MB supporters were fighting for God, His Religion and His Prophet. The MB's opponents, ostensibly in the camp of treason and unbelief because of this, were those who wanted to destroy it all. That its opponents were nearly all Muslim did not seem to matter to the MB.

I wrote a piece for *Al-Ahram*, where I argued:

> Supporters of the MB are not the only ones who have a Manichean world-view. One does not see this kind of sentiment coming from the leadership of the opposition—but, certainly, there are those who view this as a cultural war. A cultural war where the MB must fall ... so that Egypt can take her rightful place in the world. Mr Mursi winning the elections is immaterial—he should never have been allowed to run in the first place, and it is shameful that when he did run, all intelligent human beings did not vote for Ahmad Shafiq, Mubarak's last prime minister. In the new Egypt, the law must ban the MB: for otherwise, these fascistic militants will destroy Egypt.

> Neither of these perspectives was in the square between 25 January and 11 February 2011. If anything, that kind of worldview back then was present only in the regime of Hosni Mubarak—and it was precisely that worldview that the square stood in contradistinction to.

> One cannot say that the effects of these two worldviews are equal. A member of the MB is in the presidency, and its organisation all around Egypt means that the more powerful such a worldview is within, the more vicious the effects will be on the country as a whole. The sectarian messaging that is becoming more and more pervasive, describing the crisis as one where 'Islam' itself is under attack, is deeply concerning. Moreover, such messaging, if it comes from the right people in positions of authority in the MB, can affect huge numbers of people.

> One cannot say the same for the opposition. The political leadership has far less control over the protestors, who are in the streets not because al-Baradei or others asked them to—but because they spontaneously rejected President Mursi's actions and policies. That leadership has little control over them. Moreover, the truly concerning messaging does not come from the leadership anyway—it comes from far more isolated voices. Qualitatively, the rhetoric is immensely damaging—but in terms of effect, it's far more contained.'[41]

XI

At the time, I was rather frustrated by some of the coverage that festered within the international media on the goings-on in Egypt. In a flurry of exasperation, I penned a piece for the noted 'Arabist' blog. It perhaps still makes for pertinent reading—not simply as a narrative about that particular period, but also because it shows the way in which a particular type of journalism approached Egypt during that time.

There are times that myths circulate so fast, it is hard to keep track of them. In the midst of an extraordinary amount of coverage on Egypt, I was asked for my evaluation of a particular piece, recently published in what I considered to be a respectable media outlet. As I wrote my assessment, I realised that I'd seen those same problems—the same narrative—time and time again in different places. Rather than keep my assessment private, I thought I would turn it into a plea to my colleagues and friends in the media and the think-tank/policy arena.

The plea reads: please knock it off when it comes to your Egypt coverage, and check your sources and facts before you publish in the interests of being 'balanced'. Believe me: in the long run, you'll be grateful you did. ...

There seems to be a doubt that these protests were about President Mursi's decree on 22 November, as though they would have happened anyway. That's an intriguing suggestion, considering that from the 30 June 2012 to 22 November 2012, there were virtually no protests against Mr Mursi. So, for five months, despite calls for protests from pro-Shafiq elements in August, one could not really find much in the way of street action in Egypt. Odd, that.

No matter. Mr Mursi is the 'elected president of Egypt' and as such should be able to expect two things: a) that he can give himself supra-legal powers, as stipulated in the decree and b) that we constantly remind ourselves and the world that he is the 'elected president of Egypt'. Well, of course, he is the elected president of Egypt—he won the elections in June 2012, in a race where I supported his victory, and I have no regrets over that decision today.

Nevertheless, more than 48 per cent of the votes went to his opponent—and many who did vote for Mr Mursi, did so to keep his opponent out. That's not generally referred to as a strong democratic mandate: it's probably better described as a weak democratic band-aid. Mr Mursi should not have used that slim electoral victory as a sign that he could work outside of the system, as the military council had. My criticisms of that council's handling of the transition are a matter of public record: but they did have popular support for their institution, as well as their road-map. Mr Mursi did not, and would have been well-advised to have built that support by encouraging consensus, at a critical time for Egypt's transition, if he wanted to go outside the normal political and legal channels of Egypt's institutions. Instead, much of his own cabinet (let alone those outside of it) didn't seem to know about his decree before it was delivered.

There's the supposition that the opposition is a motley crew of liberal secularists, nationalists, youth groups, and holdovers from the Mubarak regime; while, of course, the president's government (all good God-fearing folk) would never have anything to do with former Mubarak supporters. How intriguing, considering the MB has been working with Mubarak-era 'remnants' for months, in order to bolster its power within the state. Fancy that.

Even more intriguing, this narrative never seems to recognise that on the opposition side, there are deeply religious Muslims (and Christians), and also Islamists like [Abd al Mun'im] Abu al-Futuh. How utterly nonsensical that might be, particularly in a country that is about 85–90 per cent Muslim, and 10–15 per cent Christian. ...

There is, however, a type of religious divide here—one that should be pointed out. One side believes it has a monopoly on what 'Islam' is, and what 'enmity towards Islam' is. For this side, there is no issue in declaring that 'their' dead are in heaven, and the dead of the opposition are in hell. ...

Tragically, polarisation in this crisis has led to deaths. More repugnant than tragic, however, has been the attempt to describe all the dead as being members of the MB. The Christian doctor who was killed was, it should be assumed, not a particularly likely candidate for an Islamist party that is tacking further and further to the right. The journalist who was killed seemed to keep his affiliations very well hidden: his fiancée and several members of his family were under the distinct impression he opposed the MB. Seeking 'victory' even in death brings a new meaning to the word 'low'.

The opposition leadership should have gone to the national dialogue [to which Mursi invited them in December 2012]. But it is somewhat easy to see why they did not feel particularly endeared to the invitation; after all, while they were being invited by one hand of the government, another hand was issuing calls from the prosecutor general's office for them to be investigated for crimes. Moreover, it did not seem they were really needed: the presidency managed to find fifty-four 'national' and 'legal' figures to participate instead. Never mind that none of them were significant leaders of the opposition or protest movement—nor that the 'representative' of the national dialogue was, actually, a presidential advisor to Mr Mursi only a few days before. Yes, he must have had the opposition's interests at heart. ...

But back to this process: the president's supporters have indicated that a lack of 'respect towards democracy' is at the heart of the opposition's motives, seeing as they rejected the referendum the president insisted go ahead. Because, of course, fifteen days is more than enough time for a population which is more than 30 per cent illiterate, is going through clashes where people have died, and from which millions of people have taken to the streets, to go through a document that has more than two-hundred articles and is confusing for even the legalistically literate… right. Very undemo-cratic of them to suggest it might be for the best of the country to reduce polarisation, rather than increase it. Naughty opposition.

But of course, they are naughty: because they should simply 'trust' the president. They should have 'trusted' the president, as his supporters sug-gested, when he gave himself freedom from judicial review—because, after all, he's a good guy, and he needs to be given time. So, when he 'commits' himself to asking the new parliament to amend disputed clauses, the opposition should 'trust' him.

Just as they should have trusted the president when he declared, after taking office, that he would not put the constitution to a referendum with-out national consensus. (Umm.)

Just as they should have trusted him when he declared he would have a Christian vice-president—and a female vice president. (Still waiting on these.)

Just as they should have trusted him when he, and the rest of his move-ment, declared that the MB would not put forward a presidential candi-date (they put forward two). Trust does not go a long way in politics at the best of times, it seems.

But that should not matter, because a majority of Egyptians, according to 'opinion polls', support the president and have supported him throughout this latest crisis. I'm perhaps somewhat dubious about this one, consider-ing that senior members of the FJP use Facebook polls to justify support levels …

There is much to criticise the opposition on. I could probably write quite a few pieces on that subject myself—but misrepresenting them does not help anyone's cause. On the contrary: Egypt, one would think, is big enough for all of them. As the Western media continues to cover this coun-try, one would also think, they might ponder upon that—and report accordingly. Just might.[42]

XII

Mursi got his constitution—albeit with a low turn out. A little under two-thirds of the vote was in favour.[43] The MB celebrated. Even those who thought that he had rushed things felt relief considering their fears that the Constituent Assembly might have been dissolved.

They might have been right about that; but if so, without being crude, so what? The power to form a new Constituent Assembly was in the hands of the presidency—if this one failed, then Mursi had the ability to simply form a new one. The question was whether or not he could form one that was genuinely diverse, and could draft a constitution that was befitting of a country that had come through a revolutionary uprising.

I remember on 27 December 2012, I was invited to meet with a noted Pakistani legal specialist, who was the guest of one of the main political figures in Egypt. He walked into the meeting, and boldly pronounced to those present, 'I have read the constitutional draft, and it is better than the one we have in Pakistan.' He said this with some kind of triumphalism. When I gently responded, 'I don't think Egyptians revolted so that they could have a constitution that was better than Pakistan's', others in the room smiled. But low expectations were soon becoming the name of the game.

The difference between Mursi's administration before his executive decree, and after it, was like the difference between night and day. Before the decree there was bad blood between Mursi supporters and opponents—but there was still a belief, permeating through the country and the political elite, that though the democratic experiment might be rocky, it could still work. Once that decree was issued, the trust quotient in Egyptian politics was abysmal. Mursi eventually backtracked on much of the decree—but he didn't reverse its effects. The Constituent Assembly had been immunised, the constitutional referendum had been called and the new constitution was to be implemented.

Mursi didn't become, despite the accusations of some, an 'Islamofascist' due to the actions he took in November and December 2012. Yet he did manage to irrevocably damage any semblance of trust that had existed between the key political players in the country. To restore it, he would have had to have done something as equally dramatic as the decree—but what? As an analyst I was often asked this. I never had a good answer, and I don't think Mursi was really interested anyway.

But if Mursi was not particularly interested in the notion of finding genuine common ground with his opponents, the political elite that represented the opposition wasn't either. There had been a window of opportunity to either get a substantial proportion of the opposition on side within a broad national consensus when Mursi was first elected, or at least to neutralise the opposition, so that it would not become resigned to the early expiration of a Mursi administration. That window closed the moment Mursi issued his executive decree granting himself supra-judicial powers.

The opposition was fragmented, which is natural in any dynamic political order, but in Egypt it became somewhat strident in its approach. By the end of 2012, there was growing dissent from within state institutions—not to the extent, it ought to be stressed, that state institutions en masse were not listening to the orders of the executive, but that sentiment was beginning to grow.

XIII

On 6 December I witnessed the consequences of this when one of the FJP offices in the Zahra al-Ma'adi district in south-eastern Cairo was ransacked. The crowd that stormed it was made up of essentially three groups. The largest was probably about 15 metres away from the office, on a grassy knoll bisecting the road. There were a few lively arguments in the crowd, to be sure, but it was peaceful and hardly confrontational. The crowd was made up mostly of young men, and a few women (some in headscarves, some not). These people looked as though they were from the area, and all seemed to be vigorously opposed to the MB. In front of the office itself were two smaller groups: one group, I believe, had been trying to keep the second from storming the office. Neither of them were MB, but I was fairly sure they were all protesters. In the midst of them were the 'Ultras', fanatic Al Ahly football club supporters who, like the MB, had played a critical role in defending Tahrir at the Battle of the Camels in 2011.

I was getting ready to leave, as it seemed all was well. Then, I turned around and saw that both groups in front of the office had moved. In the street there was someone, who appeared to be an 'Ultra', trying to agitate the crowd. I couldn't hear him, and then suddenly a young lad kicked in the door. People started cheering as the office was completely ransacked. There was no one inside and it wasn't burnt to the ground, but it was completely looted: furniture, paperwork, and everything else was taken out and hurled into the street.

There were no opposition spokespeople there, nor were there any opposition flags. This was, from what I could tell, a completely spontaneous reaction by community members against the FJP, spurred on by the 'Ultras'. The slogans that followed (swearing at the president's mother, for example), I'd never heard at any opposition rally anywhere before.

After that point, the Central Security Force (CSF) began to advance. The young men left the office and began advancing towards the CSF. The police backed down, and began to walk backwards, with an armoured vehicle. They went all the way back. I then left the area.[44]

I confirmed two things that day. The first was that at least parts of the police were still obeying orders from the presidency. The second was that opposition to the MB was spreading, and it wasn't limited to hardcore secularists in upper-elite neighbourhoods of Cairo, like Zamalek. The MB still didn't see it. But it would catch up with them. Days after the new constitution came into effect, 2013 began—the year that would change the MB forever.

6

THE SLOW-MOVING TRAIN WRECK

I think there will be a coup this July. [Mursi's] situation is pretty unsustainable.

My prediction, made to an American colleague in Cairo on 16 March 2013

Hellyer says Sunday's protests, if successful, are dangerous. 'The propensity for violence would increase. It's very bad for the story for Egyptian democracy, as it says that government can be thrown out after a year. The only way Mursi leaves is by the military forcing him out, which involves violence and social disorder.'

Interview with Bel Trew, 26 June 2013, in the *New Statesman*[1]

I

In every profession, there is a special type of arrogance. The arrogance of the analyst is that he thinks he can actually predict what is going to happen at any given point. Regardless of what we might consider to be the variables we ought to consider, there are always variables we either do not recognise at all, or fail to accurately account for. The importance of those variables has little to do with us, and everything to do with forces that are far larger and greater than our ability to predict. When we do get things right, it behoves us to be humble about it, and to recognise where we got things wrong along the way.

On 16 March, three-and-a-half months prior to the military's moves against Muhammad Mursi, I met a friend and colleague from out of town for an early-afternoon coffee. Looking back on it, Cairo was a very different place that spring. There were protests taking place fairly often, sometimes involving clashes with police, and periodically in or around Tahrir Square. There was a sense of instability or unpredictability that I recall quite vividly—as though on any given day, the roads might be closed, or I might drive inadvertently into a protest against the Mursi-led government. Things felt as though they could erupt in unforeseen ways—which became the subject of conversation with my colleague that afternoon. Early on in the year, clashes had taken place in Port Said, which resulted in the army being called in; and other parts of the country had started to heat up as well, particularly in the Nile Delta region.[2]

From March onwards, I had been writing and speaking about 'Egypt's flammable summer', which I thought was looming. I saw far too many problems bubbling up in the country—along with severe opposition to the Muslim Brotherhood (MB) from within the state, in various ministries—to be sanguine about the ability of Mursi's government to survive. So when my colleague asked me what I thought was going to happen, I answered that I thought the military would carry out a coup in July (I said the same during a public seminar at Kings College in London a month later). She was sceptical, reminding me that American law prescribed the cutting of all aid to any government that came to power via a coup, which presumably ought to cause the generals to think twice. My response to that was that the US and its allies would find every way to avoid cutting off Egypt and allowing it to drift from the Western axis, and might even package it as 'democratic' in some way.

On 3 July 2013 the military indeed carried out its coup, and predictably, the world failed to treat it as such. In the years following the coup, a number of commentators and analysts argued that a coup had been 'inevitable' the moment Mursi took office, since the odds were so massively stacked against him it was impossible for any other scenario to emerge. This idea of 'inevitability' perhaps indicates another type of arrogance endemic in my profession—because nothing is really 'inevitable' in that way. Human beings make choices. Things could have worked out differently in 2013 had different stakeholders made different choices. I didn't regard a July 2013 coup as inevitable—I just thought it was incredibly likely. How I would have liked to have been proven wrong.

My analysis was only partially correct, since I had accounted for only some of the reasons that precipitated the military's intervention.[3] I didn't, for example, perceive Tamarod (discussed later in this chapter) and the presence of widespread protests to be a critical factor— on the contrary, I expected little from Tamarod, and did not foresee large protests that would precede a military intervention. To my mind, a coup would take place in July—and specifically July—because of several factors relating to Ramadan, which was due to fall during the month of July that year. It is the most expensive month in the Egyptian calendar for Muslims. They host more guests, they go out to eat more often, and they give generously to charity: as well as playing host to the daily *iftar* (breaking of the fast), people also provide meals for the less fortunate at *ma'idat al-rahman* gatherings. With the economy failing to show signs of recovery after a tumultuous two years, and in fact continuing its tumble, Egyptians were likely to feel the pinch more during that month than any other, and perhaps to give voice to dissent more easily. Moreover, Ramadan in the unrelenting summer heat really tests the patience of those fasting. Electricity consumption during the hot months always increases due to the usage of air conditioners—and it was beginning to become apparent that severe energy cuts would hit Egyptians that year. I felt this all made for a very difficult summer ahead.

There were few among international analysts in March 2013 who agreed. Apart from my friend and fellow analyst, Michael Wahid Hanna at the Century Foundation in New York, I did not find anyone in the analytical or academic communities in the West who thought the Mursi government, unless it changed dramatically, was unsustainable and had an extremely short lifespan (a matter of weeks or months). Most thought that Mursi had successfully neutralised the military, and that as a result he'd be able to stay in office until he left it voluntarily after four years. I didn't see it that way. I saw the military's leadership as having willingly kept out of issues that pertained to governance, as long as Mursi could, at least in their perception, handle governance. That meant maintaining effective control of and stability in the country, and ensuring that the military's privileges continued. In terms of the latter, that was never in doubt from 2011 onwards. The former, however, was fast becoming uncertain.

II

I felt that in January 2013 we'd received a preview of what was to come. The police force and the government lost control of the strategic port city of Suez in the midst of civil unrest, and the army was forced to step in to restore order. In far away Cairo, during one day in particular, there were some signs of solidarity, with substantial protests in the city, the gathering of football fans at Al Ahly football club, and arson at the Police Club in Zamalek. It wasn't seen as a tipping point in Cairo, but at the time it did seem clear that the military was still more than capable of engaging directly with the populace and supplanting government. Only a month or so earlier, then-Minister of Defence Sisi had issued an invitation to host discussions between Egypt's different political forces. It was a move that indicated, unequivocally, that the military leadership continued to regard itself as having a role in the public sphere. And this was a position that wasn't unpopular with Egyptians at large. This was also something that played into my own calculations during the first half of 2013. The military and its leadership were extremely popular in Egypt. If it intervened in political life it was unlikely to be viewed with disapproval by the majority of the population—that was the nature of the Egyptian scene, whether one approved of it or not.

The military intervention in Suez appeared to be something akin to a 'mini-coup', albeit one that was acquiesced to by the Egyptian presidency. For the reasons outlined above, I wondered as early as March whether something more dramatic might happen during the summer. Dissent was growing against Mursi and the MB, from many quarters. There were those who had supported him in 2012's presidential election who now rejected him; there were those who had never wanted to give him a chance; and there were many other dissenting voices from a variety of sectors.

There were two groups competing for the cooperation of the state's bureaucracy and the more passive supporters of the former regime. The more obvious group was the anti-Mursi network; the less obvious was the Mursi administration and the MB. As one author noted, 'Mursi repeatedly accommodated the police, only to get the worst of all worlds. Citizens were outraged by continued police impunity, while police strikes and passive resistance intensified the collective violence and chaos that destabilised Mursi's rule.'[4]

The picture was perhaps even worse than that. The police force had been granted the ability to act with impunity against protesters during Mursi's year in power. Policy brutality was continuing, and revolutionary activists, as well as human rights defenders, were openly declaring that police violence was a dangerous reality.[5] One of them, Hossam Bahgat, noted in mid-February 2013 that, 'In over a decade I have not seen as many cases of male activists fully raped in policy custody as in the past few weeks.'[6] Revolutionary activists began documenting the abuse in videos, replacing the label '*kazibun*' ('liars'), with which they had referred to the military leadership, with '*kazibun bi ism al-din*' ('liars in the name of religion') to refer to the MB.[7] Some argued that the police forces that were running wild were disobeying presidential instructions. Research later showed, however, that the Mursi administration was trying to accommodate and co-opt the security sector, without engaging in reform.[8] But that didn't stop the police practically vanishing from the streets during the last months of Mursi's government. Cairo remained probably safer than most major global capitals—but the perception (and probably also the reality) of a rise in petty crime was keenly felt. That contributed, not in a small way, to the discontent with the Mursi government.

In any event, Mursi, just like his predecessors, expressed no interest in truly reforming the security sector. He only wanted to ensure it did his bidding. For a while it did—but it was naïvety of the highest order to think that it would continue to do so indefinitely. In May 2012 I was walking with the prominent liberal opposition politician Amr Hamzawy—one out of a very small handful of people who were truly political liberals, as opposed to simply paying lip service to the label. He'd just completed a panel discussing Egyptian politics, and we were both en route to a dinner. I'd known Amr since 2007, when we were both in Washington, D.C. at think-tanks on Massachusetts Avenue—he at the Carnegie Endowment for International Peace, and I at the Brookings Institution. I couldn't have dreamed that four years later we'd both be in Cairo, witnessing—and participating in—the Egyptian uprising.

As we walked from the panel's venue to Amr's car, a couple of police officers ran up to him, who recognised Amr from his many television appearances. They pleaded with him that the opposition take a more aggressive stance against Mursi. In response, Amr said that Egypt would survive, and needed to move for parliamentary elections. He also mentioned that the rest of Mursi's four-year tenure might be difficult, but that Egypt would be fine—and Egyptians needed to bear up. The look on the police officers' faces was one of disdain and shock. They pleaded with Amr, insisting that they couldn't think of tolerating Mursi's government for much longer. I wasn't sure what they thought the alternative option was. Probably they didn't know either. But it was clear they were no longer interested in the democratic experiment. For them, it was a game that was now not worth playing. To his credit, Amr disagreed, and he made that clear—but he would not be able to stand against the tidal wave that was coming.

III

In mid-April 2013, I spoke at a conference at King's College London. Ebay's Vice President and Deputy General Counsel for Global Government Relations, Tod Cohen, was also in attendance, and spoke at the conference. As is often the case with large gatherings of this nature, one of the most interesting conversations took place between scheduled discussions, the day before the panel. That day, the state funeral procession of Margaret Thatcher, Britain's former prime minister, the 'Iron Lady' of British politics, and one of the most hated figures of my father's political generation, passed right in front of King's.

As Tod and I stood on the sidelines, he asked me about Egypt, and what might happen in the coming months. I told him I frankly expected a coup in the summer. He looked at me, startled. But at that point, I had already been convinced that a military intervention of some sort was inevitable. I didn't think it was already in the works, per se, but that the way in which Egyptian politics was unfolding, it was difficult to conceive of any other outcome. The following day, at the conference itself, I made that argument in a public venue—something I had forgotten about until James Boys, an academic then at King's College, reminded me in a Tweet on 2 July: 'Hats off to @hahellyer for correctly predicting the exact date of the Egyptian military response in Egypt back in April at @KingsCollegeLon'.[9]

THE SLOW-MOVING TRAIN WRECK

All the signs were there that the military would intervene. I got the context correct, but I was not quite correct about the reasons behind the eventual decision—I presumed a military intervention would take place only after an erratic, chaotic and probably violent turn of events. I wrote the following in Egypt's *Daily News* on 19 March 2013, in a piece entitled 'Military Intervention and Egypt's Future':

> The military may be coming—and it seems like everyone knows and is waiting for it, except the Muslim Brotherhood. The irony is: they are the ones who have the most to lose.
>
> A new intervention into governance by the Egyptian armed forces is something that many in the political, social and economic elite are clamouring for. They're not all on the same page in that regard, and people ought to be honest about that. Some people just have it in for the MB, and always would have had—regardless of whether or not the MB had been successful in taking Egypt forward along the transition towards a second republic.
>
> There are others who (and let us also be equally frank in this regard) prefer a military intervention, because it removes the MB from the political playing field, thus giving them a political advantage they might not already have. Politics is hard work—and many are tempted to do away with that hard work in favour of a military intervention that would remove their adversaries.
>
> There are, however, those who are not necessarily calling for such an intervention—but are nonetheless expecting it to happen. They see the pound fall in value against the dollar; they see the supply of wheat becoming more problematic; the supply of petrol and diesel diminishing; food prices potentially rising; and looming power cuts as the summer draws closer, putting pressure on the country's electrical infrastructure.
>
> In other words: a state akin to a slow-moving train wreck. With security becoming more and more of an issue, it is not beyond the realms of possibility that that train will suddenly speed into overdrive. If the economic troubles of Egypt then turn into real threats to public order, with riots and the like, the state's security services are not likely to be able to keep a lid on it—and at that point, the military may feel obliged to intervene.
>
> People ought not to be so idealistic about what this scenario could look like. The military's conduct over the eighteen months it directly governed Egypt is a model for how not to conduct a transitional process. Indeed, much, if not most, of the problems that currently face Egypt are down to the military's mismanagement of that period. While General Sisi is, by all accounts, an extremely smart individual, it remains to be seen whether or

not he would be able to conduct an intervention that would leave the country better off than before.

Nor, it should be stated, does the military want to intervene. It doesn't. The military's standing in the country at the end of the governing period was extraordinarily good (all things considered)—but it was still markedly less than in the months after the downfall of Hosni Mubarak. The military does not want to be in that position again. Indeed, who would want to be responsible for such a mammoth task?

However, if public disorder does go beyond a certain point, it is hard to see the military simply staying on the side-lines. It would then have to deal with certain challenges.

The first is the threat to the democratic and pluralistic quotient of Egyptian politics. No matter how you slice it, an independent move by the Egyptian military means that the military continues to be above civilian control—and an intervention would almost definitely be against the elected government's wishes.

Ethically and morally, that is not a particularly good way to begin a transition. Having said that, very few people are likely to care. The military's position in the country, and in public opinion, is the envy of any political force anywhere. If it was to construct a decent enough cover story, the intervention could be packaged as 'supporting democracy'—and enough people outside and inside of Egypt would be more than willing to go along with it.

The second challenge would be how to reintroduce economic stability—a task that would require the military to deal directly with 'consensus politics'. They would need to build a consensus on economic issues with the prime political forces in the country, which command the loyalty of the expertise of the country. Would those forces work with them? Potentially, probably—there would be some whose principles would keep them back from engaging with a military junta, but that might actually encourage the military to create a proper roadmap that ensured reform and restructuring during the interim, and an exit strategy within a certain time period.

That would bring the military to the third challenge: a political roadmap that actually works. In an ideal situation, that would bring together the main presidential candidates that would be partial to such an arrangement—excluding Ahmad Shafiq. That would necessitate the involvement of Amr Moussa, to bring on board forces allied to the former regime without actually getting a hardcore '*felool*' [leftover] candidate.

Al-Baradei who has little if any grassroots support, would be important for international recognition, and international recognition of a civilian body would be necessary for macroeconomic assistance. Hamdeen Sabahi and Abu al-Futuh, if they consented to being involved, would be critical to ensuring the political roadmap had a civilian face that was genuinely bought into on the ground. Ideally, that would also mean the involvement of Muhammad Mursi—but it is difficult to consider how that would be possible if the military jumped in, as they would in this scenario.

This brings us all to that final piece of the puzzle. If public order diminishes to the point that the military feels obliged to step in, it is hard to see how they could do so while remaining acquiescent to President Mursi. On the contrary, it might be easier for the military to simply place him, and other members of the MB leadership, under house arrest. In such a scenario, can anyone really envisage that the MB would simply say 'OK'? What would their response be? Would it turn violent? No-one knows for sure—but everyone does know that Egypt is now a country that is armed on a far more widespread level than it was in the past.

The irony is—everyone sees this scenario as quite plausible, if not a certainty, except for the MB. The MB leadership is convinced it can move forward and continue in the way it has done thus far. It does not seem to realise that it is indeed in the cross-hairs. Escaping from this slow train-wreck is possible—but that all depends on President Mursi.[10]

Looking back on this piece, a few things remain striking. The first was that I was hardly the only one who saw all these signs: there were many in Cairo who saw the problems unfolding, and grew concerned. That wasn't the case among most international analysts, with some notable exceptions like the aforementioned Hanna. Nathan Brown of George Washington University, one of Washington, D.C.'s most noted Egypt-watchers, also described the Egyptian state at the time as a 'train wreck in slow motion. Well, actually, forget the slow motion'.[11]

Yet, rather than provide a constructive critique of the government, some hoped for a train wreck, while others refused to see the possibility of one. It was a staggering paradox: the MB constantly warned against the deep state, but it couldn't see that none of the steps it had taken was making life any more difficult for the deep state. On the contrary, the MB was indirectly and unintentionally enabling the deep state, as the MB steps meant the deep state found more and more allies among the MB's opposition. Deep divides no doubt remained between the Brotherhood and the ultra-conservative Salafis (though many Salafis were in the Brotherhood), but they also found new causes for agreement: a burgeoning pro-MB media generally supported the Brother-hood (or pushed, sometimes in quite aggressive terms, for something even more conservative), while Islamist groupings, never before able to exist with such ease, closed ranks around each other.

On the anti-MB side, you had figures who were openly and wholly irresponsibly calling for a military intervention. I expected the military to jump into the political fray in the summer, but I made it abundantly clear it was a bad idea. There were others who, incredibly, while laud-ing the 25 January revolution on the one hand, were openly calling for 'the military to take the lead in the country once again, until stability was restored, the economy was reformed and [the] political parties got better organised'.[12] This wasn't a revolutionary call—it was a counter-revolutionary one.

IV

Political polarisation is only part of what makes a country increasingly unstable. The conflicts between the presidency and other parts of the Egyptian state were not showing any signs of lessening—indeed, they seemed to be deepening. The Ministry of Foreign Affairs did not look like it was a part of Mursi's government: the foreign minister did not join Mursi on his trip to Russia in early 2013, and the judiciary clearly viewed Mursi as an enemy. In a cabinet reshuffle in April 2013, Mursi elevated yet more MB stalwarts, despite most having little or no expe-rience in the fields they were picked for.[13]

What became increasingly important in this context were the pres-sures induced by Ramadan in July, discussed earlier in this chapter. These pressures were abundantly clear—and many in Egypt, including myself, could see them coming.[14] Increased financial demands in a country that had a worsening economy with no short term improve-ment in sight could only mean one thing: Egypt would be particularly flammable in the summer of 2013.

Would there be a spark to set it off? It was difficult to know. To my mind, it wasn't the MB itself that was the primary source of instability; rather, the main sources of instability were in place before the revolu-tion. A set of institutions and an economy built under Mubarak's reign meant that the absence of both a 'strongman' regime and widespread fear could only result in instability. Egypt's institutions were simply not built to function without those elements; they needed widespread reform, restructuring, rebuilding, and in some cases, removal. My constant assessment was that Mursi's government should find domestic Egyptian allies who could help, through consensus, to take Egypt to its next stage of transition in that revolutionary period, if Mursi and the MB wanted Egypt to progress without things getting much worse.

Yet, despite my warnings on this front, I found it implausible that Mursi would change course. The European Union, to its credit, was involved in regular shuttle diplomacy, trying to forge an agreement between Mursi and his opposition. The aim was the formation of a national salvation government that would defuse tensions, and steer the country towards a more sustainable course, while maintaining the democratic experiment.[15] Under the proposed deal, the opposition would have reaffirmed Mursi's legitimacy, and participated in parliamentary elections later that year, which they had threatened to boycott in protest at Mursi's policies. Mursi would have formed a technocratic national unity cabinet and dismissed the partisan prosecutor general that he had appointed a few months earlier (who had raised an investigation into several opposition figures for espionage, though it was later dropped).

Sa'ad al-Katatni, a senior MB leader and head of the FJP, helped to negotiate the package, and it received backing from the US and the UK, though the European Union's envoy, Bernadino Leon, headed the foreign input. According to participants in the negotiation, the military's top brass, including Sisi, backed the deal. When Mursi reshuffled his cabinet in late spring 2013, the Europeans were startled and dismayed that his new senior officials were not remotely part of a broader coalition, but rather were from an even more pro-Islamist core. The deal they had tirelessly worked on and promoted for months was in tatters, particularly after sectarian attacks in the country left several dead, and the Coptic Cathedral came literally under fire.[16]

As we approached the summer, I wrote in one article: 'it is hard to see things in Egypt improving before they get worse. This summer in Egypt may be a sweltering one indeed, and not just because of the weather.'[17]

V

It was gearing up to be a sweltering summer indeed. By May, Mursi's government was receiving criticisms from across the political spectrum, inside and outside the country. MB supporters expressed annoyance that the government was not more dominated by MB members; former supporters of Mursi, such as the Salafi Noor Party, were becoming increasingly critical, as the government failed to deliver on their expectations; and the National Salvation Front felt that Mursi's cabinet reshuffle in May was a flawed and insufficient step to put Egypt on the right track.

Within the media establishment, Mursi was receiving an unenviable barrage of negative scrutiny. The MB and Salafi groups had succeeded in making an enemy out of Bassem Youssef, an Egyptian political satirist and one of the most popular television personalities in the Arab world. Bassem had been called for investigation by the public prosecutor, after he'd criticised the administration on the one hand, and called out ultra-conservative preachers on the other. The latter had their own television stations that were frequently full of hate speech and sectarianism—and took direct aim at Bassem. He responded in kind.[18]

The irony couldn't have been more striking. Bassem was a pro-revolutionary public figure, who voted for Abu al-Futuh in the first round of the presidential elections in 2012, and probably would have voted for Mursi in the second round. He didn't, but that was because at the time we were both travelling together in the US, producing a new television programme called 'America in Arabic', for which I was working as a subject-matter expert. For the first few months of Mursi's presidential term, Bassem tried hard to get Mursi onto his television programme, and insisted that 'criticism was not enmity'—but Mursi rebuffed the requests. Bassem's business partner, Tarek al-Qazzaz, was a scion of a noted MB family (though not a MB member himself), but amid the increasingly permissive environment for sectarianism and extremism, along with moves from the presidential palace such as the executive decree in late 2012, and the prosecutor general investigating him, Bassem went on the war path.

Outside the country, Mursi's administration lost allies and gained unfriendly cousins—if not enemies. Prime in this category was the government of the United Arab Emirates (UAE), which showed clearly

its displeasure with the MB government, while at the same time warm-
ing to other players in the Egyptian public arena. When the Grand
Imam of al-Azhar, Ahmad al-Tayyib, visited the UAE, it could not have
been a coincidence that a group of Egyptians imprisoned in Emirati
jails were released at the same time. The message was clear: if a sufficiently senior representative engaged directly with the Emirati government there might be positive results. The UAE invited Mursi to visit
Abu Dhabi but, evidently unaware of the diplomatic subtleties, he
decided not to. Had he taken up the invitation, there might have been
other dividends. At the very least, Cairo's new government would have
had one less antagonist. With an economy that was suffering so much,
Egypt needed all the friends it could get.

Mursi dispatched diplomats, and jetted around the world himself to
try and gather funds and garner investments. He came back relatively
empty handed, and part of the reason was his own attitude and the
response of the European Union and the US to it. The feeling in
European capitals was that because Egypt was 'too big to fail' the MB
was somewhat haughtily banking on the idea that their organisation, as
the ruling organisation of the country, was also 'too big to fail'. In
private discussions I had with different European officials, it became
clear that the impression being given by the MB was that if they did not
succeed, Egypt would fail. Thus, went the MB argument, the Europeans
ought to support the government economically. One irritated
European diplomat put it bluntly to me: 'This is blackmail!'

Was the MB's assessment correct? Not entirely. The reality was that,
indeed, Egypt was too big to fail for Western powers. The repercussions would have been widely felt with substantial implications for the
regional economy and prevailing security paradigms. But did that mean
that the MB itself was too big to fail? For European governments, that
was not a foregone conclusion at all; they were already becoming impatient with the government's inability to direct the country onto a more
sustainable path, economically and politically. The American government and different European administrations had expended a great deal
of energy in trying to help Egypt break the political deadlock, and
assist in the construction of a more durable economy before it was too
late to escape an economic meltdown. By May of 2013, they were not
entirely impressed with the results thus far, and as the major political

partner in the Egyptian political scene, the MB shouldered most of the blame, at least among most Western officials. At the same time, no one in the international arena saw any other scenario but the MB for the time being: Western capitals were convinced that Mursi would continue for the long haul. In that regard, they did agree with the MB—but both were wrong.

VI

On 28 April, a group of young activists, mostly Nasserites, launched an initiative called Tamarod ('Rebel') calling for early presidential elections. Within a few weeks, Tamarod claimed to have collected in excess of two million signatures, and media circles were buzzing with talk around the new grassroots campaign. Opponents claimed that Tamarod was undemocratic, and was facilitating the return to power of the former Mubarak regime.[19]

History shows that, whatever the truth was, the Tamarod initiative certainly paved the way for the end of the democratic experiment—and it could have acquitted itself better by not throwing itself so completely into the arms of the military in July. The notion of calling early presidential elections was not, however, an undemocratic one, in and of itself. In many developed democracies, snap elections happen regularly when, for example, a government fails to actually govern, or the most popular party fails to form a government supported by a majority.

Tamarod seemed to begin as a completely organic and grassroots movement,[20] but according to information uncovered later that did not last for very long.[21] The details were never fully exposed, but it seems to be the case that very soon after Tamarod managed to get a substantial number of signatures on its own, different sectors of Mursi's opposition decided it was a useful caravan to hitch themselves to. That included, crucially, elements of the Ministry of Interior,[22] oligarchs,[23] judicial figures[24] and different political parties. As time went on, more and more lauded Tamarod and joined its campaign, often unaware of (or unconcerned as to) who else was backing the initiative from behind the scenes.

Tamarod called for a mass protest on 30 June 2013, the anniversary of Mursi's presidential inauguration. By then, he was struggling to maintain his popular support. The economy was faltering. Much of the private media was hysterically rallying against him, and pro-Morsi channels were going into defensive overdrive and using hate speech. In the meantime, another type of sectarianism was rearing its ugly head: at a rally held in support of the Syrian uprising in June, Mursi shared a platform with extremist preachers, who denounced Shi'is and supported 'jihad' in Syria.[25] The rally famously saw Mursi sitting alongside released prisoners, who had once been found guilty and convicted of assassinating the late Egyptian President Anwar al-Sadat. Tragically, a few days later, several Egyptians from Egypt's tiny Shi'i minority were lynched by a mob in Giza.[26]

Seeing the president on the same platform as those preachers, without at least correcting them or rebuking them for their language, sent chills down the backs of many Egyptians; and the calls for supporting 'jihad' in Syria was probably not music to the ears of the Egyptian military. This was 2013, and the threat of ISIL had not quite reached the radar of the international media, but it was already clear to many security analysts that there were radical Islamist extremists fighting against the Syrian regime, in addition to Syrian revolutionary forces.

Regardless, Tamarod was ignored by the presidential palace. Until rather close to the date of the protests, I myself also did not consider it to have the grassroots support required to effect any kind of movement in Egypt's political fabric. I was wrong.

VII

In late June 2013, I hadn't had a proper holiday in about three years. I had planned to spend a couple of weeks abroad, and was all set to go on 29 June. However, on 20 June I had contacted my hosts and told them we might be delaying our departure, as it seemed that there could be a big protest on 30 June. I didn't feel it would be responsible to leave our neighbourhood, especially when we might have to protect it, as we did during the eighteen days of 2011.

My only intention for 30 June was to be at home. If the protests were large, there could be widespread unrest. I wasn't going to leave my home and family in the lurch. In the months and years before 30 June, I'd been on a number of protests and marches in Egypt—

sometimes as an analyst, to simply observe what was going on, but sometimes also as a participant. I often wondered after the fact if I'd betrayed some sort of academic code by participating. But I was deeply invested in and had deep convictions about Egypt's future. As the old axiom goes, *iman huwa aqd bi al-qalb wa tasdiq bi al-lisan wa al-amal bi al-arkan* (belief consists of three things: faith within the heart, proclamation with the tongue, and action by the limbs).

Nevertheless, despite my criticisms of the MB and Mursi in the year of his presidency, I was not clamouring for the success of the protests.[27] I found the National Salvation Front an ineffectual body. Moreover, they were showing themselves all too willing to engage with elements from Mubarak's former regime that had no interest in the success of Egypt's democratic experiment, as part of a broader anti-Mursi alliance. Mursi was insufficiently inclusive, that was true, but a 'zero-sum game' view was not limited only to the MB. It typified the perspective of many, although not all, of its opponents, whose interests were less about the success of Egypt's revolutionary promise of 2011, and more about simply knocking out the MB.

While I felt that early presidential elections would help to take Egypt out of its impasse (incidentally, early elections had already been called for by the opposition politicians Hamzawy and Abu al-Futuh in early 2013),[28] I was less enthusiastic about the campaign called for by the Tamarod movement. At first, it seemed unlikely to succeed, and thus to be another missed opportunity by a disparate and inadequate opposition. Also, it seemed to be an organisation that had capitalised on authentic antipathy to the Islamist movement, only to become quickly co-opted—and fairly blatantly—by other forces working within the 'deep state'. As support for the campaign increased, I began to become more concerned. The question that most worried me about the Tamarod movement as we drew closer to 30 June was: what will they do if they are not successful in pressuring Mursi to choose an alternative course?

I had no doubt that Mursi would not voluntarily call for early presidential elections, even if the entire country went out onto the streets (let alone the remarkably inflated numbers that were later reported). If Tamarod had been intent on using 30 June as a show of strength against the MB, to remind the religious right that Egypt's non-Islamist majority was still alive and kicking, that would have been one thing. But it, and the forces that publicly (and privately) backed it, had made one thing very clear: protesters would stay out until their demands were met. And that was what worried me.

Months earlier, as I discussed earlier in this chapter, I had thought there might be a military intervention in July 2013, but I hadn't linked this to Tamarod, or even to political mobilisation. Rather, I had thought that owing to the increasingly chaotic economic situation and unrest against Mursi's government, it was likely that there would be something like food riots. In such a situation, I reasoned, a repeat of what had happened in Suez earlier in the year—where the national government had lost control of security, and where the military stepped in—could easily take place, this time across the country. If it did, I wondered, would it leave the democratically elected government of Mursi in place? Or would it deem Mursi's government a liability? This was Egypt, after all: it was not as though Egypt's military had not been able to successfully pull off political intrusions before.

Before Tamarod's June protests had even began, a counter-protest was started at the Rab'a al-Adawiya[29] mosque.[30] This evolved into a sit-in that continued for weeks after the anti-Mursi protests ended (the fate of these counter-protesters is something that we will return to). On the eve of the Tamarod protests, my mind was focused on one pressing issue: would there be confrontation and conflict? Would these two groups of Egyptians, both diametrically opposed to each other, engage each other on the streets—and what would happen if they did?

Around 1 July, I was in touch with a MB official. He was later, like many other MB members, arrested and sent to jail, so I will not divulge his name. It was night, and I'd heard reports that a group of protesters from the pro-Mursi Rab'a sit-in were heading towards the presidential palace. I was deeply concerned: if that was the case, there would be blood, and a lot of it. The discourse among pro-Mursi protesters had made this conflict into one about defending Islam against the forces of evil; as for the anti-Mursi protesters at the presidential palace, they had their own exclusionary discourse too. Allowing these rival camps to come into contact with each other was a recipe for disaster.

I reached out to the official. I pleaded with him, 'Please—tell me this is not true. This is a fool's errand which will only lead to bloodshed.'

He told me to stand by, and then responded, 'False alarm. We were told that a group were about to march on Rab'a, and we sent out our guys to "greet" them. We're not going to the presidential palace yet—we have strict instructions not to do so, unless the president's safety is in jeopardy.'

My relief at the news that the MB wasn't going to send a crowd of protesters to an anti-Mursi demonstration was countered by the realisation that, as far as the MB were concerned, they could very easily do so at some future point. That still churned in my gut. There was no law. There was only vigilantism—from more than one side.

For the same was true for the anti-Mursi protesters. A group of them marched on the MB headquarters in the eastern district of Muqattam, leading to a gun battle between them and the MB. Across the country, there were skirmishes in which weapons were often brandished. I had no intention of getting involved: my only purpose in being in Cairo during those days was to observe, to actively witness, and to protect my family and my home. But as I watched, I wondered when these two opposing mobs would clash—and how many lives would be lost.

That is what I had feared from day one. It had struck me before the protests that the only way that Tamarod's campaign could realistically work would be if, indeed, those two groups did engage each other, resulting in bloodshed, which would trigger a military intervention against the sitting, and elected, president. That sort of escalation, where Egyptians would fight one another in civil strife, was not one I thought should even be contemplated. I respected friends and colleagues who insisted they had to go to the streets. But I considered their assumption that their movement was likely to win without military intervention or bloodshed to be naïve. I knew they didn't want either of those things, but as the protests began it was clear that those who had no such reservations far outnumbered cooler, more principled heads.

After the military made its ultimatum to Mursi, which I described in writing as 'not quite a coup, but pretty much',[31] several days before actually detaining him, those fears about clashes intensified. As Egypt's public arena grew increasingly tense, the seeds of a new 'war on terror' narrative started to find fertile ground among anti-Islamists, and particularly in the private media.

Somewhere along the way, the narrative switched from 'we must have early presidential elections' to 'the MB is a terrorist menace', and demonised all supporters of the president. Simultaneously, MB leaders made it clear that if they felt Mursi would come under attack in the presidential palace, they would send their supporters to intervene in what was essentially vigilante action.

Although the MB was not alone in being happy to engage in such vigilantism, the MB was in power. The sectarian discourse and incitement that came from partisans of the MB, as well as from senior members of its leadership, was especially concerning. Against the polarised backdrop, the thought of MB supporters descending upon the protests outside the presidential palace, and the ensuing violence that would inevitably take place between those forces, was deeply worrying—and those worries intensified until 3 July.

Eventually, the fateful, historic day arrived. The Egyptian military proceeded to detain Muhammad Mursi and his aides on 3 July and set into process a new 'roadmap'. That night, I was in the Intercontinental Hotel, bordering Tahrir Square, describing the night's events as a 'coup' and 'popularly backed'.

VIII

It was a label that made pretty much everyone in Egyptian politics unhappy. The word 'coup' to this day makes many opponents of the MB bristle. They insist it was a 'revolution'. Of course, the two words aren't necessarily mutually exclusive,[32] and I tended to think of the 25 January revolutionary uprising as a 'revolution' that involved a 'coup' on 11 February, for example. But a transfer of power by a military leadership is clear in its implications. As for the appellation of 'revolution', that's surely a value judgement, and in my opinion there was no revolution in Egypt that could take place with the police on your side.

Many tried to compare the 30 June protests in 2013 with those of 25 January in 2011. The protesters filling the streets certainly wanted an end to the presidency on both occasions. When the army intervened and overthrew the president in both cases, the protesters went home: they did not stay to protest the army's involvement. On the contrary, particularly in the case of the 30 June protests, many had actively called for it.

However, there were key differences. People were protesting in 2013 against an elected president who had been voted in through a genuine competition in 2012; in 2011 they were not. When people went to the streets on 25 January, they didn't have the support of more than a tiny minority of the masses—they had to win it. 30 June, on the other hand, had far more support at the outset. But there was a more critical difference. The 25 January revolution was not about Mubarak, per se, but about an insistence on building a future based on bread, freedom, social justice and human dignity. The removal of Mubarak was a necessary, but insufficient, precondition for that to happen.

No one could make this argument about the protests of 30 June–3 July. There was one demand, and it was clear: the removal of the MB from the presidency. This uprising had an objective, yes, but it lacked the spirit of the Tahrir protests. The ecstasy and joy of the 30 June protesters and supporters came only from being released, as they saw it, from the MB—but beyond that, they were simply against something, rather than for something.

Though the core group of 25 January revolutionaries were a disparate set supported by temporary allies, they did have a common vision that went beyond the removal of Mubarak. The 30 June protesters and their supporters lacked any common, pluralistic or progressive vision beyond the removal of Mursi. To be sure, some of those who backed the original revolutionary concept of 25 January decided that, despite the risks, it was important for the revolution that they be present at the 30 June protests—so that it could at least maintain something of the essence of Tahrir. In that regard, this was a continuation of the Tahrir revolution because, indeed, the goals of the revolution could never be implemented with Mursi occupying the presidency. This is a stretch, to be sure, if not utterly naïve; but it hints at the complexity of what happened during the whirlwind of events in 2013.

When the coup happened, I asked a simple question: was the removal of Mursi a good thing or a bad thing?[33] Many on both sides of the divide had easy answers—but it wasn't so easy. I wrote:

> The only way one would be able to answer, 'yes, of course it was a good thing', would be if one were certain that a military overthrow prevented

loss of life, and led to a better, stronger democracy. No one will ever know if the former is true, because we cannot assess something that was not allowed to happen.[34]

In retrospect, of course, we know that the possible answers to that question looked very different on 3 July and, for example, 14 August, when the pro-Mursi sit-ins were cleared.

Despite my criticisms and critiques of the MB, I had argued in an interview (quoted in this chapter's epigraph) a few days before 30 June that if the protests were successful, the propensity for violence would increase, and that it would be 'very bad for the story for Egyptian democracy'. I had thought it likely that the protesters could only succeed through force of arms. Nevertheless, when I later described the protests as 'popularly backed', this was accurate. Years on, most people agree that the coup was supported by a majority of the Egyptian population, even while they correctly dismiss claims that between twenty and forty million people massed on the streets in support of it.

I was relieved that the protests ended without widespread violence. If nothing else, the military's intervention meant most people went home instead of clashing in the streets. But I also wrote the day afterwards that violence, particularly against Mursi's partisans as well as from them, remained likely, and needed to be guarded against. I had no idea how prescient that would turn out to be.

I tried to be cautious about what might happen next, but my caution was grounded in concern about what events said about the story of Egyptian democracy, as well as the possible repercussions of a coup. Though there were those who opposed the military's intervention—and I had hoped alternatives were possible—I believed the military's deeds would not be resisted by a critical mass of the country's population. In that regard, as I would later observe, Mursi possessed legal legitimacy, but he lost a critical mass of popular support and—more critically—effective executive authority.

It was clear that the president's executive authority had been crippled from day one. Whether or not this is how things should have been is another issue. Within the state apparatus, Mursi had begun his office with an awkward historical albatross around his neck. For years, that bureaucracy had, in large part, regarded the MB as an enemy of the state. But for some months after Mursi took up the presidency, substantial portions of the state nevertheless played ball. The police, for example, followed orders to take action against anti-Mursi protesters during the now infamous clashes outside the presidential palace in December 2012.

By 30 June 2013, though, the state was more or less in open rebellion against the presidency.[35] So was Mursi's own government: within hours of the 30 June protests, non-MB cabinet members began to resign en masse.[36] Within days, many of his ministers had deserted him on the grounds of his unwillingness to compromise. In fact, just days before the military removed him Mursi's government was already dysfunctional. One can argue he was partly to blame for that; one can also argue that any president from outside of the traditional Egyptian elite would have faced the same fate. There is evidence for and against both these arguments. In any case, by this time Mursi's government was existent almost only in name.

Mursi certainly did himself few favours. On the night of 1 July, after the army had issued its ultimatum for the various political factions (including the presidency) to 'move forward', he gave a speech lasting over forty minutes that only reinforced in the minds of his opponents that no workable compromise would be forthcoming.[37] From the pro-Mursi camp's perspective, that was wholly natural; Mursi was the elected president, after all. But those who opposed him saw the momentum on the street and, with most sectors of society seeming to be against Mursi, they expected him to acquiesce in some fashion. Instead, Mursi's speech only repeated, almost *ad nauseum*, protestations about his 'legitimacy', and cast aspersions on all those who opposed him, even going so far as to say he would spill his own blood if needed. The proportion of the population that supported the MB, as well as a substantial number of even his own ministers, began to desert him.

With his trademark finger patronisingly pointed at the audience, the defiant Mursi, like Mubarak before him, did little to console people by convincing them that he was actually listening: 'There is no alternative to legitimacy, the constitutional legitimacy, legal legitimacy and electoral legal legitimacy that produced an elected president for Egypt for the first time in its history.'[38] Videos immediately began circulating online mocking Mursi's overuse of the word 'legitimacy'—reportedly repeated fifty-seven times in just that speech—and his long-winded and repetitive rhetorical style that had long been a source for political satire. Except this time many people found it more sinister than funny.

At street level the Egyptian public was in a gloomy political mood. Repeated opinion polls carried out by Gallup and Tahrir Trends showed that the Egyptian public was losing confidence in the MB and Mursi. Moreover, the research showed that same public losing confidence in all political forces. Despite this, one institution had managed to keep its standing with the Egyptian population during 2012 and 2013: the Egyptian military. Irrespective of the calamitous transitional process that its leadership had presided over in 2011 and 2012, the military retained an impressive status in the eyes of the Egyptian public. Recurrent nationwide face-to-face interviews confirmed that nine out of ten Egyptians expressed confidence in the military almost through the entire post-Mubarak transition until 3 July 2013.

That support for the military, justified or not, would indelibly define not only the events of 30 June–3 July, but also all political events in Egypt from those days until the time of writing.

That is not to say that the military never lost at least some support. The revolutionary camp that was responsible for the original 2011 protests soon lost faith in the military's ability to steer Egypt in the right direction after Mubarak's ousting. But given the positive portrayal of the military in the national media and the educational system, and the general desire for stability amid a tumultuous economic situation, research consistently showed that the military could always count on around eight out of ten Egyptians to give it support, throughout the period of 2011–13.

IX

No side in Egypt resisted the temptation to craft inaccurate narratives in the aftermath of the coup.[39] The pro-Mursi camp, whether in Egypt or abroad, pushed a bizarre narrative of the previous year. At its best, it promoted Mursi as a model democrat, a man who did nothing to deserve the animosity that so many in Egypt felt towards him, even after having backed him and the MB in presidential and parliamentary elections. His failings, if any, were limited to incompetence, aggravated by his opponents' willingness to see him fail, and perhaps some rashness. The extra-legal decree suspending judicial review, the nature of the constitutional writing process, the rushed constitutional referendum, the prevailing nepotism, the crackdown on media personalities and activists opposed to him, combined with the toleration of—and acquiescence to—sectarian and violent incitement were all somehow swept under the rug, as though they were irrelevant to the 'larger' democratic project. After all, Mursi won at the ballot box, so the rest is collateral damage or, according to some narratives, didn't even happen.

Meanwhile, much of the anti-Mursi camp did not fail to remind all observers of all of the above. That was all well and good, but when it came to pointing out the structural issues that Mursi had to face down, they minimised them entirely. Indeed, in the years since 2013, the narrative in much of this camp has been that the 'deep state' of Mubarak collapsed during the 25 January revolutionary uprising, and that Egypt essentially began from a clean slate. That, of course, is a fallacy: the 'deep state' and former Mubarak networks did not collapse. They simply took a beating, which is why they failed to mobilise around parliamentary elections properly; but by the time presidential elections came around, they had regrouped and struck back, leading to a split decision between Mursi and Mubarak's last prime minister, Shafiq. To underestimate their power was and is foolhardy—but, alas, it seems that even the MB itself did that.

The narratives of the 30 June protests were equally polarised. For a large segment of the pro-Mursi camp, the protests were engineered and the numbers did not reach very substantial proportions; Mursi had at least as many supporters as opponents in the population; and no matter what he did, his forceful overthrow was assured. As one protestor told Mada Masr: 'It will be over my dead body that the army returns. The president said that his blood is a small price for upholding legitimacy. Our blood does not have a higher price than that of the president.'[40]

On the other hand, for many of Mursi's opponents, the mobilisation was entirely organic, the numbers exceeded 33 million (a preposterous number),[41] and Mursi rebuffed every single attempt by his opponents to reach a compromise. Reports of violence started by pro-Mursi supporters, real and exaggerated, filled the local news. Other reports spoke of a festive atmosphere in Tahrir Square, in contrast to angry pro-Mursi crowds a few miles away at the presidential palace. The set up left little room for the fostering of nuance. As another protestor told Mada Masr, 'He [Mursi] is not going to go down without a fight. He is so persistent and there will have to be bloodshed. Nothing in what he does is presidential.'[42] In Egypt, then, truth really is the greatest victim.

In reality, parts of both narratives reveal the truth. The protest movement plugged into an existing swell of anti-Mursi sentiment, due to popular dissatisfaction with his performance, and then the movement was aided and abetted by different sectors of society who gave it amplification in the media, as well as providing financial assistance. But the reality of the amplification did not mean that it had not already been there: a critical mass of Egyptians were unhappy with Mursi's rule.

Mursi did have the chance—actually, several chances—to defuse the situation, right up until the end, and could even have stayed in office. It was still in his hands, but he refused to do so, thinking that he would be able to hold on, regardless of popular pressure, as well as the organised forces against him.

Given the infancy of Egypt's democractic experiment, which had not yet delivered what Egyptians had expected it to (their expectations being vastly unrealistic), the overwhelming public support for the military, and the immense unpopularity of the MB and other political forces, things seemed rather clear on 3 July. A coup by the military had taken place, and whether one liked it or not it was clear that the majority of the population acquiesced. Nevertheless, even at this point, prior to any state crackdown against the MB and ensuing dissent, as well as militant and terrorist ruptures, it was clear that Egypt had just entered a very treacherous phase of its modern history.

As the night of 3 July ensued, and for weeks afterwards, I wondered: what other scenarios could have been worked towards? It was clear on the one hand that the status quo could not have continued. For, to recap, the state was in full rebellion against the presidency, and many Egyptians had mobilised against Mursi. A substantial number of ministers had resigned, and it seemed inevitable, based on the statements of all sides, that if the standoff continued there would be bloody clashes between the parties. Something had to give. What would it be?

People asked—and still ask—what were the alternatives? Even before 3 July, I saw no hope for any outcome that would be good for

Egypt while all sides played a zero-sum game. For Egypt's transition to democracy to survive, at least one of the power pivots in the country would have to compromise. No one was interested in that, because they were all interested in winning—and so, at least in my assessment, Egypt lost.

That night, as I completed my interviews, I walked across the Qasr al-Nil bridge. I hadn't put a foot into Tahrir Square during the 30 June protests. On the bridge, I found someone who had been in the square, and who now was in a state of shock. A friend and political activist, he had participated in the protests, but when the military had removed Mursi, he had been gobsmacked at the public's reaction.

'Don't they remember last time?' he asked me. 'How can they be carrying policemen on their shoulders, when on this same bridge the police were shooting at us in 2011?' I didn't have an answer for him.

In politics, very few things can be genuinely described as 'inevitable', because the variables keep changing. As I have said, Mursi could have chosen different courses of action, most fundamentally by constructing a vigorous and consensus-based front against the former regime's counter-revolutionary forces. But in order to have done so, he would have had to himself rebel against the MB leadership, and thus have been a wholly different type of political actor—one that was skilled in the art of compromise and negotiation. Mursi was Mursi, despite bizarre claims to the contrary. He certainly wasn't a Mandela, as noted Egyptian pro-revolutionary writer, Belal Fadl, forcefully pointed out.[43] I had made a similar argument.[44]

But the demise of the Mursi presidency, in the manner in which it took place, was nothing to cheer. Some might have temporarily rejoiced in Mursi's departure—but at what cost did his exit from the presidential palace come? The democratic experiment was suspended, and its reinstitution was going to be ever more difficult, even if all sides wanted it. And patently, not everyone did want it.

In 2012, millions of Egyptian citizens voted in Muhammad Mursi to allow for the continuation of the Egyptian revolution of 2011. He should not have had to bear that responsibility, a responsibility he never wanted, was wholly unprepared for, and had little interest in, at least in the sense of the 'revolution' that was born in the Square of Liberation in January 2011. Field Marshal Tantawi could have laid down the groundwork far more easily, and constructively, if he had taken appropriate steps in early 2011. But he also had no interest in that.

The only ones who did have an interest in it were those in the revolutionary camp that was forged in 2011. For this group, whose political consciousness was forged in those eighteen days, the 'revolution' had just begun. A few years later, all that remained of that larger-than-life story was an echo of the promising roar it once was—and the revolutionaries went into a post-traumatic trance.

X

As 30 June approached, it was prudent to presume that a voluntary departure of Mursi from the presidency was unlikely. However, most revolutionaries, somewhat naïvely, mobilised. They assumed that the military was an institution already neutralised, or aligned with the MB. The revolutionary camp did not propose alternatives to mobilisation, except to not mobilise: some never protested, and others demobilised in defiance after they saw the military threatening interference. But in the end, revolutionaries either stayed home or ingenuously persisted in the notion that Mursi's voluntary departure was plausible. Many accuse the revolutionaries of turning into 'faux liberals' at this time, those whose principles were all secondary to hatred of the MB. There were indeed cheerleaders for the military, those who would later justify or remain silent in the face of the most horrendous abuses—I didn't see the bulk of the revolutionary camp, though, as falling into that category.

The roots of the revolutionaries' failures were discussed in Chapter 2. They failed in 2012 to coalesce around a presidential candidate. While during the 25 January uprising they mobilised for something, the revolutionaries had neither a plan nor a cohesive message to continue to rally 'for' and instead became homogenised by what they stood 'against'.

The presidential election that resulted from the revolutionaries' failure to back a single candidate produced a president that they eventually, and correctly, opposed. Pro-revolutionary figures were the first to demand presidential elections: a laudable, democratic escape route from the prevailing political impasse, with revolutionaries endorsing the demand en masse. However, when the National Salvation Front, the key political opposition umbrella, backed the Tamarod group's call for protests, the revolutionaries should have focused more intently on pressing Front members to distinguish themselves and the Front from more insidious forces, as well as interrogating exactly who Tamarod and its backers were. With the revolutionaries failing to constitute a cohesive force of consensus, a 'plausible alternative' to military intervention was never agreed upon.

In short, at a time that they could have made a critical difference, the revolutionaries did not realise the need to take the initiative. As the protests to fulfil the democratic demand for presidential elections drew nearer, it was only a small group of revolutionaries that were dubious about the outcome. The rest merely made various public calls against military intervention, when they should instead have focused on holding the National Salvation Front to that anti-intervention principle as a condition of support, and established protocols to be followed in the event that an intervention happened. But, in all fairness, they didn't have much leverage to insist on one course of action or another.

The revolutionaries had little effective control over, or responsibility for, the protests. Had the revolutionaries been silent and stayed at home on 30 June, the size of the protests drawn from the broader anti-MB constituency would have seen the same outcome. Here, effective power and the power of the responsibility to provide alternatives diverge. Through the media and mobilisation, the revolutionaries were significant agitators who provoked responses from non-revolutionary forces. Generally, though, those responses only affected the speed at which the post-Mubarak transitional plan developed. Most of the time, the revolutionaries had no effective power to cause the plan to actually change direction.

Nevertheless, as the inheritors of the revolutionary moment of Tahrir, the revolutionary camp had another kind of power. It had the power—but also then the responsibility—to provide genuinely viable options and contingencies, even if it lacked the ability to implement such alternatives. It failed to do this at acute junctures. The reluctance of so many of them to engage in formal politics—and the undermining and even ridicule of those of the revolutionaries who did seek a political path—contributed to a lack of cohesion and inability to relay a message. By refusing to participate even in political parties like the

THE SLOW-MOVING TRAIN WRECK

Egyptian Social Democratic party, and other relatively more pro-revo-lutionary networks, they became unable to capitalise on the power they had harnessed in the square.

The revolutionaries weren't necessarily morally inconsistent in this regard. Inconsistency existed during those days and weeks in 2013, to be sure, but it came from other quarters. Some of my friends in the diplomatic corps were consequently flabbergasted to see how Egypt's ambassadors in the foreign service turned 180 degrees the day Mursi was ousted, and without so much as a colouring of the cheeks, began spouting the kind of dogma and vitriol against him that would have been unthinkable twenty-four hours earlier. They seemed not to notice how opportunistic and insincere this made them look. The same with many of Egypt's journalists. As Warren Buffett said about the crash of 2008, 'When the tide goes out fast, you suddenly get to see who's been swimming naked'. It goes without saying that the sight in Egypt's case was decidedly unedifying.

But while some of them might have even been revolutionaries them-selves once upon a time, such 'faux liberals' put the revolutionary camp in their crosshairs as well. The revolutionary camp's failures were not in its converting to a 'faux liberalism' which excused human rights viola-tions—rather, it was through the failure to deliver alternate choices.

Few revolutionaries would ever have opposed the departure of Mursi from the presidency, with most harbouring concerns about the military coming back to the centre-stage of Egyptian politics. However, on 3 July, revolutionaries effectively abandoned the field to the gener-als, albeit for varying reasons. Some impetuously lauded the military, thinking they could control it if it got out of line. However, probably the majority of revolutionaries were not swept up by the popular, gull-ible exhilaration over the military's return. Some expressed cautious optimism about the involvement of figures like Muhammad al-Baradei in the post-Mursi cabinet. They felt such figures would restrain more dastardly influences, bringing about an inclusive, civilian-led transition that would include the MB and others. Others stayed on the sidelines, harbouring concerns about the military's role. Yet, those concerns did not immediately result in the revolutionaries en masse standing up to the military, going to the streets, or providing any plan or strategy to deal with the new reality.

Within a couple of weeks, there were a few revolutionaries who even expressed a circumspect optimism about the new political dispensation. Police brutality in July, let alone August, as well as the call to 'mandate' the military to 'fight terrorism', soon dispelled that restrained confidence. Some revolutionaries began to protest against both the MB and the military in July—but they were few, and before long, security concerns meant protesting became tactically nonsensical. Yet, once again, they failed to imagine a practicable alternative.

The revolutionaries had genuinely and publicly opposed any role for the military—but they found themselves yielding to that role in the event, without providing an alternate path. It would be unfair to describe them as 'military cheerleaders', who put aside notions of fundamental rights, as did so many others. Nor, as I have said, could the revolutionary camp have affected the outcome on 3 July, one way or the other—but they had a responsibility to be relevant, nonetheless.

The sum of the revolutionary camp's concerns and discomfort led to it being either naïve or virtually inept in the run up to and the aftermath of 30 June. It should have rallied behind alternatives—a referendum on the military-led roadmap; a new roadmap altogether—but no viable options were seriously considered and mobilised for. That is where the real failure of the revolutionary camp after Mursi's departure lies: naïvety, and the shirking of the responsibility to demand alternative courses of action.

But if the revolutionary camp failed in certain ways, it was at least not responsible for the shedding of blood. But there would be blood. There would be more blood than I could ever have expected in Egypt. Historians will no doubt record the long-term ramifications and consequences of this to Egypt—likely in the range of decades, rather than simply months.

PART 3

THE AFTERMATH OF THE ABORTION
OF THE EXPERIMENT

7

'WEEKS OF KILLING'

'The international community can't really just let everything slide here. There is far too much to be lost. We just have to hope that they see that if the security state re-establishes itself, it's bad for everyone—Egypt included.'

'They killed a thousand people in a day. And the world basically rolled over. Do you think they care?'

Conversation between a leading human rights activist and the author in Cairo, September 2013

I

About a hundred years after the passing of the last prophet of Islam, in around 717 A.D., a woman called Rabi'a was born in Basra, in the south of present-day Iraq. She became one of the most famous saints in Sunni Islam, and as result there is more than one mosque in the Muslim world that bears her name. One of them is Masjid Rab'a al-Adawiyya in Nasr City, in the northeast of greater Cairo.

Before the 30 June protests began, Cairo's streets were already tense and there were some violent clashes between pro- and anti-Mursi groups. Mursi had given a speech on 27 June that made it abundantly clear he had no interest in engaging with the opposition (as discussed in the previous chapter), and accused his opponents of being in cahoots with drug dealers and criminals. The speech had an electrifying effect on both sides: it encouraged the opposition to dig in and prepare for large-scale protests, while it spurred the pro-Muslim Brotherhood (MB) camp into establishing a sit-in in solidarity with the beleaguered president. The latter formed a coalition called the National Alliance for Legitimacy, which included the Freedom and Justice Party, the Wasat Party (which was made up of more centrist Islamists), the small Watan Party of the Salafis, and the Building and Development Party of the Gama'a al-Islamiyya group, which had been considered a terrorist organisation in the 1990s. The site of their sit-in was to be the Masjid Rab'a al-Adawiyya and its environs.

This sit-in became the MB's main show of force during the 30 June protests, and for about six weeks after that.[1] It was deeply worrying to have two large groups of people, especially with mutually contradictory aims, on the streets of Cairo. You had anti-Mursi protesters in Tahrir and around the presidential palace. And you had pro-Mursi protesters in Nasr City. Another pro-Mursi sit-in was set up in al-Nahda Square, in the western part of Cairo, in front of the iconic main hall of Cairo University, on 1 July, mostly controlled by more radical protesters. Over the course of the first few weeks after the military ousted Mursi, both sit-ins were accused of widescale abuses—including violently clashing with residents and abusing opponents—by independent media outlets like Mada Masr[2] as well as human rights organisations such as Amnesty.[3]

Tensions were not just tensions: the raw friction led to blood from very early on after the military took power.[4] Opponents (both state forces and non-state forces) and supporters of the MB clashed only a few days after 3 July. The security forces did little to defuse or even de-escalate the situation, and dozens died.[5] Security forces fired on MB supporters camped outside the Republican Guards headquarters, the place where Mursi was rumoured to be held, on 7 July. British journalist Patrick Kingsley wrote a comprehensive exposé of that first mass killing for the *Guardian*.[6] Based on eye-witness accounts, his report stated that fifty-one Mursi supporters had been killed by the state forces.

Towards the end of July, there were more reports of mass killings. On 24 July, then-Defence Minister Sisi, who had led the military in its overthrow of Mursi, issued a call to the Egyptian people on national television. If anyone had been in any doubt that Adli Mansur, the

Supreme Court judge who had been sworn in as interim president, was secondary to another power, that speech would have dispelled any such illusion. Sisi called for a mass rally and a mass protest under the banner of his being granted a 'mandate' to 'fight terrorism'.[7]

It was a startling development. When Sisi had overthrown Mursi on 3 July, he had not struck me as a particularly unique figure. He had come across as a younger, more animated version of the former defence minister, Field Marshal Tantawi—nothing more. But there was something that quietly niggled at me.

A few days after the coup I saw him in a short clip on national television, where he'd been addressing a group of military officers off the cuff. He had no prepared notes or teleprompter, and he spoke well. It wasn't poetry, with verse and rhyme, but his tone, approach and mannerisms came across as calming. I was already extremely sceptical of the military, especially after the previous two years, and didn't find myself sympathetic. But as Sisi wrapped up his comments, something occurred to me. 'If I think he's, analytically and objectively speaking, "calming", then how much more might others think of him given the popularity of the military?' That was what concerned me. If Sisi wanted an open political role—unlike Tantawi, who preferred pulling the strings behind the scenes—then with that kind of gift of the gab before the camera, he could be very perilous indeed.

On 24 July I saw a wholly different Sisi. In full regalia, and sunglasses that made him look like a Latin American military autocrat, Sisi called for the 'mandate'. I had hoped, perhaps beyond hope, with cautious optimism shared by others like Human Rights Watch,[8] that there still existed the possibility, however meagre, of the military overseeing even a flawed regeneration of the democratic experiment, and allowing civil society to focus on calling the authorities to account. There would be much the military leadership would have to do, including ending what was already a crackdown on senior MB leadership figures, and investigating abuses by the military and the police forces. But once that speech was given, even low expectations were dashed even further.

It's important to note that the speech calling for a mandate to fight terrorism did not happen in anything remotely like a vacuum. There were clashes in early July between pro- and anti-Mursi protesters in Giza, near one of the major sit-ins in support of Mursi; the television coverage and commentary from both sides of the divide was deeply polarising and incendiary; officials and public figures joined in to rile up supporters even further rather than to appeal for calm.[9] The environment was primed—and not for anything positive.

Against that backdrop, Sisi's declaration was even more irresponsible than it would have been normally. As minister of defence, he had no business engaging in populist politics of any nature, let alone issuing a call to protest. Moreover, given the tensions that were palpable all across Egypt, such a call could only be interpreted in one fashion: as asking for a show of force and mobilisation of military supporters against MB backers. This was happening at the same time as the pro-Mursi camp was conducting marches around Cairo—and I worried greatly that two adamantly opposed sides would meet in a massive conflict.

They didn't. But on the evening of 26 July, after the main rally was over, a group of Mursi supporters moved out of their encampment in Nasr City, and started heading west along Nasr Street. They encountered the security forces, who opened fire. At least seventy-four MB supporters were killed,[10] with witnesses claiming that snipers from government forces were responsible.

Until this point, I'd stayed away from the Nasr City sit-in. On 27 July I decided I should go there. As an analyst, I didn't feel wholly able to understand the sit-in's context without at least visiting it. I also wanted to verify precisely where the killings had taken place—the MB had argued that a group of their supporters had moved west in a 'natural enlargement' of the sit-in, which appeared peculiar. Looking on the map didn't really tell me very much, so I went off to Nasr City.

II

The normal route to the sit-in would have taken me through Nasr Street itself, where the coffin of former President Anwar al-Sadat lies, marking the place where he was assassinated. The road that day was completely blocked off by the security forces, as well as the pro-Mursi protesters. So, I drove into Nasr City from the southern side of it, rather than the east. Due to the tension in the air, there were few if any cars around, and I arrived in good time, opting to park around 200 metres from the edge of the sit-in. I walked down Tayaran Street, somewhat surprised that my car hadn't been stopped when I'd driven so close. After all, this was, according to the national media, a 'terrorist stronghold'—a claim I did not believe, but one that I nonetheless expected to have resulted in security checkpoints and the like from the state.

There were no checkpoints. On the contrary, I saw trucks full of supplies entering the sit-in, via the same road I drove down. The only security checkpoints to speak of were those belonging to the protesters. At the entrance of the sit-in, there were Mursi supporters (reportedly, MB members) politely patting down people as they came in.

I walked through, and my mind flashed back to 2011. It wasn't a flattering comparison. If Tahrir in 2011 represented the diversity of Egypt, then Rab'a in 2013 represented homogeneity. This was clearly a pro-Islamist sit-in, and not much else. That didn't make me feel remotely unsafe as I walked through, and I didn't witness any weapons in Rab'a, although the pro-Mursi sit-in at al-Nahda in the east of Cairo would likely have been different. But the atmosphere at Rab'a bore no resemblance to what I remembered of Tahrir. I almost felt as though I was walking through a parallel universe—one where Mursi was surely going to be reinstated in short order, and the military would listen to the demands of the 'people'. For those in Rab'a, victory was assured—they only needed to be steadfast.

I came across the Rab'a stage. Safwat Higazi, a radical pro-Mursi preacher, was there, riling up the audience as was to be expected. This was the same Higazi whom the British government had banned from entering the UK years before for hate speech, and who had threatened opposition protesters in the run up to the 30 June protests by saying: 'The president, Dr Mursi, is a red line, which means who ever sprays Mr Mursi with water, we will spray with blood.'[11] In a move that aptly exemplified one of Mursi's failures throughout his year in power, he had, incredibly, appointed Higazi to the National Council of Human Rights a year before, despite the latter's long record of incitement to sectarianism, radical rhetoric, and complete lack of experience in the human rights field.

That the MB allowed such a preacher on a stage that they controlled was unfortunate but part of a pattern. The discourse in the MB camp was intensifying—Higazi was only one example—and it was all aired on international satellite television. Al Jazeera Mubasher Masr, an

Arabic-only channel of the Qatari-owned Al Jazeera network, dedicated huge amounts of airtime to covering the stage and amplifying its message. It had the effect of shocking a substantial amount of Egyptians, who were already being fed a regular diet of demonisation and dehumanisation by anti-MB stations and programmes. But it also had the inverse effect of emboldening MB supporters.

The media narratives on both sides of the divide that summer were truly distasteful to say the least, although only one side had mass firepower. The pro-Mursi camp had Al Jazeera (particularly Al Jazeera Mubasher Masr) on international satellite stations to promote its message through, although the local Egypt-based channels such as Hafiz had been taken off the air. Pro-military talk-show hosts and programmes were keen to insist that the sit-ins were essentially Tora Bora in the middle of Cairo, denouncing MB supporters as terrorists who deserved no mercy. The dehumanisation extended to others as well, in a nasty Egyptian version of chauvinistic nationalism, veering on xenophobia. Rumours of Palestinian and Syrian participants in the sit-ins sent some media outlets into a collective frenzy, although the reality was that the overwhelming majority of participants were Egyptians. The damage, however, was done.

As far as large sectors of the pro-Mursi side was concerned, they were God's people, and their opponents were enemies of God's religion. Sectarian discourse against Christians was rampant, as well as against Muslim Egyptians who didn't agree with the MB. Some senior MB figures said some rather idiotic things, such as Muhammad al-Baltagi's statement that if Mursi were to be reinstated then the violence in Sinai by radical Islamists (which had flared up after Mursi's detention but was part of an ongoing battle since the start of the uprisings in 2011) would end. Baltagi was making a predictive statement, fuelled by rootless bravado, but it convinced many in Egypt that there was an indelible link between the MB on the one side, and extremists in the Sinai on the other—ominously, men who were killing Egyptian soldiers and security personnel.

None of this boded well. That was clear as day: the national discourse was not just polarised, but was hanging by a thread.[12] Egypt desperately needed de-escalation before someone did something utterly irresponsible and destructive.

To its credit, at least a few actors in the international community tried to assist in that needed phasedown. During Mursi's tenure, the most active international actor involved in negotiations between Egypt's different factions had been the European Union, under Catherine Ashton,[13] the High Representative for Foreign Affairs and Security Policy. Due to that track record, the European Union, particularly via its special representative Bernardino Leon, managed to crystallise certain negotiation processes, backed by diplomats from the US, Qatar and the United Arab Emirates. But they were not successful.

On 7 August 2013, I attended a dinner with one of the senior European officials and some Egyptians involved in trying to encourage de-escalation between the military government and the MB. It was a very sombre evening. As soon as he arrived, the official began expressing his pessimism at the likelihood of a deal being struck, and conveyed his dissatisfaction at both the government, as well as the MB. The MB seemed convinced that the vast majority of the population was on its side, and thus it did not need to compromise with the military-backed interim government. In government quarters, the hawks were circling, and space was fast disappearing for the likes of Muhammad al-Baradei and Ziyad Bahaa al-Din, vice-president for international affairs and deputy prime minister, respectively, at that time.

These two politicians were trying desperately to find a way out of the impasse, and al-Baradei thought he'd managed to secure an agreement with the MB that would downgrade the tensions. The outline of the deal was simple: certain high profile members of the MB leadership who'd been arrested would be released, and the MB in turn would wind down its numbers at the Rab'a and the Nahda sit-ins. Unfortunately, al-Baradei couldn't lock in the agreement of the military and the security establishment. Later, officials involved in the negotiations would make clear that it was the state that chose to allow the negotiations to break down. The MB was admittedly unrealistic, but it was the state that had pulled the plug,[14] and with hardliners in the security establishment urging a swift and decisive end to the crisis.

At that dinner two of Egypt's most noted human rights defenders and I sat dolefully. Our message was united: though we'd all been highly critical of the MB during its year in power, we all vigorously opposed the idea that the security forces should forcefully disperse the

Rab'a sit-in. Such a move would lead to tremendous bloodshed, we were sure, and the repercussions would haunt Egypt for a long time. On a separate occasion, Heba Morayef, of Human Rights Watch, had said clearly that there should be no forcible dispersal of the sit-in. Morayef noted on 1 August:

> We know based on our work in Egypt over the last two years that when the police try to disperse sit-ins, they consistently use excessive force and kill unarmed protesters—137 people were killed in the past month alone. We've said there should be no forcible dispersal of the sit-in. All it takes is one stone thrown from the protesters for the violence to escalate, and even when the Interior Ministry swears it will only use birdshot, we've seen them use live gunfire again and again.[15]

She was right. We were right. I wish we hadn't been right. But we were. And Egypt went down a very dark road just days later.

III

This chapter is named 'Weeks of Killing',[16] which is the title of a report written by the Egyptian Initiative for Personal Rights, relating to the summer of 2013. Another report, 'All According to Plan', was compiled by the US-based Human Rights Watch.[17] All independent human rights organisations came to more or less the same conclusions. The forced dispersal of the pro-Mursi sit-in at Rab'a on 14 August 2013 was the largest killing of Egyptian civilians by Egyptian security forces in modern times. This wasn't Egypt's Tiananmen Square—it was worse. As Human Rights Watch argued: 'the killings not only constituted serious violations of international human rights law, but likely amounted to crimes against humanity, given both their widespread and systematic nature and the evidence suggesting the killings were part of a policy to attack unarmed persons on political grounds'.[18]

I was at home on 14 August, and was shaken awake by my wife urgently telling me, 'It's begun! They started clearing the sit-ins!' My stomach churned. My senses went on red alert. After six weeks of extensive polarisation and mutual dehumanisation, there was only one way this was going to end.

There is no better way to describe what occurred that day than to reproduce what Human Rights Watch and the Egyptian Initiative for Personal Rights separately stated. Human Rights Watch said:

On 14 August, authorities used deliberate and indiscriminate lethal force to disperse the two sit-ins, where protesters had remained encamped for 45 days, resulting in one of the most bloody incidents of mass unlawful killings of largely peaceful protesters in recent history. While Egyptian security forces have repeatedly since 2011 used excessive force to respond to demonstrations, the August 14 dispersals were unprecedented in the scale of sheer brutality.

By the end of that day, the police in concert with the army had killed at least 904 people during the dispersals, at least 817 from Rab'a and 87 from al-Nahda, including women and children. In September, Prime Minister al-Beblawy told the Egyptian daily *Al-Masry al-Youm* that the death toll from the Rab'a and al-Nahda square dispersals on August 14 was 'close to 1,000.' Ten members of the security forces were also killed—eight in Rab'a and two in al-Nahda. Although some protesters were armed and shot at the police, Human Rights Watch concluded that they were few in numbers, based on 132 interviews with protesters, local residents, medics, and journalists from both incidents, and review of hours of video footage.

Following its year-long investigation, Human Rights Watch has further concluded that the government used disproportionate force, failed to take measures to minimise loss of life, and knowingly opened fire on unarmed protesters with live ammunition, therein committing serious violations of international human rights laws. The systematic and widespread nature of the deliberate and indiscriminate killings, coupled with evidence indicating that the government anticipated and planned to engage in mass unlawful killings, i.e. murder, and that they fit into a consistent pattern of protester killings, indicate that the violations likely amount to crimes against humanity.[19]

In similar vein, the Egyptian Initiative for Personal Rights recounted:

[Our] report finds that security forces failed to plan for the dispersal of the sit-in with a view to minimising human casualties, imposing collective punishment on every person in the area, especially after some protestors—a small number by most accounts—used firearms and exchanged fire with police.

Sources for the report said that security forces used unlawful lethal force in more than one case, targeting a large number of protestors without evidence that they possessed weapons. In most cases, there were no actual safe exits to protect protestors who wished to leave the site without facing attempts by residents of nearby buildings to harass them.

The report notes that MB leaders made no effort to minimise the number of their supporters at the sit-in when the dispersal began or explain the serious danger facing them. Testimonies and other evidence indicate that a number of protestors used firearms, but it is difficult to determine the time they began to use live ammunition or the amount of ammunition used. It appears that several protestors used bricks, Molotov cocktails and primitive homemade shotguns while a fewer number used live ammunition and shot at police forces, killing several policemen. It is clear from eyewitness testimony and journalists' accounts, and the comparison of casualties on both sides that the overwhelming majority of the protestors at the sit-in were unarmed and that Rabia was not an armed sit-in in the way that the sit-in at al-Nahda was. Moreover, the Ministry of Interior's official statement that police forces had found ten automatic weapons and 29 shotguns confirms that this level of violent intervention and lethal force was unwarranted. Video footage also shows that many of those killed constituted no threat at all and that indiscriminate shooting by police for long periods killed many innocents, some while they were trying to escape or hide.[20]

This was a massacre—an absolutely unnecessary and unbelievably tragic one. And it shocked many of us to the core. The Egyptian authorities argued that the sit-in had been an armed terrorist stronghold in Nasr City, but for six weeks the state had left the 'stronghold' alone. When I had visited it, I had seen vehicles with supplies freely coming in and out, experiencing no observable problems from state security forces. If this had been a 'terrorist stronghold', surely the state would have stopped such vehicles from entering. Or water and electricity might have been cut from the area. Or, indeed, wouldn't the state have established a security perimeter around the area, so as to reduce the numbers coming into the sit-in? Why would the Egyptian state leave a 'terrorist stronghold' to operate so freely for six weeks? After the uprising in 2011, massive concrete blocks had been put all around Tahrir Square's entrances and elsewhere downtown to curb mobility. Why hadn't that been done around Rab'a, if it was such a massive threat to national security?

Unless, of course, it wasn't.

But Rab'a also wasn't a Tahrir-type locus calling for democracy and human rights, as MB supporters have been wont to argue since it was established and thereafter, including since the forced dispersal. The sit-in was about power: the MB had it before the coup, and they wanted it back. The discourse of the sit-in and Mursi partisans after the dispersal has rarely been about 'human rights'; instead it has been far more about rank political chauvinism dressed in Islamist jargon. These people were not the inheritors of the 25 January revolutionary uprising, nor were they the Muslim equivalents of Mandela's African National Congress. Previously, MB supporters had shown that they were quite willing to shoot back, as in the defence of their headquarters at Muqattam on 30 June.[21] The excerpts above from Human Rights Watch and the Egyptian Initiative for Personal Rights also provide claims that there was a small minority in Rab'a who had weapons.

Nonetheless, that could never justify the decisions taken by Egypt's security forces, nor their conduct during the summer at other points, or indeed at other times in the post 2011 era. Rab'a was undeniably the worst of the state-led killings of Egyptian civilians in the post-Tahrir period, but it wasn't the only one. There were more than a dozen, as declared in the following statement, signed by Egypt's top human rights organisations:

> List of incidents in which security forces have killed protesters since January 2011:
>
> 1. October 6, 2013, at least 57 protesters killed in dispersal of marches headed from Dokki and Ramsis towards Tahrir Square, police and armed forces deployed, no reported police deaths, no investigation of security forces wrongdoing;
> 2. August 16, 2013, at least 120 people and two police killed in clashes at the epicenter of protests in Ramsis Square and in marches en route, police deployed, no investigation of police for wrongdoing;
> 3. August 14, 2013, MB sit-ins al-Nahda and Rabi'a al-Adawiya, police deployed, up to 1000 protesters according to the prime minister and 9 police killed, no investigation of police for wrongdoing;
> 4. July 27, 2013, on Nasr Street in Cairo, police deployed, 95 protesters and one policeman killed, no investigation of police for wrongdoing;
> 5. July 8, 2013, outside the Republican Guard Club headquarters in Cairo, military deployed, 61 protesters, one military and one police officer killed, no investigation of military for wrongdoing;
> 6. July 5, 2013, outside the Republican Guard Club headquarters in Cairo, military shoots five protesters dead, no investigation of any military personnel.
> 7. January 2013, outside Port Said prison, police killed 46 people over three days, two policemen killed, investigation started but no one referred for trial. Police killed nine people in Suez. No prosecution of any officers.

8. January 2013, police kill two protesters during protests, one outside the presidential palace and one downtown. No prosecution of any officers.
9. November 2012, Tahrir square area, two killed during Muhammad Mahmoud anniversary;
10. December 2011, outside Cabinet in Cairo, military deployed, 17 killed, no investigation;
11. November 2011, Muhammad Mahmoud Street, police deployed, 51 protesters killed, one police officer serving three-year sentence after captured on video shooting protesters in the eye, no other investigation of security forces;
12. October 2011, Maspero, 27 Coptic Christian protesters killed, three soldiers sentenced by military tribunal to 2 and 3 year sentences for driving APCs that killed protesters, no investigation of shooting deaths of 13 protesters; and
13. January 2011, Cairo, Alexandria, Suez and other cities, 846 protesters killed in squares and near police stations, according to the most conservative estimates, two policemen serving time.[22]

Accountability was a word often used in Egypt, and was seen as necessary in the aftermath of the 25 January revolutionary uprising. But, ultimately, there was not even an attempt to introduce real accountability. Indeed, on some levels, a particular concept of accountability was co-opted and politicised to *favour* those in power. Societies are fortunate when public upheavals or political events, which require accountability, only affect their current generation. History shows that there are some things that endure far beyond one generation. Societal traumas take a long time to heal, and require careful, delicate reconciliation processes. Otherwise, the scabs keep coming off. Unfortunately, most in Egypt—apart from a few rare individuals—were not that focused on healing in the early years after Tahrir.

Rab'a

After Rab'a, Egyptian state news insisted the police cleared the camps 'in a highly civilised way' and, in the words of the interior minister, maintained 'the highest degrees of self-restraint'.[23] Other supporters of the violent dispersal of Rab'a were more upfront: 'We are in a state of war', Alaa al-Aswany, one of Egypt's premier novelists, told the *Guardian* in defence of the clearance. 'They are a group of terrorists and fascists'.[24] Pro-crackdown media largely downplayed the violence and dehumanised the Brotherhood, for example asserting that they used women and children as human shields.

It is obvious that none of the major players have not been interested in accountability or reform on a wide scale—not even those who have suffered as a result of the absence of these things. The parties have been purely interested in their own power, and the call for accountability was a threat to everyone's power. For Egypt has known so many traumas in the past few years that there are few who do not feel vulnerable in the face of calls for accountability. And without having healing processes in place, all Egyptians can be assured that those traumas will continue to haunt them for many more years to come.[25]

8

THE RISE OF SISI

'It looks like Egypt has come full circle. Autocratic regime, democratic experiment, then autocratic regime.'

'Regime? You think this is a regime? That's quite a compliment.'

Conversation on a Cairo street, 2015

I

On 1 July 2015 I gave a talk at Queen Mary University in London on the then-current condition of the Muslim Brotherhood (MB) and, such as it was, the Egyptian state. I had last given a talk at another London university three months earlier. That year, Abd al-Fattah al-Sisi had gone from being General Sisi, Minister of Defence, to field marshal, and then to president.

There were those in 2015 who insisted that that had been the plan all along: that from the moment Sisi became Minister of Defence in 2012, appointed officially by President Mursi, his scheme was to lead a coup against the MB, and to become president himself. I did not find that scenario convincing: it vastly overestimated the capability of the Egyptian military establishment to foresee events and to account for all the variables. From the very first day of the post-Mubarak transition, it was abundantly clear the military leadership under Tantawi was approaching political developments with more of an ad hoc approach, and could not see any further ahead than the short term future. With regards to Sisi, the situation wasn't that different.

When Sisi first became the real power in Egypt on 3 July 2013, he didn't outlaw the MB, or call for its disbandment. The titular head of the interim cabinet, Adli Mansur, offered the MB seats in cabinet. Whether this was a genuine offer or not (the MB would never have accepted and Mansur probably knew that), it did indicate a particular narrative at a particular time. That's important to note, because things were in flux for months, and transformed many times as the political arena deteriorated.

This is not evidence of a plan put into operation, so much as evidence that a plethora of political forces were jockeying for the power to define the new political dispensation. It eventually became clear what that new dispensation would look like. A 'war on terror' became not only the narrative of certain private media stations, but the state's own account.[1] The image of the MB as the root of all terrorism became no longer one only promoted under the surface by different political factions. It became the official line. But on 3 July, that wasn't quite the case: it was developed against the backdrop of later events, though many are now wont to forget that. It was certainly the design of certain forces, particularly the security establishment, and an 'eradication' tendency within the military itself, that surged post-July 2013.[2] But it took time.

Indeed, many of Cairo's staunchest international critics first gave it a chance. On the day Mursi was arrested, Human Rights Watch, a firm critic of Mursi's government and then of Sisi's, issued a press release with a title that declared: 'Judge Government on Respect for People's Rights'.[3] It was not a blanket rejection or acceptance of the change of power in a coup which saw an elected but unpopular president unseated. Rather, it was a demand that any political dispensation had to uphold fundamental human rights. Much of the world's political elite and the watchful media were on the same page at the time. But, unfortunately, Cairo lost the opportunity to show that the overthrow of Mursi would lead to a more positive reboot of the preceding three years.

When Tantawi took over in February 2011, there was no great clamouring around him as a political figure: the popular support for the resignation of Mubarak had manifested itself in support for the military as an institution, and its leadership. Things were very different when it came to Sisi in July 2013. Almost immediately, a cult of personality surrounded him. He was much younger than Tantawi, and more engaging with the media. When Mursi was overthrown, for instance, Sisi surrounded himself with public figures when he made the announcement. When Mubarak departed the presidential palace, Tantawi wasn't on that kind of platform. He didn't even make the announcement himself, or any of the army statements to come until much later in 2011. But there was a question that remained in July 2013: who exactly had taken power? Outside the top brass of the military, few had a deep relationship with Sisi, and when analysts tried to understand what made him tick, they were left empty-handed.

There was the thesis that Sisi wrote when he was a student at the United States Army War College in 2006, which many devoured as 'evidence' that he was a 'radical Islamist', since he wrote about Islam and how respect for religion would be at the bedrock of any democratic government in the Middle East. What he wrote was typical of a conservative Egyptian Muslim, and did not make him an Islamist. On the contrary, Sisi was an Egyptian conservative, a statist who believed firmly in the supremacy of the Egyptian state and its institutions.

Sisi might have simply turned out to be a more public-relations-friendly version of Tantawi. But his personality cult took on a life of its own in the Egyptian public sphere, especially since only one narrative was allowed on air. The national television stations that were aligned to the pro-Mursi camp were suspended, forcing Al Jazeera Arabic and Al Jazeera Arabic Mubasher to broadcast only from Doha.[4] (The suspended stations were full of incitement to extremism or violence, to be fair, but the pro-military and anti-MB stations were also full of other types of appalling rhetoric, and were left alone.) And, as mentioned, three weeks after the coup Sisi delivered a speech that Tantawi would never have made, calling for the Egyptian people to give him a 'mandate' to fight 'terrorism'.

In Cairo, there were suspicions that Sisi's call was a direct message to the MB, telling it that if it thought it could mobilise the masses, Sisi and the state could mobilise far more. Perhaps the hope was that this would cause the MB to buckle and capitulate to the new political dispensation. If so, it did not work. But I also wondered what the speech said about Sisi himself. Western diplomats reported that Chuck Hagel, the US Secretary of Defence, had been conveying rather disturbing messages about Sisi. Hagel and Sisi had been talking on a near daily basis, and over the first couple of weeks after Mursi had been detained, the scuttlebutt was that Sisi's demeanour and attitude had changed. If he was a younger version of Tantawi on 3 July, he was apparently gradually beginning to get puffed up by the personality cult building around him, a cult promoted by much of the Egyptian media and the military's supporters.[5]

When he appeared on television on 24 July with sunglasses and full braided military regalia, it boded badly for the future of Egypt. The following year, unsurprisingly, Sisi announced his resignation from the military. He claimed that he was answering the 'call of the people' by announcing his presidential candidacy. In 2014, riding a wave of populism, after an election that was harshly criticised for not being open, Sisi became president.[6]

II

The six months before that election were rather textbook. If the first month after the military took over was one of flux and dynamism—where room existed for compromise, negotiation and mediation—that all ended after the Rab'a massacre. From then on, the path was clear. This was a new Egyptian republic in the making, and its leadership had to rewrite the history of the previous two years in order to construct a new public discourse.

In the 'new Egyptian republic', the 25 January revolution was still called a 'revolution'. It could not be otherwise: the military had, after all, intervened and forced Mubarak from office. That couldn't be rewritten. But following Mubarak's overthrow, so the story went, the Egyptian people had been caught off guard as the deceptive, if not treacherous, MB had made all sorts of false promises. Many Egyptians trusted these claims at first, but later came to believe that the MB was a terrorist group in democratic garb. The 'Egyptian people', according to this narrative, eventually took to the streets for another revolution, to 'correct' the path taken after the first one, and so the 30 June revolt was born.

This narrative was, of course, full of holes. While many had criticisms of the MB during Mursi's year in power, there was never any suggestion from the Egyptian military, or Sisi himself, from 2011 until rather late in 2013, that the MB was a terrorist organisation. No one ever asked, for example, how, if the MB was truly a terrorist organisation, the former chief of military intelligence, Sisi, could have accepted an invitation to serve as Mursi's Minister of Defence.

Such questions were buried. Mursi, along with scores of the senior MB leadership, were referred to trial for a variety of offences ranging from incitement to espionage. The Freedom and Justice Party was banned. The MB was proscribed as a terrorist organisation. Official Egyptian statements on terrorist activities in the country were prefaced with mention of the 'terrorist MB'. After 3 July I recall hearing on Cairo's cacophonous radio stations that the MB were responsible for almost every calamity that had fallen upon Egypt. For instance, the Maspero massacre—which had been carried out by military personnel against a largely Christian group of protesters in October 2011[7]—was now, apparently, the fault of the MB. The killing of *shaheed al-Azhar, shaykh al-thawra* ('martyr of the Azhar, shaykh of the revolution') Emad Effat had been carried out by the MB; though, at the time, it seemed far more popular in the public arena that a sniper from the security forces had taken him out.

Egypt's political space was beginning to shrink in this new 'war on terror'. About five months after Mursi had been pushed from power, the interim president had passed a law to 'regulate' protests. The new law banned public assembly without specific permission from the security establishment, allocated the power to cancel, postpone or forcibly break up any protest to the Ministry of Interior (rather than the judiciary), and further restricted freedom of assembly, peaceful strikes and sit-ins, even if they did not constitute a threat to the security of citizens, or to private or public properties.[8]

What it meant was that for the first time in post-Tahrir Egypt, Egyptians did not have the right to protest. Yet before that point, protest had been intrinsic to the Egyptian polity. It was inconceivable to imagine the momentous years of 2011–13 in Egyptian history without taking into account the notion of protest. Any Egyptian law had to take that very much as a starting point: that Egyptians not only had the right to protest, but that such a right was inherent to the nature of the Egyptian political landscape. This was something that Egyptians had paid for with their blood, their sweat and their tears.

But now the new post-2013 political dispensation had snatched that right away. Instead, the Egyptian interim government—ignoring even the objections of its own deputy prime minister and others—had drawn up a law that took little notice of this important historical legacy. This law was to be problematic owing to the amount of power it provided the Ministry of Interior. It went beyond being a headache—it was a disaster—and was supported and justified by many, if not all, of the political elite of Egypt.[9]

The basic function of the rule of law is, all things considered, to protect the rights of citizens from the state, not the other way around. In Egypt there was a need for the law of free protest to act as a check against those state institutions that were still in need of reform. The new protest law seemed, instead, to communicate that the state was in need of protection from its citizens, and that their collective right to protest against the state had to be restricted.

The context was clear: the Ministry of Interior had a troubling history, to say the least, with regards to engaging with protesters. Invariably, abuses were reported by leading human rights organisations, and such reports continue, with abuses now being in some contexts worse than they were even under the Mubarak-era of impunity. Those abuses were often the impetus for protests in the first place. The law, therefore, needed to establish clear limitations, and preferably punitive measures, on the Ministry of Interior, rather than to give it the ability to effectively organise (and thus possibly marginalise or neutralise) protests.

Another aspect of the context was the political backdrop. It was troubling enough that unjustifiable restrictions were legalised, but they were then selectively (and thus politically) enforced. In a country in the midst of a deeply polarised and tense political transition, any measure that was designed to silence peaceful, critical voices had to be challenged on the basis that it would prolong rather than help overcome instability. Where citizens feel enfranchised and free to express their views subject to the use of non-violent means, a country's political institutions become respected and entrenched. Where citizens feel they live in a country where authoritarianism is legalised, those same institutions lose their respect, and instability becomes more likely. Egypt, of all countries, ought to have known that—but the law went ahead anyway.[10]

By the time the law had been implemented, there had already been thousands—perhaps even tens of thousands—of arrests of MB supporters. The passing of the protest law brought more arrests, including of many of Egypt's famous revolutionary activists, such as Alaa Abd al-Fattah, Ahmad Maher, Sana Seif, Yara Sallam, and Mahinur al-Masri. They were all referred for jail time under the protest law.[11] The objections of human rights and civil rights activists, as well as a smattering of political actors and large parts of the international arena, went unheard.

On the flip side, human rights organisations complained that police officers could expect an easy ride from the country's judiciary. Gamal Eid, the head of the Arabic Network for Human Rights Information wrote on Twitter that, 'In the city of Alexandria, the same justice released Wael El-Komi, a defendant accused of killing thirty-seven martyrs [during the eighteen days of uprising in 2011], and sentenced fourteen girls to eleven years [due to involvement in pro-Mursi protests].'[12]

III

The early years of the post-Mursi political dispensation are characterised by three main factors. The first was continuing security concerns through the country. While the narrative of a 'war on terror' remained problematic, as it failed to take fundamental rights as the core of any successful, comprehensive counter-terrorism strategy, that did not mean a militant threat from opponents of the authorities was not real and present.

The question was where that threat came from. Geographically, it started in the Sinai Peninsula, particularly with a group called Ansar Bayt al-Maqdis (Supporters of Jerusalem). That radical group had been in operation since at least early 2011, and by some estimations went back to the pre-revolution era.[13] But it did benefit in the aftermath of the uprising, both due to the Supreme Council of the Armed Forces and the MB.

In 2011, Tantawi oversaw the release of a massive number of radical Islamists from jail, presumably under the assumption that a new political reality was in place. The accusation after 30 June 2013 was that Mursi, as an Islamist, had been responsible for such prison releases, but the record is clear, as per the excellent investigative work of the likes of Hossam Bahgat.[14] Mursi did indeed release some radicals, but Tantawi did too, and his releases exceeded those of Mursi. Where Mursi managed to outdo Tantawi was in his willingness to engage and be seen with former violent radicals: in his last cabinet reshuffle in 2013, before his overthrow, he appointed a member of the Gama'a al-Islamiyya group to the governorship of Luxor. Considering Luxor had been the site of a militant attack in the 1990s by Gama'a al-Islami-yya, where many civilians had been killed, it was an abundantly impru-dent move, to say the least.

In both Tantawi and Mursi's times, Ansar Bayt al-Maqdis and other radical groups managed to organise and rally together in a way that wouldn't have been possible in the Mubarak era. Ansar Bayt al-Maqdis didn't regard the military or the MB as allies any more than the most extreme Islamists in Syria regard President Erdogan of Turkey as a friend, but they also saw no reason to target them in the early stages of their build up of strength. The likes of the so-called 'Islamic State' (ISIL) did not target Turkey to begin with (even though they regarded Turkey's leadership as apostates), since Turkey was not interfering directly with their activities. When that changed, Turkey became a tar-get. The same happened in Egypt: Ansar Bayt al-Maqdis engaged in small skirmishes in 2011–13, but when the military overthrew Mursi in 2013, they saw it as a direct attack on their broader Islamist project, even though they considered Mursi and the MB as more or less sell-outs—al-Ikhwan al-Muflisun (the Bankrupt Brotherhood)—to what they regarded as the evil ideology of democracy.

Would the violence in the Sinai have happened without the removal of Mursi? It's entirely possible. Turkey's Erdogan was not opposed to Islamism at large as a political ideology at all, but eventually Turkey became a target as the result of diverging political priorities between Ankara and ISIL. That had not yet happened in Egypt by June 2013, but considering that these particular extremists had no particular loyalty to Mursi, and regarded the MB as renegades anyway, it is unlikely Egypt would have managed to steer clear of their wrath for long.

What is most certainly true, however, is that the overthrow of Mursi lent huge credibility to the narrative of extremist Islamists, as they pur-sued recruitment strategies. For years, the MB had argued that the main mechanism for pursuing change would be through gradual means and the ballot box. There were certainly exceptions to this rule, especially when one looked beyond Egypt into the wider MB universe: Syrian MB leaders had engaged in an armed struggle in the early 1980s, culminating in a brutal and ruthless crackdown by Hafiz al-Assad at Hama. In the aftermath of the Libyan uprising, Libyan MB leaders refused to recognise the outcome of the 2014 election, and aligned themselves with extremist Islamist militias, putting to rest any notion they prioritised the ballot box and democratic means above all else. But taking all that into account, the mainstream of MB ideology foresaw that effective organisational capacity, combined with slow but steady work via existing political systems, would ultimately deliver the best results.

That was obviously complete anathema to the extremists of the likes of ISIL. In 2011, many commentators had speculated about the demise of extremist Islamism as a social alternative, on the basis that Egypt had shown that real change against autocrats and dictators could come about by largely peaceful means. But by 2013, at least in the extremist Islamist camp, that argument was dead, and groups such as Ansar said 'I told you so' at every turn. That no doubt assisted them greatly in their recruitment strategies, and probably siphoned off many novices, who might have previously thought the MB was a better option.

This phenomenon no doubt only intensified as the conflict in the Sinai intensified, particularly given the harsh measures that the Egyptian military used in the peninsula. Western allies continuously advised Cairo, in private, that the struggle in the Sinai had to be considered as a counterinsurgency, and that they ought to rely on classic counterinsurgency strategies. Instead, so the Western critique went, the army seemed to treat it more like a typical ground war against a foreign invader. That might have worked had it really been fighting a foreign invader, but it wasn't: the militants were nearly all Egyptian, and many of them were from the local population. Counterinsurgency recognises the need to bring the local population on board for intelligence purposes, or at the very least, to avoid turning them into a recruitment source for the enemy.[15]

It wasn't just the Sinai where security was an issue. In Egyptian cities, including greater Cairo, a number of extremist groups coalesced in the aftermath of Rab'a. The threat of those militants was exceptionally stark—moreso because they were relatively disconnected. The official state narrative was that these groups were armed wings of the MB answering to the MB leadership at large, and while there was no evidence to substantiate that claim, the MB itself was going through very difficult times.[16]

Following Rab'a, demonstrations and protests calling for Mursi's reinstatement continued, but they progressively dwindled in size and impact. The pro-Mursi protest movement then engaged in what it considered to be 'defensive violence'. The Egyptian media, anti-MB as it was, needed few excuses to roast the MB. The angry rhetoric the MB indulged in did not help to distinguish it from extreme groups either— domestically or internationally. The international lobbying effort led by the Egyptian Revolutionary Council, a pro-MB group based in Turkey made up of Egyptian exiles, had little political impact. The new political dispensation headed by President Sisi in Cairo had become accepted, rightly or wrongly, on the international scene, especially against the backdrop of the extremist Islamist threat emanating from Syria and Iraq.

The strategy of protest within Egypt and lobbying outside it persisted for some time. It was based on an assessment by the MB that the majority of Egyptians supported them, still looking back to the electoral success it had enjoyed in 2011 and the narrow election victory of Mursi in 2012. It was an assessment few analysts considered as valid in 2013, and certainly not thereafter but, given that calculation of widespread support, the strategy seemed to be worthwhile. Yet, the MB continued to become weaker, not stronger. While Sisi's political dispensation faced a broad array of challenges, the chances of Mursi being reinstated via prolonged protests became more and more remote.

The old guard of the MB, which had controlled the leadership for years, had been attempting to hold the group together around the above strategy. But the younger ranks grew impatient. For them, the violent dispersal of the Rab'a al-Adawiyya sit-in in August 2013 (which, as discussed in the previous chapter, Human Rights Watch had described as likely being a crime against humanity)[17] was probably the defining moment of their political lives. Many of them, if not the majority, supported escalating the confrontation with the authorities.

The old guard prioritised the continued cohesion of the group above all else, but also tried to reduce the possibility of escalation that the younger ranks were seeking. At the same time, it didn't have the sort of control over the younger ranks it once did. Most of the top MB leaders were in jail or outside the country.[18] The younger ranks were not operating as though the leadership was completely AWOL, but the control structures between the top tier and the fourth tier, which had been so active on the ground, had been broken.

Moreover, the old guard permitted, and in some cases even encouraged,[19] a more aggressively belligerent rhetoric through the MB media, which only fed into the sense that confrontation was desirable. That sort of rhetoric began prior to the 30 June protests against the MB in 2013 and only deepened thereafter. The rhetoric on the anti-MB side became at least as equally distanced from the notion of reconciliation.[20]

This escalationist tendency was not only in ascendance within the MB, but also on the ground. In 2015, a group of 150 Muslim preachers issued a statement declaring that the time had come for a more aggressive posture vis-a-vis the Egyptian authorities—although it was unclear if all signatories had actually signed it. The language could have been easily interpreted as support for the violent targeting of Egyptian officials such as police, army and judicial personnel. MB representatives publicly praised the declaration,[21] further indicating the presence of an escalationist tendency within the group.

Vague terms like 'resistance' and 'by all means necessary' were used in the MB's various media, but their language may have been elastic precisely to ensure that all elements that made up the MB support base felt included. The English statements were obviously directed towards the international media and Western capitals, so these emphasised, for example, 'nonviolence,' and 'democracy', unlike Arabic-language statements. This also wasn't a new trend: back in 2012, when protestors attacked the US Embassy, a sarcastic Twitter 'fight' broke out between the MB and the embassy, after the latter pointed out that the former's statements in English were substantively different than its statements in Arabic.

The Arabic statements contained more inflammatory language, but the discourse was also aimed at an entirely different audience. An increasingly pliable definition of 'violence in self-defence' seemed ever more likely to take hold. By 2015, there were signs that isolated members of the MB had taken it upon themselves to engage in rather unsavoury activities without being restrained by the old guard—which may no longer have had the capacity, let alone the will, to restrain them anyway.

The old guard, however, was not down and out by any means, but its fate was directly linked to how the Egyptian government would respond, and a cynical strategy in that regard began to unfold in mid-2015. Shortly after the rift between the 'old guard' and the escalationist tendency within the MB became a matter of public knowledge, with opinion pieces and press releases being issued on different platforms sympathetic to the MB, the security forces arrested several senior MB old guard leaders. It surprised many analysts that anyone from the top level of the MB was even at large on Egyptian territory. Anyway, their arrests appeared difficult to put down to coincidence.

Their detention seemed to ensure that the more radical voices in the group were freer to pursue whatever escalation they wanted, even if it turned out to be violent. That, in turn, was likely to lead to an even harsher crackdown by the Egyptian authorities, and also provide a modicum of validation for Cairo's argument internationally that the MB en masse had become a terrorist organisation.

There were those that argued that the transformation of the MB into a more radical group was inevitable, and that the blame for that had to be laid at the door of the Egyptian government's immense crackdown. But there were choices, for both the MB and the Egyptian authorities. Those supporting the escalationist tendency on the ground in Egypt's MB might have chosen to become political vigilantes, but they could equally have pursued more reasonable options. The April 6 Youth Movement, for example, did not endorse the declaration of the 150 Muslim preachers. Rather, it condemned it as 'an incitement to violence', which was destructive to any peace among Egyptians.[22] April 6 had itself suffered significant losses since June 2013, but its position on the call had still been a principled one.

The Egyptian state could have formed policies that made it easier— or harder—for more reasonable voices, or at least less radical voices, to be heard among the MB's ranks. Ultimately, it was the individual responsibility of every MB member to choose his or her own path,[23] but those members were also Egyptian citizens, and they were, first and foremost, the responsibility of the Egyptian state. Unfortunately, it did not appear in 2015 as though wisdom was in particularly high supply in either camp—though, one camp was supposedly responsible for the country at large.

IV

The second factor that characterised post-Mursi Egypt was the deterioration of human rights generally, across the board, against the backdrop of its 'War on Terror'. That earned Egypt a spotlight internationally, particularly during the 28th Session of the United Nations Human Rights Council, when the country was subjected to the Universal Periodic Review. That review serves as a peer-assessment process during which states and civil society organisations provide information and analyse the overall human rights performance of a given country.[24] Technically, Egypt accepted most of the recommendations offered at the session, but rights groups and critics complained that 'the contrast between the promises made at the UN by the Sisi government and the reality on the ground, suggests scepticism is a wiser position'.[25]

Scepticism seemed not only a wise position, but also the only reasonable position. The protest law was still in force, and there was no suggestion it would be amended or scrapped; civil society organisations and human rights groups faced deeper and more wide-ranging restrictions; and the excessive use of force by the security forces continued unabated, with virtually no accountability.

Many of Egypt's most noted human rights organisations failed to attend the Universal Periodic Review itself, citing fear of reprisals by the Egyptian state.[26] Tens of thousands of citizens were mentioned by various human rights groups as being detained—the precise number being difficult to establish owing to the lack of transparency from the Egyptian state in allowing independent monitors access.[27] In 2015, groups such as the International Federation for Human Rights (FIDH) continued to condemn 'the prevailing impunity and failure of the authorities to hold officials, police and army officers accountable for the use of excessive force against protesters', and noted that hundreds of individuals were still on 'death row'.[28] The military court system continued to apply to civilians, a procedure entrenched in the country's constitution, with over 3,000 civilians being tried in military courts between April and

December 2014, and a counter-terrorism legislative regime implemented by decree of the presidency in 2015, leading to concerns that exceptional measures were becoming normalised.

Against this background, the economy—the third factor—began to recover sluggishly after Sisi's government ordered mega-projects, such as the expansion of the Suez Canal and reforming the energy sector. Critics wondered if such projects would lead to sufficient stimulus within the economy, particularly while more urgent structural reforms were left unattended.[29] The final results of this approach will make themselves more clearly known in years to come. In the meantime, Egypt's military elite have retained much of their Mubarak-era economic hold, significantly withstanding pressures to privatise or redistribute their many factories and industries, which further entrench their political weight, as academics like Zeinab Abul Magd and others have diligently documented.[30]

Despite political and economic instability, and inherent social volatility, there continues to be, at the time of writing, a sense of wary, if not weary, resilience as Egypt approaches the fifth anniversary of Tahrir. There has been a peculiar combination of phenomena in tension with each other. The same conditions that existed in late 2010—which later led to the eruption in 2011—have intensified. The youth bulge is still there. Indeed, according to some demographers, there are two youth bulges waiting to impact the country.[31] The economy was continuing to deteriorate as the time of writing, and requires widescale public, private, and military reforms, as well as substantial investment. The security sector is in direr need of reform than it has ever been, and accountability for all the abuses that have taken place since 2011, and before, remains a remote possibility. The human rights situation has worsened substantially, and the political arena is more polarised than it has ever been before. The military roadmap might have been fulfilled, in that a new constitution, a new presidency and a new parliament have been voted on—but under what conditions? A fully fair and open political environment, or one that was defined in terms of a 'war on terror', with all the narrowing qualities that go along with that?

Be that as it may, there was little expectation at the beginning of 2015 that Abd al-Fattah al-Sisi's political dispensation was going away anytime soon. Michael Hanna described the situation succinctly as 'sustainable instability':

However, while Egypt as a country will continue to suffer various kinds of instability, the regime of President Abdel Fattah el-Sisi remains firmly ensconced for the foreseeable future. The irreparably fragmented state of political opposition, ferocious levels of state repression, societal fatigue, fear of state collapse, regional disorder, and a lack of demonstrable leadership alternatives act as inhibiting factors for dissent and outward opposition and, these elements have come together to create an environment of sustainability, despite the obvious and expanding forms of instability that plague, and will continue to plague, Egypt. [32]

The point is that Sisi does not preside over a regime—that would be overestimating its structure. The elements that make up his political dispensation appear almost sovereign entities unto themselves. In the post-Mursi reality, different state institutions sought—with varying degrees of success—to implant their authority over their own autonomous zones on the one hand, and extend it further around the state on the other. Some further exploited constitutional autonomy granted to them in the process of implementing the post-Mursi 2014 constitution. The military is certainly the most powerful of these institutions, but a formidable Ministry of Interior, and the wider security establishment, follows its example. The judiciary is another institution that sees itself as a partner of the presidency and other institutions, rather than as part of a cohesive, republican and presidential state. Sisi has a theoretical veto power within many parts of the state—perhaps all of it, even—but practically speaking, that power does not always filter down. Moreover, the presidency does not always use its veto: to do so requires the expenditure of internal political capital, within the system. Hanna continues:

While a certain amount of communication and coordination among the institutions of the state does occur, outside observers should not assume that the institutions are tethered to a top-down decision-making process. The various institutions of state share common views and assumptions, but individuals within these institutions still have wide latitude to exercise authority in many instances. This has clearly been the case with the public prosecutor and the judiciary, which have at times made decisions that created foreign relations problems for the regime. The al-Jazeera English case, in which journalists were convicted of terrorism-related charges, is the most high-profile example of this phenomenon, which escalated without top-level authorisation. However, continued cooperation among the organs of state is highly valued by the regime, which limits the appetite of the executive branch to unwind decisions that it does not agree with.[33]

Nevertheless, the power of state institutions, a population that is politically and economically exhausted by years of upheaval, the popular support for the state establishment, and the fragmentation of any genuine opposition force, all make it entirely likely that Sisi will remain in power for quite some time. The nature of his dispensation, however, bears within it a very dangerous risk: should his state crumble in any significant way, the results would be immeasurably chaotic.

In 2011, the military intervened on the part of the protesters, and removed Mubarak. This coincided with its own agenda. Similarly in 2013 with Mursi. Following 2013, I was asked many times—by media, by analysts, and by political figures—whether or not I expected another revolutionary uprising. I cautioned against any sort of prediction in this regard; if nothing else, 2011–13 had taught me to be circumspect. But one question clearly needed to be asked: if there was an uprising in Egypt again, would the military be looked upon as an institution that would go against the presidency? Would the military be at odds with a presidency led by Sisi, one of their own?

I found that difficult to imagine, unless the relationship between the presidency and the military establishment weakened over time, as happened with Mubarak. But I feared that any potential uprising would not be the result of political mobilisation seeking negotiated political ends. Rather, it would be what the economic elites in Cairo were so dreadfully afraid of: a 'hunger revolution'. In a country where there is such a disparity between the rich and the poor, such an eruption is a very real fear.

Internationally, though, there are few countries who are willing to take serious steps to involve Egypt in a multilateral enterprise of reform. There have certainly been many countries willing to lobby Egypt unilaterally about different aspects of what they have seen as detrimental to Egypt's short-term or long-term prospects. But none of them have been willing to engage in a multilateral effort. Cairo has fobbed off many a unilateral attempt; multilaterally, particularly with the right partners, there might have been a different outcome. But the interest simply hasn't been there. The rise of ISIL has taken up much of the bandwidth of policy establishments in the Arab world and the West—and Egypt has been on the 'right' side of that particular conflict.

Has Egypt come 'full circle', five years after the 25 January revolutionary uprising? Not quite. There are members of the security establishment who fled the country in the aftermath of that uprising, but returned a few days before the 30 June protests because they knew that the MB's time was up and they wanted to stake their claims to new roles in the post-30 June reality. Objectively speaking, they made a strategically smart—if not utterly cynical—call. But they need to realise, like all of us, that an Egypt of the future is never going to be the Egypt of 2010. The question is: what it will be instead?

CONCLUSION

THE GENIE IS OUT

'I'm not sure where I should end it. It's taken a long time to write. It's almost heart wrenching. But I still don't know where to end it.'
'End it at Shaimaa. End it where this all began.'
'And where it might begin again?'
'Oh, it never ended. And they have only themselves to blame for what comes next.'

Conversation at Cimatheque, Cairo, May 2015

Why is it that all the good people die in this country?

Bassem Sabry, 24 March 2013

I

Writing a book is never an easy endeavour. I agreed with my publisher to write this book in April 2014, and I had in mind to give it to him a few months later. I'm not sure how I thought that would happen. We eventually settled on a new deadline for delivery of the manuscript, which gave me two more years to write it. One of the reasons for the delay, as I look back through my correspondence, was the passing of one Egyptian whom I knew well. His name was Bassem Sabry.

He was my friend, and as I write these lines I'm in Cape Town, at the base of Table Mountain, which Bassem visited on his last international trip, just weeks before his passing. When Bassem visited Cape Town in early 2014, he felt truly honoured to have received the invitation; he was a columnist for a renowned website on the politics of the Middle

189

East, Al-Monitor, and was representing it in the city during a conference. He was so proud.

On 29 April 2014, I met a couple of friends who I had known in Cairo (and who had been the reason I loved the Madinat al-Qahira, the 'city victorious') but who had moved away from the city. We hadn't met up in a long time, and were chatting about how so many of our friends had left Cairo. Our point was simple: if they all left, what would become of this grand city? If they were all gone, then what would this city still mean to us? Then the phone rang, and to my shock I learned that my friend, colleague and comrade, Bassem Sabry, had also gone.

We talked about how so many people in Egypt seemed to have gone mad over the past year or so, such was the destructive, disagreeable and detestable polarisation that had dominated so much of Egypt's discourse. But Bassem hadn't gone mad. Bassem had been entirely consistent unto himself. And that was a great comfort to so many people who looked at the behemoths of division and saw despair. They saw despair until they spoke with someone like Bassem Sabry.

At a time when Egypt sorely needed voices to reject polarisation and hatred, Bassem was one of the few who insisted on standing for loftier ideals. He believed in a better Egypt for all Egyptians and worked tirelessly, quietly and without credit, in pursuit of that goal. Bassem and I often talked about hope—hope in this country and hope in its people and hope in its future. Many had given up all hope. But Bassem hadn't given up. We talked about people feeling Egyptian—and Bassem inspired in others a joy and hope in being Egyptian.

Bassem began writing through his blog and then for some of the most prestigious outlets on Arab politics in the world. Over the course of the Egyptian revolution he marked out a space as one Egypt's most balanced commentators. He had never given in to extremes, even when everyone else around him was more than happy to.

I met Bassem through the revolution of 25 January. Both of us believed in that revolution's potential for making Egypt great, and I'll be forever grateful that Tahrir allowed me to meet people like Bassem. It is both the revolution's and Egypt's loss that he is no longer here to fight for it. And fight for it he did, with all his heart.

But he didn't struggle for it with his ego, as so many did. He fought with his heart, which is why he was so incredibly discreet about the work he had actually done, behind so many different scenes and in so many bizarre situations. He was adamantly private about his political affiliations in his work because he truly wanted there to be as few barriers as possible between him and his readers. In an Egypt where schism is the norm, Bassem was one of a kind. He wanted, so much, to be the non-partisan commentator that was so rare, and which we all saw was so needed in the public sphere.

We were both in Tahrir Square during the protests in 2011, and later talked about the prospects for a new Arab political ideology, one that would be true to the Arab world's heritage, but which would be vibrant and dynamic, beyond the failures that Egypt had already seen and experienced.

We often talked about his political work behind the scenes, and some of the difficult decisions he had to make and the quandaries he found himself in.

Yet he agilely traversed those scenarios, avoiding the limelight, even though he could have easily become an even more famous public figure. He called his blog 'An Arab Citizen', even though he knew that this was more of an aspiration than a reality. He wanted to help to build that concept of citizenship, where all Egyptians and all Arabs could genuinely claim that there was an equitable and just social contract between the ruled and the ruler—where, indeed, they were citizens. That was Bassem's work and mission.

It did come at a price. Bassem was a great optimist and was deeply pained by the experience of 2013. The anguish he felt, as he saw Egyptian turn on Egyptian, troubled him tremendously. He lived to see the revolution that so many Egyptians of his generation wanted to be a part of—but he was also profoundly distressed to see the failure of Egyptians to live up to it.

I never had any doubt that if the revolution arose again, Bassem Sabry would be, as he always had been, right in the thick of it—hidden, yet paradoxically in plain sight, giving so much of himself without anyone knowing about it.

The very last time I saw Bassem, he visited me at home. He always found great joy in playing with my young daughter. He insisted that I prepare myself for the days ahead when he would teach her Latin, philosophy, astrophysics and all sorts of subjects that he would learn in

order to teach her to be a 'renaissance woman'. My daughter, incidentally, was not even four years old, but that didn't stop Bassem from
planning. We all left the house together. I put my daughter in her car
seat and then went over to say goodbye to Bassem. He was about to
walk away, when my little girl told her mother, 'I want to kiss Bassem
goodbye'. I don't think I have ever heard her say that about anyone. He
came back and she kissed him goodbye.

On Wednesday 30 April 2014 we buried my dear friend. We had all
gathered at the Mustafa Mahmud mosque for his funeral prayer. For a
young man of thirty-one, so many people were there and from so many
different walks of life. The condolences received came from across the
political spectrum, and from around the world. He was not just an
Egyptian analyst; he was a globally respected one, and, more importantly, a globally loved one. Public figures from across the political
spectrum in Egypt and internationally publicly mourned his passing.

When his funeral prayer finally took place in Sixth of October, a suburb west of Cairo, I thought there would only be a handful of us. There
had been complications about where the prayer would actually be held,
owing to some paperwork concerning the releasing of the body. But the
procession of cars and people that I saw on that Wednesday evening I
cannot remember seeing before, except perhaps on television. From far
and wide, people drove for hours to reach Bassem.

When the funeral prayer was over, we walked to his final resting
place. He was placed in the ground and his friends and family suppli-
cated for his soul. As the grave was sealed, I placed the last pieces of
soil on it, and swept up the remaining pieces of earth. For some time I
couldn't quite let go of the door of the crypt.

At a time when Egypt sorely needed voices that rejected destructive
polarization and mutual hatred, Bassem was one of the few that insisted
on standing for far loftier principles. He believed in a better Egypt for
all Egyptians and worked tirelessly, often very quietly and without
taking credit, in pursuit of that goal.

It is my loss that I did not meet Bassem sooner. He was, as Al-Monitor
put it, among the most incisive and respected analysts of contemporary
Egyptian politics[1]—but for me, he was, most of all, my friend.

Strangely, when he died I was rendered emotionless. Around me,
Bassem's many friends were tearing up, or breaking down—he had

passed away in a tragic accident, and it was extremely sudden. My pressing concern was to ensure that he found his way to his resting place, and that those of his friends who were traumatised about his passing had at least one person to console them. I wanted to ensure there had been no foul play at work, and my investigations, together with those of others, showed that Bassem's death had, indeed, been an accident.

When friends of Bassem mention how sad they are that he is no longer with us, a part of me always reaches out through the sorrow and reminds them, as I remind myself, that we were immensely fortunate to have known him, and that rather than mourning his passing, we should take not only solace, but inspiration from the memories we had of his sterling commitment.

When he passed away, friends and comrades told me, 'It's like we're being reminded that the revolution itself has passed on'. This helps explain why Bassem is so significant to me as I ponder the aftermath of the 25 January revolutionary uprising. The revolution has, indeed, passed on. But rather than lament that, as so many are wont to do, it befits all of us who fought for it and believed in it to remember that we are privileged to have been there. And for those of us who participated, even in some insignificant way, the 25 January revolution continues to provide lessons and principles that remain pertinent.

II

As the memories of Tahrir recede further into history, and the revolutionary fervour that was so palpable in 2011, right through till 2013, becomes difficult to recall, the question that many ask is simple: was it worth it? Wouldn't things have been better if Mubarak had simply remained in office, and all this revolutionary nonsense had been sealed in a box and thrown into the Nile?

It is a legitimate question—but it is usually pointed in the wrong direction.

As I've indicated before, on 24 January 2011, a day before the Cairo protests began, I penned a piece for an Arab world newspaper, *The National*, with the title, 'Youth need vision, not revolt'.[2] It was essentially an argument against uprising, not because I had any sympathy for Mubarak's regime, but because I didn't think it could possibly work out well. I began my piece by recalling an incident that occurred during the inaugural address of the second caliph, Umar al-Faruq ibn al-Khattab: 'a person in the crowd promised: "If we find you crooked, we will correct you. With our swords!" To which the new ruler replied, "Praise be to God, who created among our people someone who is able to correct the crookedness of Umar."'[3] My supposition was that there were imperatives that could lead to the correction of a ruler—and that at the bedrock of traditional Muslim societies, despite the oligarchies, those correctional imperatives still existed in principle. The question was what kind of corrections would be appropriate given the prevailing circumstances. The answer depended on two main factors: the sort of ruling administration that was in place, and the kind of civil society there was to question and correct it, as per Caliph Umar's declaration.

When I looked at Egypt on 24 January, I could not see a civil society capable of calling the regime to account—precisely because the regime, and regimes before it, had so unreservedly crippled civil society. And thus, all there could be was chaos. Yet, in spite of my fears, the eighteen days did not turn out to be a mass panic. The country did not go up in flames. On the contrary. Tahrir was not perfect by any stretch of the imagination, but the way in which Egyptians conducted themselves during those eighteen days of uprising was truly revolutionary. And inspiring.

Crucially, however, the question of 'was Tahrir worth it?' should never be asked of the protesters in the square. Rather, it should be asked of those who refused to listen to those in the squares and the streets of Egypt.

The point is that throughout the post-uprising period, right through the democratic experiment that came to an end in the summer of 2013, the forces of the revolutionary camp were never in power. That is not to say that they should have been: no person has some kind of divine or innate right to rule, even if they are right. Plato's argument for a philosopher king has some merits, but creates far more problems than it solves. The revolutionary camp had many if not all of the right instincts—but instincts alone were never going to be sufficient for ruling a country.

Their lack of executive power means that sticking blame for Egypt's woes primarily on the revolutionary protestors, as many after 2011

CONCLUSION

have done, is nonetheless absurd. Perhaps, as I mentioned before, the largest specific failure that one could genuinely hold the revolutionary camp to account for, in terms of strategic deficiencies, was its inability to promote a single leader. That cost the country a great deal in 2012. If, for example, Hamdeen Sabahi and Abd al-Mun'im Abu al-Futuh had pooled their campaigns into a single one, their combined share would have exceeded 38 per cent of the voting population (of course, though, the differences between the two candidates complicated matters greatly). That would have placed their combined campaign in the final runoff against either Mursi or Shafiq, and it is difficult to imagine Mursi or Shafiq beating either of them under those circumstances.

Perhaps a rehabilitation of Amr Moussa in that election, working alongside the revolutionary figures, might have been something to explore. To be sure, he had served the forces of the previous regime, but he embraced the need for change, even if insufficiently. That might have stabilised a pro-revolutionary ticket enough to take Egypt through the first stage of its democratic experiment: a full term of a president elected democratically in a relatively open, free and fair race might have been possible.

But if the revolutionary forces were unable to do what was necessary, they at least wanted to do what was inkeeping with the progressive and pluralistic spirit of the revolutionary uprising. The Muslim Brotherhood (MB), the largest political force in the country once Mubarak's party imploded, may make claims today that it wanted the revolution to be a success, but few revolutionaries will agree. History does not bear out the MB's claims. The movement was politically opportunist in the most typical and ordinary way. It jumped onto the revolution bandwagon as a way to increase its own power. Its own impulses were far from pluralistic, whether in political or religious terms, and at every point its desire for political power outweighed its commitments to the revolutionary cause. It even led, in a number of areas, to collaboration with and co-option of elements of the former regime.

The MB did, nevertheless, adhere to the basic rules of the democratic game—and one can argue over whether they did so only because they thought it would serve their interests. But the Egyptian MB neither had the foresight nor the inclination to go beyond that, unlike its corresponding numbers in Tunisia, where the Ennahdha party compromised in order to maintain the democratic experiment. When Ennahdha compromised, it benefited. The democratic experiment benefited. The entire country benefited. But the Egyptian MB was trapped in its own bubble, and it couldn't prick itself out of it. As Ahmad Maher, a revolutionary activist, said from his jail cell:

> In general, they [the Muslim Brothers] refuse to recognise that they made any mistakes while in power. They are saying that the protests of 30 June 2013 were not due to popular outrage but to a Western Crusader conspiracy against Islam and the MB. They are still in denial about what happened. On the whole, I don't think that there is serious reflection or any flexibility among the MB. This means that the solution is still far off. How can there be a solution without serious reflection—not just about their practices while in power, but also a reconsideration of the theory itself? This is what they refuse to do. They claim that they did not make mistakes but rather that the world conspired against them.[4]

The force that precipitated the abortion of the democratic transition in Egypt was the most powerful one of all—the military. It was to the military that the people had turned to take the country through its transition to democracy. The Supreme Council of the Armed Forces, under Tantawi, could have constructed a roadmap that would have done just that; indeed, one of the great ironies of Egypt's revolution is that if 11 February 2011 had looked more like 3 July 2013, the transition might have had a far better chance of succeeding.

If Tantawi had gathered a group similar to the one Sisi gathered on 3 July—with the addition of the MB—the transition might have looked very different indeed. Moreover, if the post-3 July 2013 roadmap had been implemented in 2011, with some minute changes, a great deal of suffering might have been avoided. Economic restructuring could have taken place at a time when the transition to democracy was incredibly popular, and if the massive support that the Gulf provided to Sisi after 2013 had taken place in 2011, the economic crash could have been ameliorated.

Instead, the military leadership oversaw a decrepit blueprint from 2011 to 2012, something that they changed in an ad hoc fashion, and which could only ensure that minor changes in the country would happen in the most unsystematic and inoperable manner. Had the military enacted reforms in the security sector alone (something the MB also failed to do), Egypt might have been saved a great deal of blood-shed in later years.

III

But the reality is that in the aftermath of the revolutionary uprising, the four main forces—the revolutionaries, the MB, the old regime, and the military—acted precisely as one would have expected based on their strengths, weaknesses and overall characteristics. No one expected the old regime of Mubarak to suddenly become revolutionary—that would have been nonsensical. When it came to the revolutionaries, no-one should have expected them to organised enough to lead a democratic transition, or even to participate within it at senior levels: it was almost miraculous that they had been able to achieve what they did in early 2011, and for that alone they deserve a spot in history.

On the question of the MB: while it would be unfair to call the Egyptian MB a cult, it is arguably an exceedingly narrow clique pander-ing to a deeply limited worldview. For the MB to have become an organisation genuinely engaging in pluralistic politics in the same way that Christian Democratic parties in Europe do, was possible, but not without massive internal change. It would have had to have become something like the Strong Egypt Party led by Abu al-Futuh, a former senior MB leader himself, or the Ennahdha Movement of Rashid al-Ghannushi in Tunisia, which predominates within the Tunisian MB trend. But that was not the MB of Egypt, and it performed in the only way it knew how. Maher, revolutionary activist par excellence, noted in an interview: 'I think that trusting the military and the MB was naïve, because each of them have a plan and their own interests. They each tricked us and broke all their promises. Each of them are authori-tarian and think that they have the absolute truth.'[5]

If a pluralistic and progressive trend within the MB was rare, it at least existed as a minor grouping within it at the dawn of the uprising. In the military leadership of 2011, who was interested in converting Egypt's autocratic regime into a pluralistic democracy that would stand on the strength of its accountable institutions? It pursued the interests of the military, as it saw them; and it, just like the MB as well as the revolutionaries, identified its interests as the 'interests of Egypt'. The revolutionaries acquitted themselves a lot better morally only because they had revolted against the existing order, and weren't interested in partisan power.

But as historians look back on the Tahrir revolution, it will seem copiously clear that there was, indeed, someone who could have made all the difference. He could have averted it all if he had simply chosen to recognise that the people of Egypt wanted change. He could have been a player in implementing that change, and even avoided account-ability for himself in the new order; that would have been a price worth paying had it averted bloodshed and bedlam. But Mubarak, long before he was imprisoned by the military, appears to have been held captive by the delusion of power. That is a great pity. But as questions of culpability continue to swirl around in the annals and corridors of universities, think-tanks and policy establishments the world over, let the question be posed not to the revolutionaries, who only wanted the chance to say their piece. Let the question be posed to the one who was the president of Egypt: 'Mr Mubarak, was it truly worth it?'

IV

For months after the military abortion of the democratic experiment in 2013, almost every time I engaged with non-Egyptians (whether based in Egypt or not) I was asked, 'Where have they all gone? Where are all those young activists from the 25 January revolution?' The cyni-cal among them reckoned those activists had 'sold out', and had become cheerleaders for the military, despite having protested against the military in late 2011 and much of 2012. The idealists were just left confused, because they did not have a clue where these 25 January activists had disappeared to. The truth was, many of those activists also did not know where they themselves were. But they were still there, and I reckon their part in Egypt's story is not yet over.[6]

During Mursi's year in office, the position of these activists was weak; they operated in an arena in which no-one was overwhelmingly dominant. As the year progressed, the MB found itself preoccupied with an ongoing vendetta against forces of the former regime. In the process, it managed to alienate even those activists who had supported Mursi over Shafiq. None of this strengthened the hand of the revolutionary camp, but it did inadvertently provide limited space for the revolutionaries to operate in certain quarters, while the MB and Mubarak's old networks battled each other.

The revolutionaries correctly saw the state's 'war on terror' as counter-revolutionary, a polarising and divisive influence on Egyptian society, and rejected with contempt the violent dispersal of the pro-Mursi Rab'a sit-in. Parts of the revolutionary forces were cautious about supporting the military and the interim government on 4 July 2013, but that was very short-lived. After the state's dispersal of Rab'a, it would have been difficult to find a supporter of the revolution who was pro-military in any way.

So 'where are they?' In the post-Mursi period, the state has monopolised the width and the breadth of the political arena, and there has been little effective opposition. With such overwhelming support for the current military backing the interim government, those who offered critiques—even if they had proven their non- or anti-MB 'credentials'—were being depicted by parts of the Egyptian media as 'fifth columnists', who were akin to or even worse than the MB (who were at least 'open' about who they were).

In this context, a few decided to take something of a sabbatical from political activism. They were cynical about a society that seemed so overwhelmingly polarised between either pro-military and pro-state forces on the one hand, and the Islamists of the MB on the other, which had weakened the revolutionary impetus so much that it allowed the space for a military-backed regime to take over. Others insisted that the time for struggle was now, and found the struggle continuing in different mediums and fashions—whether it was in the human rights community, pockets of the media, or other surviving sections of civil society.

It's probably true, though, that most pro-25 January activists have, at the time of writing, found themselves in a limbo between these two positions. They do not see the revolution as 'dead', but they do see it as in 'deep freeze'. They see a choice. One can resign oneself to the idea that there is no point in working for change. Or, one can remind oneself that, just as it did under Mubarak, the cause for 'bread, freedom, social justice, and human dignity' remains intact—even if it has to be propagated for the time being from the margins, and even if the real political alternative has yet to be adequately articulated and formulated.

For these activists, aspiring to such principles did not start on 25 January, and nor did it end on 3 July. As Maher put it in 2015:

> When I re-read about the events or read about the history of revolutions, I realize that the radical demands were sometimes excessive, romantic or unrealistic, especially since our camp was not united and did not have sufficient power. Many revolutions only succeeded in agreeing on peaceful transition between two sides or after transitional justice, or after agreement on a gradual transition of power. I'm not speaking about a specific situation, but I think I was very romantic and a dreamer. I think that if I knew that truth about the regime or the truth about certain people, I certainly would have thought differently.[7]

The political dispensation that put Abd al-Fattah al-Sisi at the helm in 2014 seemed impervious to attempts at reform, at least in the short-to-medium term. Sisi was a military man who went from the Ministry of Defence directly to the presidential office, and it appeared he tried to run his presidency like he was in a military barracks. The idea that he might respond positively to ideas of gradual but real reform was shortsighted. As of mid-2016, Sisi still enjoyed wide support from state institutions, had a significant proportion of the population continuing to back him, and the international community continued to give him a wide berth. There didn't appear to be much incentive for reform.

At the same time, there has been no choice for revolutionary activists but to attempt to exploit any small efforts at reform. With mass mobilisation totally out of the question, the only other options have been diminutive attempts at holding back the tide of authoritarian practices, or simply to pack it in. The latter, in truth, was never really an option for the revolutionary camp.

There may yet be a pronounced need for that revolutionary camp, because in the aftermath of the revolutionary uprising, and particularly after the abortion of the democratic experiment, there arose a new threat to Egypt. Extremists in Egyptian prisons and on the streets of Egyptian cities continue to look for recruits, and the policies of the Egyptian state make their job a lot easier now. The revolutionary camp, one hopes, can fashion alternatives that will channel the desire of Egyptians for change into more positive, peaceable avenues. If they fail to do so, then only more iron-fisted authoritarianism is likely; if they succeed in presenting a viable alternative, they might save a generation from the desperate clutches of extremism, from a variety of perspectives and directions. The uncomfortable reality is that, quite simply, politics is not the be all and end all of real and genuine change in any society. If there is not a cultural or intellectual awakening of some sort, then all the politics in the world won't achieve much. That kind of awakening relies a great deal on education—of the political elites and of various sectors in society, young and old. A simple top-down or a bottom-up approach will be insufficient. But, alas, such work is difficult, takes a lot of time, and happens in the background, painstakingly, where there is little in the way of glory or recognition. But ultimately, this is the lesson of history: individuals, even small groups of them, can and do make a phenomenal difference in societies.

Alas, this sort of change could take many years to unfold. The Arab Awakening of 2011 is not dead, but the 'spring' has given way to winter; a winter that the authoritarians of the Arab world in general stimulated, by resisting positive and gentle change when it was possible. The original authoritarian pact of the 'security state' in exchange for 'rights and freedoms' led to the 2011 uprising in the first place. The continuation of that pact, newly packaged but essentially identical, does not mean that a new uprising is imminent. But it does mean that tensions under the surface will cause the pressure cooker to heat up, and it is imperative the tensions are dealt with before the lid blows.

V

On the eve of the fourth anniversary of the 25 January revolutionary uprising, a thirty-one-year-old woman from Alexandria was marching near Tahrir Square, in remembrance of the uprising. She was a poet, a mother and an activist. The demonstration was organised by her party, the left-wing Socialist People's Alliance. For her troubles, she was killed by a twenty-four-year-old police gunman near Tala'at al-Harb square.[8]

Shaimaa al-Sabbagh typified so much of what was right—and her death so much of what was wrong—about the years between the 2011 uprising and the day she died. Shaimaa had supported the revolution in 2011 and she'd protested against the military. She'd backed the protests in 2013, but hadn't supported the massacres that took place later that summer. But what happened on that fateful January day in central

Cairo was that a member of the security forces shot her in the back with a shotgun. After she was buried, the conspiracy mill of Cairo's upper-class elite and the pro-military establishment tried to back every explanation but the obvious one: that a peaceful citizen of Egypt could walk down a street in central Cairo and be shot dead by a security establishment that was meant to protect her.

But in the wake of her death, public pressure grew. It should have grown much earlier—Shaimaa was certainly not the first peaceful protester to be killed by the Egyptian security forces—but, nonetheless, it grew. In June 2015, as a result of that pressure, a police officer was sentenced to fifteen years in a maximum-security prison. It was a small victory, compared to the many hundreds of deaths that have still not been investigated properly, their perpetrators not brought to justice, but it was a victory. By February 2016, however, a retrial had been called—justice, it seems, deferred. Again.[9]

Early in the post-Mursi era, in the autumn of 2013, I saw one of the revolutionary activists, and asked him, 'So, what now?' He smiled and said, 'You know, I always felt I did not do enough for Egypt while Mubarak was in power. I get to make up for it now.' In a way, that was the same kind of spirit that I discovered in George Orwell's *Homage to Catalonia*, where he reflected on his time in a struggle that rocked him to his core, as Egypt's struggle did to me:

> This war, in which I played so ineffectual a part, has left me with memories that are mostly evil, and yet I do not wish that I had missed it. When you have had a glimpse of a disaster such as this ... the result is not necessarily disillusionment and cynicism. Curiously enough the whole experience has left me with not less but more belief in the decency of human beings.[10]

There is always a temptation when it comes to engaging with the Arab world, to fall into one of two camps, to choose one evil over another, and to accept the argument of those who claim, 'Support *me*, or you are supporting *him*.' But it is a false choice. Stratagems and political dynamics may well often place one in the situation of dealing with people one does not want to deal with—but that's not the issue. When one has a clear and transparent way of identifying what one supports, it will become far easier to identify who one supports, especially when the going gets tough. What happened in Egypt after its revolutionary uprising has happened, and cannot now be changed—but one can hope that mistakes are learned from for the future, because the future is one thing that does remain.

However marginal the thought of the maverick middle trend is, it has remained. While much of Egypt, whether pro-military or pro-MB, might regard the revolutionaries as traitors to their interpretation of the 'cause', these post-Tahrir activists still have a lot more to give. One day, Egypt might realise that while these revolutionary activists were imperfect, they were the most honourable manifestation of the promise that was Tahrir Square—and none have provided Egypt with a better vision than that promise.

The eighteen days is not a 'something' that could be realised—a political force that could envisage taking power in some shape or form. But the days at Tahrir might still inform a political position, because Tahrir embodied a respect for pluralism and fundamental rights that are crucial for the enduring sustainability of any polity that seeks to protect the people of this country and the region. Indeed, I'm not sure that Tahrir is a reified political force of any sort anymore. But for me, it is at least a representation of honesty, a 'home', as it were, of a type of sincerity. It is such for many of this generation of Arabs.

It is not some sort of utopia. Rather, the memory of 2011's uprising is—or could be developed into—an inspiring source of principles by which the Egyptians judge themselves. To do otherwise—to avoid the principles—can more often than not simply be just a form of bigotry. Or, as former Bush speechwriter and *Washington Post* columnist Michael Gerson once put it, the 'soft bigotry of low expectations'.[11] Egyptians cannot fall prey to the negative idea that because they've never properly tasted democracy, they will never be able to eat of its fruit. When I wrote this book, I imagined someone reading it 200 years from now. What state would Egypt be in then? That's entirely open.

Egypt's constitution now talks about the 25 January revolution, and it also talks about the 30 June revolution. As I've mentioned, the appellation of 'revolution' is, essentially, a value judgement. I suspect that historians and analysts will debate endlessly how best to describe those events. I've come to the conclusion that the uprising of 25 January hasn't been successful yet, and that an opportunity was squandered in a sordid power struggle.

I've never doubted 25 January was a revolutionary uprising. Its promise continues to reinvigorate at least some Egyptians to struggle for a brighter future—and miraculously, that small revolutionary core still remains resilient. Even as many of their number grow pessimistic and cynical, they still aspire for that better future, and if one chance has been lost, I reckon another will emerge. Egypt's youth—who happen to constitute the overwhelming majority of the Arab world's largest population—are unlikely to have it any other way. They know they are meant to have rights and they know that those in power can be held accountable. After Tahrir that awareness cannot be erased.

Any opening for genuine, progressive change in Egypt towards a more inclusive, democratic political culture, with more meaningful provisions for fundamental rights, is likely to take much more time to materialise. In the meantime, there is much for the revolutionary camp to consider if it is to properly address the failings of its infancy. It can still play the role that it rightfully ought to, if it stays true to the spirit of the eighteen-day uprising, and the transformation it seeks.

To adopt viable political positions, as well as to advance a cohesive critique, requires a real vision—underpinned by a genuine political philosophy—which is concerned with the next ten, twenty and thirty years. Developing such a political project—one forged by the lessons of the eighteen days and the history of the last four years—remains a vital issue. Otherwise, any future opportunity that presents itself will be squandered, as Egyptians, and Arabs generally, fall victim to the false choice different types of authoritarianism. Egyptians and Arabs deserve, and can do, much better.

The next generation of Egyptian activists will need support, as well as skills training and creativity. Other constructive and peaceful models of activism need to be considered, as activists look for different ways to pursue their aspirations. Some institutions of this current generation may fade away into the annals of history—perhaps our next generation may even be so impatient as to discard them. But others can develop, and lay down fruitful seeds for the future.

Finally, the revolutionaries must remain cognisant of what has so distinguished Tahrir. The core of the 25 January revolutionary uprising was speaking truth to power, but with dignity. That is what stirred the soul of a nation. While the revolutionary camp may embrace certain political personalities, movements or ideas, it ought to never make the mistake of confusing its mission with that of just acquiring power for its own sake. Otherwise, its notions of social transformation will become transient, and will meet the same fate as those political projects that have so failed us in world history.

The revolutionaries need to be resourceful, focusing on the greater goal of constructively building a better society. Their time may indeed come, though it is not here today. When it does come, they could do worse than return to what made the eighteen days of 2011 so special. If they would be revolutionaries then they must be 'revolutionary' and have a spirit of compassion infused with tolerance, and a noble vision of inclusive, not exclusive, nation-building. They must be revolutionary not in the sense of a 'revolution' that seeks to tear down and destroy, but rather in the sense of being true to noble principles, which are not subjective. Certainly, in this day and age, that would be a 'revolution' in and of itself.

The inheritors of the 25 January revolutionary moment not only have the ability to do so much more for Egypt and beyond, but that inheritance means they also have an obligation to do so in the interests of all.

Those tumultuous eighteen days that Egyptians lived in 2011, with their epicentre in the Square of Liberation, remain as evidence of potentials and possibilities—perhaps beyond our current imaginations. We may not get those same days back—but history is thus testament that much remains possible. If there would be Egyptians that would wish to betray that potential, thus giving a hollow victory to those who wanted to destroy Tahrir, then they need do little else than simply stop trying to change things for the better. But if there would be Egyptians who would honour the memories of the fallen, then try again, and again, they must. They would thus show distinction, not only paying tribute to the memories of those who have since passed from the scene, but also paying tribute to their own selves in the process.

NOTES

PROLOGUE

1. There are other books that might be pertinent: in particular, Jack Shenkers' *The Egyptians: A Radical Story*. There is also Reem Abou El-Fadel's *Revolutionary Egypt: Connecting Domestic and International Struggles*, as well as others. This work also prioritises the political questions over the economic dynamics, which other recent scholarship, like the work of Zeinab Abul Magd on the military economic elite, have importantly documented.
2. Samuel P. Huntington, *The Clash of Civilizations and the Remaking of World Order*, New York, NY: Simon and Schuster, 1996.
3. H. A. Hellyer, 'Youth need vision, not revolt, in the Muslim world', *The National*, 24 January 2011, http://www.thenational.ae/thenationalconversation/comment/youth-need-vision-not-revolt-in-the-muslim-world, last accessed 2 Nov. 2015.

1. THE EIGHTEEN DAYS OF TAHRIR

1. Hellyer, 'Youth need vision, not revolt, in the Muslim world', *The National*, 24 January 2011, http://www.thenational.ae/thenationalconversation/comment/youth-need-vision-not-revolt-in-the-muslim-world, last accessed 2 Nov. 2015.
2. '*Kifaya*' means 'enough'.
3. Reem Abou El-Fadl, ed., *Revolutionary Egypt: Connecting Domestic and International Struggles*, London: Routledge, 2015.
4. Kareem Fahim, 'Death in Police Encounter Stirs Calls for Change in Egypt', *New York Times*, 18 July 2010, http://www.nytimes.com/2010/07/19/world/middleeast/19abuse.html?_r=0, last accessed 16 Feb. 2016.
5. Mike Gigio, 'How Wael Ghonim Sparked Egypt's Uprising', Newsweek,

13 Feb. 2011, http://europe.newsweek.com/how-wael-ghonim-sparked-egypts-uprising-68727, last accessed 16 Jan. 2016.

6. Rania Abouzaid, 'Did Prison Breakout Reveal a Plan to Sow Chaos in Egypt?', *Time*, 16 March 2011, http://content.time.com/time/world/article/0,8599,2059301,00.html, last accessed 16 Feb. 2016.

7. Ursula Lindsey, 'Revolution and Counter-Revolution in the Egyptian Media', Middle East Research and Information Project, 15 Feb. 2011, http://www.merip.org/mero/mero021511, last accessed 16 Feb. 2016.

8. Sharif Abdel Kouddous, 'Live from Egypt: The True Face of the Mubarak Regime', Democracy Now, 2 Feb. 2011, http://www.democracynow.org/2011/2/2/live_from_egypt_the_true_face_of_the_mubarak_regime, last accessed 16 Feb. 2016.

9. 'Remembering Sheikh Emad Effat', Egyptian Chronicles, 22 Dec. 2014, http://egyptianchronicles.blogspot.co.uk/2014/12/remembering-sheikh-emad-effat.html, last accessed 16 Feb. 2016.

10. 'Egypt from Tahrir to Transition', Abu Dhabi Gallup Center, http://www.gallup.com/poll/157046/egypt-tahrir-transition.aspx, last accessed 23 June 2016.

11. P. Gerbaudo, *Tweets and the Streets: Social Media and Contemporary Activism*, London: Pluto Books, 2012.

12. Ahmad Younis and Mohamed Younis, 'Most Egyptians Believe Continued Protests are Bad for the Country', Gallup, 28 Nov. 2011, http://www.gallup.com/poll/151001/egyptians-believe-continued-protests-bad-country.aspx, last accessed Feb. 17 2016.

13. For more see Stephen Maher, 'The Political Economy of the Egyptian Uprising', *Monthly Review*, 63, 6 (Nov. 2011), http://monthlyreview.org/2011/11/01/the-political-economy-of-the-egyptian-uprising/, last accessed 28 Sept. 2015.

14. Osama Diab, 'New Egypt, New Media', The Guardian, 10 March 2011, http://www.theguardian.com/commentisfree/2011/mar/10/egypt-media-newspapers-mubarak-propaganda, last accessed 22 Feb. 2016.

15. Miriam Berger, 'What's Next for Egypt's Media Moguls and the Military?', Egypt Source, 28 April 2015, http://www.atlanticcouncil.org/blogs/egyptsource/what-s-next-for-egypt-s-military-and-media-moguls, last accessed 22 Feb. 2016.

16. 'Freedom of the Press: Egypt', Freedom House, 2012, https://freedomhouse.org/report/freedom-net/2012/egypt, last accessed 22 Feb. 2016.

17. 'Meet Asmaa Mahfouz and the vlog that helped spark the revolution', YouTube, 11 Feb. 2011, https://www.youtube.com/watch?v=SgjIgMdsEuk, last accessed 22 Feb. 2016.

18. Robert Brym, Melissa Godbout, Andreas Hoffbauer, Gabe Menard and Tony Huiquan Zhang, 'Social media in the 2011 Egyptian uprising', *British Journal of Sociology*, 65, 2 (2014).
19. Adel Iskander, 'A year in the life of Egypt's media: A 2011 timeline', Jadaliyya, 26 Jan. 2012, http://www.jadaliyya.com/pages/index/3642/a-year-in-the-life-of-egypts-media_a-2011-timeline, last accessed 22 Feb. 2016.

2. THE PLAYERS EMERGE

1. 'Kifaya: The Origins of Mubarak's Downfall', *Egypt Independent*, 12 Dec 2011, http://www.egyptindependent.com/news/Kifaya-origins-mubaraks-downfall, last accessed 22 Feb. 2016.
2. Neil MacFarquer, 'Egyptian Voters Approve Constitutional Changes', *New York Times*, 20 March 2011, http://www.nytimes.com/2011/03/21/world/middleeast/21egypt.html, last accessed 16 Feb. 2016.
3. H. A. Hellyer, 'Power, the January 25 revolutionaries, and responsibility', Mada Masr, 24 January 2015, http://www.madamasr.com/opinion/power-january-25-revolutionaries-and-responsibility, last accessed 23 June 2016.
4. 'The New Arab Debates with Tim Sebastian', 9 April 2013, uploaded 25 April 2013, https://www.youtube.com/watch?v=An6-_lZeSb8, last accessed 16 Feb. 2016.
5. 'Egypt's Constitutional Referendum Results', Jadaliyya, 25 Dec. 2012, http://www.jadaliyya.com/pages/index/9234/egypt%E2%80%99s-constitutional-referendum-results, last accessed 16 Feb. 2016.
6. Lina Atalla, 'Back to the Margins', Mada Masr, 29 June 2013, http://www.madamasr.com/opinion/back-margins, last accessed 16 Feb 2016.
7. '"We will not allow for return of Mubarak officials or military"': Opposition groups', AhramOnline, 28 June 2013, http://english.ahram.org.eg/NewsContent/1/64/75151/Egypt/Politics-/We-will-not-allow-for-return-of-Mubarak-officials-.aspx, last accessed 19 Oct. 2015.
8. Stephen Glain, 'Fault Lines in Egypt's Muslim Brotherhood', *The Nation*, 12 Sept. 2011, http://www.thenation.com/article/162970/fault-lines-egypts-muslim-brotherhood#, last accessed 19 Oct. 2015.
9. Mariz Tadros, *The Muslim Brotherhood in Contemporary Egypt: Democracy Redefined or Confined?*, Durham: Routledge, 2012, p. 38.
10. Jack Shenker, 'The Muslim Brotherhood uncovered', *The Guardian*, 8 Feb 2011, http://www.theguardian.com/world/2011/feb/08/egypt-muslim-brotherhood-uncovered, last accessed 19 Oct. 2015.

11. Nathan Brown, 'Landmines in Egypt's Constituional Roadmap', Carnegie Endowment for International Peace, 7 Dec. 2011, http://carnegieendowment.org/2011/12/07/landmines-in-egypt-s-constitutional-roadmap, last accessed 16 Feb. 2016.

12. H. A.Hellyer, 'How Morsi let Egyptians down', *Foreign Policy*, http://mideastafrica.foreignpolicy.com/posts/2013/08/02/Morsis_disappointing_year, last accessed 19 Oct. 2015. H. A. Hellyer, 'Egyptians Shifted to Islamist Parties as Elections Neared', Gallup, 24 January 2012, http://www.gallup.com/poll/152168/egyptians-shifted-islamist-parties-elections-neared.aspx, last accessed 19 Oct. 2015.

13. Tadros, *The Muslim Brotherhood in Contemporary Egypt*, p. 42.

3. ON DEMOCRACY AND REVOLUTION

1. '78% of Egyptians want Mubarak brought to justice,' *The Egyptian Gazette*, 6 Aug. 2011, citing the Abu Dhabi Gallup Centre, http://www.masress.com/en/egyptiangazette/20230, last accessed 19 Oct. 2015.

2. Hossam Bahgat and Soha Abdelaty, 'What Mubarak must do before he resigns', *Washington Post*, 5 February 2011, http://www.washingtonpost.com/wp-dyn/content/article/2011/02/04/AR2011020404123.html, last accessed 27 Oct. 2015.

3. Ellen Knickmeyer, 'In Egypt, a Son is Readied for Succession', *Washington Post*, 11 Oct. 2007, http://www.washingtonpost.com/wp-dyn/content/article/2007/10/10/AR2007101002436.html, 16 Feb. 2016.

4. 'Egypt: SCAF Apologizes For Clashes With Protesters', Stratfor, 26 February 2011, https://www.stratfor.com/sample/situation-report/egypt-scaf-apologizes-clashes-protesters, last accessed 27 Oct. 2015.

5. Hossam Bahgat, 'The Mubarak Mansions', Mada Masr, 20 May 2014, http://www.madamasr.com/sections/politics/mubarak-mansions, last accessed 16 Feb. 2016.

6. Ahmed Younis and Mohamed Younis, 'Most Egyptians Believe Continued Protests Are Bad for Country', Gallup, 28 Nov. 2011, www.gallup.com/poll/151001/egyptians-believe-continued-protests-bad-country.aspx, last accessed 19 Oct. 2015.

7. H. A. Hellyer, 'Egyptians Shifted to Islamist Parties as Elections Neared', Gallup, 24 Jan. 2012, http://www.gallup.com/poll/152168/egyptians-shifted-islamist-parties-elections-neared.aspx, last accessed 22 Feb. 2016.

8. Mohamed Younis, 'Egyptians' Views of Government Crashed Before Overthrow', Gallup, 2 Aug. 2013, http://www.gallup.com/poll/163796/egyptian-views-government-crashed-overthrow.aspx, last accessed 22 Feb. 2016.

9. 'Islamist MPs Clash in Egypt Over Call to Prayer', Reuters, 7 Feb. 2012, http://af.reuters.com/article/commoditiesNews/idAFL5E8D75UP20120207, last accessed 16 Feb. 2016.

10. 'This House believes for the sake of democracy Egypt should postpone elections', http://www.thedohadebates.com/debates/item/index964a.html#539, last accessed September 2015. (Sami el-Erian, senior Muslim Brotherhood leader, made this statement on international television on 14 March 2011.)

11. Amira Howeidy, 'Meet the Brotherhood's Enforcer', AhramOnline, 29 March 2012, http://english.ahram.org.eg/NewsContent/1/64/37993/Egypt/Politics-/Meet-the-Brotherhood%E2%80%99s-enforcer-Khairat-ElShater.aspx, last accessed 19 Oct. 2015.

12. El-Sayed Gameledine, 'Muslim Brotherhood's second man El-Shater arrested: security official', AhramOnline, 6 July 2013, http://english.ahram.org.eg/NewsContent/1/64/75815/Egypt/Politics-/Muslim-Brotherhoods-secondman-ElShater-arrested-Se.aspx, last accessed 13 July 2016.

13. Ibid.

14. I explored this in more depth in 'The Muslim Brotherhood in Egypt: Power is a double edged sword', Huffington Post, 13 April 2012, http://www.huffingtonpost.com/ha-hellyer/the-muslim-brotherhood-in_b_1408820.html, last accessed 19 Oct. 2015.

15. Also spelled 'Amre'.

16. Ahmed Younis and Mohamed Younis, 'Most Egyptians Plan to Cast Ballots in Presidential Election',Gallup, 16 Feb. 2012.

17. Jeffrey Fleishman and Reem Abdellatif, 'Egypt election boycott gains momementum', Los Angeles Times, 11 June 2012, http://articles.latimes.com/2012/jun/11/world/la-fg-egypt-election-boycott-20120611, last accessed 22 Feb. 2016.

18. 'Shafiq and Morsi confirmed for Egypt runoff', Al Jazeera, 28 May 2012, http://www.aljazeera.com/news/middleeast/2012/05/2012528125146103967.html, last accessed 22 Feb. 2016.

19. Salma Shukrallah, 'Once election allies, Egypt's "Fairmont" opposition turn against Morsi', AhramOnline, 27 June 2013, http://english.ahram.org.eg/NewsContent/1/152/74485/Egypt/Morsi,-one-year-on/-Once-election-allies-Egypts-Fairmont-opposition-.aspx, last accessed 19 Oct. 2015.

20. Matthew Weaver, 'Muslim Brotherhood's Mohammed Morsi wins Egypt's presidential race', The Guardian, 24 June 2012, http://www.theguardian.com/world/middle-east-live/2012/jun/24/egypt-election-results-live, last accessed 20 Oct. 2015.

21. Passant Rabie, 'The Curious Case of Ahmed Shafiq', Mada Masr, 6 Oct

2015, http://www.madamasr.com/sections/politics/curious-case-ahmed-shafiq, last accessed 22 Feb. 2016.

22. 'Muslim Brotherhood's Mohammed Morsi wins Egypt's presidential race', *The Guardian*, http://www.theguardian.com/world/middle-east-live/2012/jun/24/egypt-election-results-live, last accessed 20 Oct. 2015. 'Speculation at fever pitch ahead of Egypt result as ElBaradei meets Tantawi says @elfoulio', GuardianNews, https://audioboom.com/boos/859810-speculation-at-fever-pitch-ahead-of-egypt-result-as-elbaradei-meets-tantawi-says-elfoulio, last accessed 20 Oct. 2015.

23. Paul Sedra, 'The Church, Maspero, and the Future of the Coptic Community', Jadaliyya, 19 May 2012, http://www.jadaliyya.com/pages/index/4735/the-church-maspero-and-the-future-of-the-coptic-co, last accessed 22 Feb. 2016.

24. Momen el-Husseiny, 'The "Maspero Crime": Accounts against the Counter-Revolution's Power, Media, and Religion', Jadaliyya, 31 Oct. 2011, http://www.jadaliyya.com/pages/index/3022/the-maspero-crime_accounts-against-the-counter-rev, last accessed 22 Feb. 2016.

25. Hatem Maher, 'Election's "nightmare" scenario leaves Egypt Revolutionaries in shock', AhramOnline, 26 May 2012, http://english.ahram.org.eg/NewsContent/36/122/42909/Presidential-elections-/Presidential-elections-news/Elections-nightmare-scenario-leaves-Egypt-revoluti.aspx, last accessed 22 Feb. 2016.

26. I wrote on this issue for *The National* (UAE): 'Brotherhood turns to politics at cost of regional credibility', 5 April 2012, http://www.thenational.ae/thenationalconversation/comment/brotherhood-turns-to-politics-at-cost-of-regional-credibility#full, last accessed 20 Oct. 2015.

27. 'Profile: Kamal al-Helbawy, a Defector of Conscience', Mohamed Elmeshad *Egypt Independent*, 9 March 2012, http://www.egyptindependent.com/news/profile-kamal-al-helbawy-defector-conscience, last accessed 16 Feb. 2016.

4. DEMOCRACY, ISLAMISM AND ISLAM

1. Jack Stuart, 'The Egyptian Revolution: Was it Hijacked?', https://academic.aucegypt.edu/independent/?p=4063, last accessed 19 Oct. 2015.

2. Alaa Abd El Fattah, 'Jan 25, 5 Years On: The Only Words I can Write Are About Losing My Words', Mada Masr, 24 Jan. 2016, http://www.madamasr.com/opinion/politics/jan-25-5-years-only-words-i-can-write-are-about-losing-my-words, last accessed 16 Feb. 2016.

3. Patrick Kingsley, 'Ahmed Seif el-Islam, Leading Light of Egypt Human Rights, Has Died', *The Guardian*, 27 Aug. 2014, http://www.theguardian.

com/world/2014/aug/27/egypt-lawyer-ahmed-seif-el-islam-dies-age-63, last accessed 16 Feb. 2016.

4. H. A. Hellyer, *Muslims of Europe: The 'Other' Europeans*, Edinburgh: Edinburgh University Press, 2009.

5. George Makdisi, *Rise of Colleges: Institutions of Learning in Islam and the West*, Edinburgh: Edinburgh University Press, 1984; *The Rise of Humanism in Classical Islam and the Christian West: With Special Reference to Scholasticism*, Edinburgh: Edinburgh University Press, 1990; *Religion, Law, and Learning in Classical Islam*, Volume 347 of *Collected Studies*, London: Variorum, 1991, (originally a Ph.D dissertation, Indiana University, 1984).

6. Aftab Malik, *The Broken Chain: Reflections upon the Neglect of a Tradition*, Bristol: Amal Press, 2001.

7. Hamid Algar, 'Wahhabism: A Critical Essay', New York: Islamic Publications International, 2002; Natana J. Delong-Bas, *Wahhabi Islam: From Revival and Reform to Global Jihad*, Oxford: Oxford University Press, 2002; Madawi Al-Rasheed, *A History of Saudi Arabia*, Cambridge: Cambridge University Press, 2002; David Dean Commins, *The Wahhabi Mission and Saudi Arabia*, London: I.B. Tauris, 2006.

8. 'Afghani, Jamal al-Din al', Oxford Islamic Studies Online, http://www.oxfordislamicstudies.com/article/opr/t243/e8, last accessed 20 Oct. 2015.

9. Mark Sedgwick, *Muhammad Abduh*, London: OneWorld, 2009.

10. H.A. Hellyer, and Nathan J. Brown, 'Leading From Everywhere: The History of Centralized Islamic Religious Authority', *Foreign Affairs*, 15 June 2015, https://www.foreignaffairs.com/articles/2015-06-15/leading-everywhere, last accessed 26 Oct. 2015. Also see: http://carnegieendowment.org/2015/06/16/leading-from-everywhere/ianw, last accessed 26 Oct. 2015.

11. Ali Muhammad As Salabi, *Omar Al Mokhtar Lion of the Desert (The Biography of Shaikh Omar Al Mokhtar)*, London: Al-Firdaus, 2011.

12. Bouyerdene, Ahmed, *Emir Abd El-Kader: Hero and Saint of Islam*, Indiana: World Wisdom Books, 2012.

13. 'Egypt's Grand Mufti decries identification of political leaders with prophets', AhramOnline, 11 February 2014, http://english.ahram.org.eg/NewsContent/1/64/93964/Egypt/Politics-/Egypts-Grand-Mufti-decries-identification-of-polit.aspx, last accessed 27 Oct. 2015.

14. 'The Draft Constitution' from the Hizb ut Tahrir website, http://www.hizb-ut-tahrir.org/PDF/EN/en_books_pdf/15_Muqaddimat_V1_Eng_07.05_.2013_.pdf, last accessed 19 Oct. 2015.

15. Ibrahim el-Houdaiby, 'From Prison to Palace: the Muslim Brotherhood's challenges and responses in post-revolutionary Egypt', Fride and

Hivos, 2013, http://fride.org/download/WP_117_From_Prison_to_ Palace.pdf, last accessed 19 Oct. 2015.

16. Barbara H.E. Zollner, *The Muslim Brotherhood: Hasan al-Hudaybi and Ideology*, London and New York: Routledge, 2009.

17. Parts of this section come from writing I published on the websites of RUSI and Brookings. See H. A. Hellyer, 'What Role do Egyptians Want for Religion?', Brookings Institute, 8 Sept. 2013, http://www. brookings.edu/research/opinions/2013/09/18-egypt-brotherhood-restrictions-hellyer, last accessed 16 Feb. 2016.

18. H. A. Hellyer, 'What Role do Egyptians Want for Religion?', Brookings Institute, 8 Sept. 2013, http://www.brookings.edu/research/opinions/2013/09/18-egypt-brotherhood-restrictions-hellyer, last accessed 16 Feb. 2016.

19. Ibid.

20. Ibid.

21. Ibid.

22. Ibid.

23. H. A. Hellyer, 'Egypt Killed Islam in the West', *Islamic Monthly*, 18 Dec. 2014, http://theislamicmonthly.com/egypt-killed-islam-in-the-west/, last accessed 16 Feb. 2016.

24. Cornel West, *Prophetic Thought in Post-Modern Times*, Monroe, ME: Common Courage Press, 1993. Also see: Ashley Kanan, 'What is Cornel West arguing when he argues for "prophetic thought?"', E-Notes, 28 Nov. 2009, http://www.enotes.com/homework-help/what-cornel-west-arguing-when-he-argues-prophetic-119485, last accessed 27 Oct. 2015.

25. Ibid.

5. THE RISE AND FALL OF THE FIRST DEMOCRATICALLY ELECTED PRESIDENT

1. H.A. Hellyer, 'Meet Egypt's Mr Mursi: a president without checks and balances', Al Arabiya, 24 November 2012, http://www.alarabiya.net/views/2012/11/24/251527.html, last accessed 20 October 2015.

2. 'Egypt Border Guards Killed in Sinai Attack', Al Jazeera, 5 Aug. 2013, http://www.aljazeera.com/news/middleeast/2012/08/20128518 3958163902.html, last accessed 16 Feb. 2016.

3. Sara Salem, 'Morsi and the Military in Egypt's Transition', Muftah, 21 August 2012, http://muftah.org/morsi-and-the-military-in-egypts-transition/#.VehrftOqqko, last accessed October 2015.

4. Kareem Faheem, 'In Upheaval for Egypt, Morsi forces out Military Chiefs', *New York Times*, 12 Aug. 2012, http://www.nytimes.com/2012/

08/13/world/middleeast/egyptian-leader-ousts-military-chiefs.html?_
r=0, last accessed 20 Oct. 2015.

5. Abdel-Rahman Hussein, 'Egypt Defense Chief Tantawi Ousted in
Surprise Shakeup', *The Guardian*, 13 Aug. 2012, http://www.theguard-
ian.com/world/2012/aug/12/egyptian-defence-chief-ousted-shakeup,
last accessed 16 Feb. 2016.

6. Zeinab Abul-Magd, 'The Army and the Economy in Egypt', Jadaliyya,
23 December 2011, http://www.jadaliyya.com/pages/index/3732/
the-army-and-the-economy-in-egypt, last accessed 20 Oct. 2015.

7. 'Egypt and Morsy proved "pivotal" in Gaza cease-fire talks', CNN,
22 Nov. 2012, http://edition.cnn.com/2012/11/20/world/meast/
egypt-gaza-morsy/, last accessed 20 Oct. 2015.

8. 'Update: Public Prosecutor Refuses to Leave his Position', *Egypt
Independent*, 10 Oct. 2013, http://www.egyptindependent.com/news/
update-public-prosecutor-refuses-leave-his-position, last accessed 16 Feb.
2016.

9. 'Egypt prosectuor-general to remain in office', Al Jazeera English,
13 October 2012, http://www.aljazeera.com/news/middleeast/2012/
10/20121013135626371129.html, last accessed 20 Oct. 2015.

10. This section is partially drawn from an article I penned for Ahram
Online on 16 October 2012: 'Mr President: The Revolution Continues!
Or Does it?', http://english.ahram.org.eg/NewsContentP/4/55747/
Opinion/Mr-President-The-Revolution-Continues-Or-Does-it.aspx, last
accessed 20 Oct. 2015.

11. Nathan Brown, 'Egypt's Constitutional Conundrum', Carnegie Endowment, 9 Dec. 2012, http://carnegieendowment.org/2012/12/09/
egypt-s-constitution-conundrum, last accessed 16 Feb. 2016.

12. 'Egypt court suspends constitutional assembly', BBC, 10 April 2012,
http://www.bbc.co.uk/news/world-middle-east-17665048, last accessed 20 Oct. 2015.

13. Ibid.

14. 'Egypt parties end deadlock over constitutional panel', BBC, 8 June
2012, http://www.bbc.co.uk/news/world-middle-east-18360403, last
accessed 20 Oct 2015.

15. Nada Hussein Rashwan, 'Egypt's constituent assembly convenes Tuesday
with future still in doubt', AhramOnline, 27 June 2012, http://eng-
lish.ahram.org.eg/NewsContent/1/64/46274/Egypt/Politics-/Egypts-
constituent-assembly-convenes-Tuesday-with-.aspx, last accessed 20 Oct
2015.

16. 'Egypt supreme court calls for parliament to be dissolved', BBC,
14 June 2012, http://www.bbc.co.uk/news/world-middle-east-1843
9530, last accessed 20 Oct. 2015.

17. Kareem Fahim, 'Egypt's Military and President Escalate Their Power Struggle', *New York Times*, 9 July 2012, http://www.nytimes.com/2012/07/10/world/middleeast/egypt-tension-after-order-to-recon-vene-parliament.html?_r=2&pagewanted=all, last accessed 20 Oct. 2015.

18. 'Morsi pledges respect for Egypt court rulings', Al Jazeera, 11 July 2012, http://www.aljazeera.com/news/middleeast/2012/07/201271 11171531842973.html, last accessed 20 Oct. 2015.

19. Abdel Hafez, Ahmed, 'As Vote Nears, Constituent Assembly May Have Quorum Problem', *Egypt Independent*, 29 Nov. 2012, http://www.egyptindependent.com/news/vote-nears-constituent-assembly-may-have-quorum-problem, last accessed 16 Feb. 2016.

20. 'The Middling Muslim Brothers', Baheyya, 20 July 2013, http://baheyya.blogspot.co.za/2013/07/the-middling-muslim-brothers.html, last accessed 20 Oct. 2015.

21. 'Egypt: The president's new powers', Al Jazeera, 24 Nov. 2012, http://www.aljazeera.com/programmes/insidestory/2012/11/2012 112482649205402.html, last accessed 20 Oct. 2015.

22. Zeinobia Azeem, 'Is Egypt's Shura Council Constitutional?', Al-Monitor, 29 April 2013, http://www.al-monitor.com/pulse/originals/2013/05/egypt-shura-council-constitutional.html#, last accessed 22 Feb. 2016.

23. 'Egypt's President Mursi assumes sweeping powers', BBC, 22 Nov. 2012, http://www.bbc.co.uk/news/world-middle-east-20451208, last accessed 20 Oct. 2015.

24. Ibid.

25. 'Video: Egyptians Storm Muslim Brotherhood HQ in Alexandria', *The Telegraph*, 23 Nov. 2012, http://www.telegraph.co.uk/news/world-news/africaandindianocean/egypt/9699221/Egyptians-storm-Muslim-Brotherhood-HQ-in-Alexandria.html, last accessed 16 Feb. 2016.

26. Yasmine Salweh and Edmund Blair, 'Egypt's Morsi to meet with judges over power grab', *Christian Science Monitor*, 26 Nov. 2012, http://www.csmonitor.com/World/Latest-News-Wires/2012/1126/Egypt-s-Morsi-to-meet-with-judges-over-power-grab-video, last accessed 20 Oct. 2015.

27. David Kirkpatrick, 'Pressure Grows on Egyptian Leader After Judicial Decree', *New York Times*, 25 Nov. 2012, http://www.csmonitor.com/World/Latest-News-Wires/2012/1126/Egypt-s-Morsi-to-meet-with-judges-over-power-grab-video, last accessed 20 Oct. 2015.

28. Ibid.

29. 'Youth of anti-Morsi parties reject coalition with Mubarak "remnants"', AhramOnline, 28 Nov. 2012, http://english.ahram.org.eg/NewsCon-

tent/1/64/59355/Egypt/Politics-/Youth-of-antiMorsi-parties-reject-coalition-with-M.aspx, last accessed 20 Oct. 2015.

30. Cornelis Hulsman, 'A Conversation with Egypt's Aboul Fotouh', Middle East Institute, 16 Oct. 2013, http://www.mei.edu/content/conversation-egypts-aboul-fotouh, last accessed 20 Oct. 2015.

31. 'New Arab Debates to argue whether the Opposition has let Egyptians down', 4 April 2013, http://www.newarabdebates.com/en/news/announcements/new-arab-debates-to-argue-whether-the-opposition-has-let-egyptians-down/, last accessed 20 Oct. 2015.

32. H. A. Hellyer, 'The rewriting of Egypt's recent events', Al Arabiya, 11 Dec. 2012, http://english.alarabiya.net/views/2012/12/11/254412.html, last accessed 20 Oct. 2015.

33. Mohammed Adam, 'Right and Left, Protests With and Against Morsy in Cairo',Egypt Independent, 8 Dec. 2012, http://www.egyptindependent.com/news/right-and-left-protests-and-against-morsy-cairo, last accessed 16 Feb. 2016.

34. H.A. Hellyer, 'A Better Egyptian Constitution', Foreign Policy, 6 Dec. 2012, http://foreignpolicy.com/2012/12/06/a-better-egyptian-constitution/, last accessed 20 Oct. 2015.

35. Jano Charbel, 'Wednesday's Papers: Presidential palace besieged, constitutional crisis, and media blackout', Egypt Independent, 5 Dec. 2012, http://www.egyptindependent.com/news/wednesday-s-papers-presidential-palace-besieged-constitutional-crisis-and-media-blackouts, last accessed 16 Feb. 2016.

36. 'El Baradei, Sabbahi and others to be investigated for "espionage"', Egypt Independent, 4 Dec. 2012, http://www.egyptindependent.com/news/elbaradei-sabbahi-and-others-be-investigated-espionage, last accessed 20 Oct. 2015.

37. 'Egypt: Investigate Brotherhood's Abuse of Protesters', Human Rights Watch, 12 Dec. 2012, https://www.hrw.org/news/2012/12/12/egypt-investigate-brotherhoods-abuse-protesters, last accessed 20 Oct. 2015.

38. Kristen Chick, 'Egypt's Copts lash out at government's anti-Christian rhetoric', Christian Science Monitor, 12 April 2013, http://www.csmonitor.com/World/Middle-East/2013/0412/Egypt-s-Copts-lash-out-at-government-s-anti-Christian-rhetoric, last accessed 20 Oct. 2015.

39. 'Egypt: Investigate Brotherhood's Abuse of Protesters', Human Rights Watch, 12 Dec. 2012.

40. Ahdaf Soueif, 'Egypt's Hopes Betrayed by Morsi, The Guardian, 9 Dec. 2012, http://www.theguardian.com/commentisfree/2012/dec/09/egypt-hopes-betrayed-mohamed-morsi, last accessed 22 Feb. 2016.

41. H.A. Hellyer, 'The irony in Egypt's political crisis', AhramOnline, 9 Dec. 2012, http://english.ahram.org.eg/NewsContent/4/0/60117/

Opinion/The-irony-in-Egypts-political-crisis-.aspx, last accessed 20 Oct. 2015.

42. H. A. Hellyer, 'From Cairo to London to DC: please, knock it off', The Arabist, 15 Dec. 2012, http://arabist.net/blog/2012/12/15/from-cairo-to-london-to-dc-please-knock-it-off.html, last accessed 23 June 2016.

43. Leila Fadel, 'Morsi Wins and Loses After Egypt Passes Draft Constitution', NPR, 22 Dec. 2012, http://www.npr.org/sections/thetwo-way/2012/12/22/167878598/constitution-vote-seen-as-referendum-on-egyptian-brotherhood, last accessed 16 Feb. 2016.

44. Some of my reflections that day are archived in a piece I penned for the Muftah website on 7 Dec. 2012: 'A First Hand Account: The Storming of the FJP's Office in a Cairo Suburb', http://muftah.org/a-first-hand-account-the-storming-of-the-brotherhoods-party-headquar-ters-in-cairo/#.Vem5HtOqqko, last accessed 20 Oct. 2015.

6. THE SLOW-MOVING TRAIN WRECK

1. Bel Trew, 'A Make or Break Moment for Egypt's Morsi', New Statesman, 26 June 2013, http://www.newstatesman.com/politics/2013/06/make-or-break-moment-egypts-president-morsi, last accessed 17 Feb. 2016.

2. Hamza Hendawi, 'Egypt Braces for More Violence After Court Confirms Death Sentences for Port Said Footballer Rioters', The Independent, http://www.independent.co.uk/news/world/africa/egypt-braced-for-more-violence-after-court-confirms-death-sentences-for-port-said-foot-baller-rioters-8527528.html, last accessed 17 Dec. 2016.

3. H. A. Hellyer, 'Egypt's Sweltering Summer Ahead', Al Arabiya, 30 April 2012, http://english.alarabiya.net/en/views/news/middle-east/2013/04/28/Egypt-s-sweltering-summer-ahead.html, last accessed 20 Oct. 2015.

4. 'The Middling Muslim Brothers', Baheyya, 20 July 2013, baheyya.blogspot.co.za/2013/07/the-middling-muslim-brothers.html, last accessed 20 Oct. 2015.

5. Robert Mackey, 'Policy Brutality, Catalyst for Egypt's Revolution, Continues Under Morsi', New York Times, 21 Feb. 2013, http://thelede.blogs.nytimes.com/2013/02/21/police-brutality-catalyst-for-egypts-rev-olution-continues-under-morsi/, last accessed 20 Oct. 2015.

6. Bahgat tweeted as such on 16 Feb. 2013, at 11.23 pm, Cairo time, https://twitter.com/hossambahgat/status/302891072370126848?ref_src=twsrc%5Etfw, last accessed 20 Oct. 2015.

7. Aaskar Kazeboon, 'Interior Ministry Violence', YouTube, 20 February

2013, https://www.youtube.com/watch?v=FA7VXWwPTR8, last accessed 20 Oct. 2015.

8. Karim Medhat Ennarah, 'The End of Reciprocity: The Muslim Brotherhood and the Security Sector', *South Atlantic Quarterly*, 113, 2 (2014), pp. 407–418.

9. A tweet from James Boys on 2 July 2013, https://twitter.com/james-dboys/status/351993456568188928, last accessed 20 Oct. 2015.

10. 'Military Intervention and Egypt's Future', H.A. Hellyer, *Daily News Egypt*, 19 March 2013, http://www.dailynewsegypt.com/2013/03/19/military-intervention-and-egypts-future/, last accessed 20 Oct. 2015.

11. Nathan Brown, 'Train Wreck Along the Nile', *Foreign Policy*, 10 July 2012, http://foreignpolicy.com/2012/07/10/train-wreck-along-the-nile/, last accessed 17 Feb. 2016.

12. Dalia Ziada, 'As Turmoil Grows in Egypt, Army Rule finds new support', *The National*, 24 March 2013, http://www.thenational.ae/the-nationalconversation/comment/as-turmoil-grows-in-egypt-army-rule-finds-new-support, last accessed 14 July 2016.

13. Sarah El Deeb, 'Egypt Appoints 9 Ministers in Limited Reshuffle', Associated Press, 7 May 2013, http://news.yahoo.com/egypt-appoints-9-ministers-limited-reshuffle-094416551.html, last accessed 17 Feb. 2016.

14. Hellyer, 'Egypt's Sweltering Summer Ahead'.

15. Paul Taylor, 'Egypt's "road not taken" could have saved Morsi', Reuters, 17 July 2013, http://www.reuters.com/article/2013/07/17/us-egypt-protests-mediation-idUSBRE96G0C120130717, last accessed 20 Oct. 2015.

16. 'Egypt's Coptic pope criticises Morsi over cathedral attacks', Ahram Online, 9 April 2013, http://english.ahram.org.eg/NewsContent/1/64/68830/Egypt/Politics-/Egypts-Coptic-pope-criticises-Morsi-over-cathedral.aspx, last accessed 20 Oct. 2015.

17. Hellyer, 'Egypt's Sweltering Summer Ahead'.

18. Stephen Kalin, 'Here are the jokes that got Bassem Youssef, the "Jon Stewart of Egypt," arrested', Quartz, 8 April 2013, http://qz.com/71678/this-is-what-bassem-youssef-the-jon-stewart-of-egypt-actually-said-to-get-himself-arrested/, last accessed 17 Feb. 2016.

19. Basil El-Dabh, 'June 30: Tamarod and Its Oponents', Middle East Institute, 26 June 2013, http://www.mei.edu/content/june-30-tamarod-and-its-opponents, last accessed 17 Feb. 2016.

20. Hend Kortam, 'Kefaya says Tamarod campaign is not under auspices of Kefaya movement', *Daily News Egypt*, 30 April 2013, http://www.dailynewsegypt.com/2013/04/30/kefaya-says-tamarod-campaign-is-not-under-auspices-of-kefaya-movement/, last accessed 20 Oct. 2015.

21. Sheera Frenkel and Maged Atef, 'How Egypt's Rebel Movement Helped Pave The Way For A Sisi Presidency', http://www.buzzfeed.com/sheerafrenkel/how-egypts-rebel-movement-helped-pave-the-way-for-a-sisi-pre#.nqnpLLaLpw, last accessed 20 Oct. 2015.

22. Asma Alsharif and Yasmine Saleh, 'The real force behind Egypt's "revolution of the state"', Reuters, 10 Oct. 2013, http://uk.reuters.com/article/2013/10/10/uk-egypt-interior-special-report-idUKBRE99908720131010, last accessed 20 Oct. 2015.

23. David Kenner, 'Egypt's Bloomberg outlasts his Islamist enemies', Foreign Policy, 10 July 2013, http://foreignpolicy.com/2013/07/10/egypts-bloomberg-outlasts-his-islamist-enemies/, last accessed 20 Oct. 2015.

24. Ben Hubbard and David Kirkpatrick, 'Sudden Improvements in Egypt Suggest a Campaign to Undermine Morsi', New York Times, 11 July 2013, http://www.nytimes.com/2013/07/11/world/middleeast/improvements-in-egypt-suggest-a-campaign-that-undermined-morsi.html?_r=0, last accessed 20 Oct 2015.

25. 'Egypt: Lynching of Shia Follows Months of Hate Speech', Human Rights Watch, 27 June 2013, https://www.hrw.org/news/2013/06/27/egypt-lynching-shia-follows-months-hate-speech, last accessed 20 Oct 2015.

26. H. A. Hellyer, 'The Scourge of Sectarianism in Egypt', Foreign Policy, 26 June 2013, foreignpolicy.com/2013/06/26/the-scourge-of-sectarianism-in-egypt/, last accessed 20 Oct. 2015.

27. I went into some detail on these points in a two-part essay for Al Arabiya, 'Egypt: Revisiting June 30th and July 3rd', 30 June 2014 and 3 July 2014, http://english.alarabiya.net/en/views/news/middle-east/2014/07/03/Egypt-Revisiting-June–30-and-July-3-Part-II-.html; http://english.alarabiya.net/en/views/news/middle-east/2014/06/30/Egypt-Revisiting-June–30-and-July-3-Part-I-.html, last accessed 20 Oct. 2015.

28. H. A. Hellyer, 'Egypt: Inevitable consequences of June 30', Institute for Social Policy and Understanding, 11 Nov. 2013, http://www.ispu.org/content/Egypt_Inevitable_consequences_of_June_30_by_HA_Hellyer, last acessed 17 Feb. 2016.

29. Alternatively spelled 'Adaweya' or 'Adawiyya' or 'Adawiyah'. 'Rab'a' is also alternatively spelled 'Rabi'a' or 'Rab'iah'.

30. 'Live Updates: Hundreds of thousands attend rallies in Cairo; clashes in Alexandira', AhramOnline, 28 June 2013, http://english.ahram.org.eg/NewsContent/1/0/75134/Egypt/0/Live-updates-Hundreds-of-thousands-attend-rival-ra.aspx, last accessed 17 Feb. 2016.

31. H. A. Hellyer, 'Not Quite A Coup: but pretty much', Foreign Policy,

1 July 2013, http://foreignpolicy.com/2013/07/01/not-quite-a-coup-but-pretty-much/, last accessed 21 Oct. 2015.

32. 'Excuse me Sir, is it a coup?', Mada Masr, 5 July 2013, http://www.madamasr.com/sections/politics/excuse-me-sir-it-coup, last accessed 17 Feb. 2016.

33. H. A. Hellyer, 'How the June 30 uprising wasn't the January 25th revolution', Al Arabiya, 21 July 2013, http://english.alarabiya.net/en/views/news/middle-east/2013/07/21/How-the-June-30-uprising-wasn-t-the-January–25th-revolution.html, last accessed 21 Oct 2015.

34. Ibid.

35. Nancy Messiah, "Morsi Government Resignations', Egypt Source, 22 May 2013, http://www.atlanticcouncil.org/blogs/egyptsource/morsi-government-resignations, last accessed 17 Feb. 2013.

36. 'Egypt Ministers Resign Amid Unrest', Al Jazeera English, 1 July 2013, http://www.aljazeera.com/news/middleeast/2013/07/201371122823125310.html, last accessed 17 Feb. 2016.

37. David Kirkpatrick and Ben Hubbard, 'Morsi Defies Egypt Army's Ultimatum to Bend to Protest', New York Times, 2 July 2013, http://www.nytimes.com/2013/07/03/world/middleeast/egypt-protests.html?_r=0, last accessed 17 Feb. 2016.

38. Robert Mackey, 'July 2 Updates on Egypt's Political Crisis', The Lede Blog: New York Times, 2 July 2013, http://thelede.blogs.nytimes.com/2013/07/02/latest-updates-on-egypts-political-crisis/?_r=0, last accessed 23 Feb. 2016.

39. H. A. Hellyer, 'On Egypt, the truth is the greatest victim', Foreign Policy, 12 July 2013, http://foreignpolicy.com/2013/07/12/on-egypt-the-truth-is-the-greatest-victim/, last accessed 21 Oct. 2015.

40. Ola Gala and Lina Attalah, 'Protestors remain polarized as army deadline nears', Mada Masr, 3 July 2013, http://www.madamasr.com/news/protesters-remain-polarized-army-deadline-draws-near, last accessed 23 Feb. 2016.

41. Ruth Alexander, 'Counting Crowds: Was Egypt's Uprising the Biggest Ever?', BBC, 16 July 2013, http://www.bbc.co.uk/news/magazine-23312656, last accessed 17 Feb. 2016.

42. Ola Gala and Lina Attalah, 'Protestors remain polarized as army deadline nears'.

43. Belal Fadl, 'Mohamed Morsi is no Nelson Mandela', al-Araby al-Jadeed, 2 June 2015, (http://www.alaraby.co.uk/english/comment/2015/6/3/mohamed-morsi-is-no-nelson-mandella), last accessed 21 Oct. 2015.

44. H. A. Hellyer, 'Mursi is no father of the Nation', Al Arabiya, 12 Aug. 2013, http://www.hahellyer.com/articles/mursi-is-no-father-of-the-nation-al-arabiya/, last accessed 21 Oct. 2015.

7. 'WEEKS OF KILLING'

1. 'Varied Reactins to Rabea Violence', Mada Masr, 28 July 2013, http://www.madamasr.com/news/varied-reactions-rabea-violence, last accessed 17 Feb. 2016.
2. Mohamad Salama Adam, 'From inside the Brotherhood Nahda sit-in', Mada Masr, 24 July 2013, http://www.madamasr.com/sections/politics/inside-brotherhood-nahda-sit, last accessed 28 Oct. 2015; 'Bodies of 11 torture victims recovered from sit-ins, claims ministry', Mada Masr, 29 July 2013, http://www.madamasr.com/news/bodies-11-torture-victims-recovered-sit-ins-claims-ministry, last accessed 28 Oct. 2015; 'Conflicting reports about Brotherhood sit-in violence', Mada Masr, 23 July 2013, http://www.madamasr.com/news/conflicting-reports-about-brotherhood-sit-violence, last accessed 28 Oct. 2015; Al Abdel Mohsen, 'An account of abuse at Raba'a', Mada Masr, 28 July 2013, http://www.madamasr.com/news/conflicting-reports-about-brotherhood-sit-violence, last accessed 28 Oct. 2015.
3. 'Egypt: Evidence points to torture carried out by Morsi supporters', Amnesty International, 2 August 2013, https://www.amnesty.org/en/press-releases/2013/08/egypt-evidence-points-torture-carried-out-morsi-supporters/, last accessed 28 Oct. 2015.
4. 'Egypt: Deadly Clashes at Cairo University', Human Rights Watch, 5 July 2013, https://www.hrw.org/news/2013/07/05/egypt-deadly-clashes-cairo-university, last accessed 28 Oct. 2015.
5. 'Egypt: Threat of Escalating Street Violence', Human Rights Watch, 7 July 2013, https://www.hrw.org/news/2013/07/07/egypt-threat-escalating-street-violence, last accessed 21 Oct 2015.
6. Patrick Kingsley, 'Killing in Cairo: the full story of the Republican Guards' club shootings', The Guardian, 18 July 2013, http://www.theguardian.com/world/interactive/2013/jul/18/cairo-republican-guard-shooting-full-story, last accessed 21 Oct. 2015.
7. Patrick Kingsley, 'Egypt's Army Chief Calls for Show of Support from Citizens', The Guardian, 24 July 2013, http://www.theguardian.com/world/2013/jul/24/egypt-army-chief-support-citizens, last accessed 17 Feb. 2016.
8. 'Egypt: Judge Government on Respect for People's Rights', Human Rights Watch, 3 July 2013, https://www.hrw.org/news/2013/07/03/egypt-judge-government-respect-peoples-rights, last acccessed 21 Oct. 2015.
9. Miriam Berger, 'With Morsi Out, Uphill Battle for Independent Media Intensifies', Egypt Source, 17 July 2013, http://www.atlanticcouncil.org/blogs/egyptsource/with-morsi-out-uphill-battle-for-independent-media-intensifies, last accessed 17 Feb. 2013.

10. 'Egypt: Many protesters shot in head or chest', Human Rights Watch, 28 July 2013, https://www.hrw.org/news/2013/07/28/egypt-many-protesters-shot-head-or-chest, last accessed 21 Oct. 2015.

11. Reem Abdellatif and Matt Bradley, 'Egyptian Moves to Detain Brother-hood Leaders', *Wall Street Journal*, 10 July 2013, http://www.wsj.com/articles/SB10001424127887323740804578597321211486136, last accessed 21 Oct. 2015.

12. Sara Carr, 'On Sheep and Infidels', Mada Masr, 8 July 2013, http://www.madamasr.com/opinion/sheep-and-infidels, last accessed 17 Feb. 2016.

13. Elizabeth Day, 'How Baroness's gift for consensus opened the door to Mohamed Morsi', *The Guardian*, 4 August 2013, http://www.theguardian.com/politics/2013/aug/04/baroness-ashton-morsi-secret-meeting;, last accessed 28 Oct. 2015; Catherine Ashton, 'The Challenge for Egypt', *New York Times*, 23 July 2013, http://www.nytimes.com/2013/07/24/opinion/global/ashton-the-challenge-for-egypt.html?_r=2&assetType=opinion, last accessed 28 Oct. 2015.

14. Paul Taylor, 'West warned Egypt's Sisi to the end: don't do it', Reuters, 14 August 2013, http://uk.reuters.com/article/2013/08/14/uk-egypt-protests-west-idUKBRE97D16E20130814, last accessed 28 Oct. 2015.

15. Heba Morayef, 'Dispatches: All it takes is one stone', Human Rights Watch, 1 Aug. 2013, https://www.hrw.org/news/2013/08/05/dispatches-all-it-takes-one-stone, last accessed 28 Oct. 2015.

16. 'Weeks of Killing', EIPR, 18 June 2014, http://eipr.org/en/report/2014/06/18/2124, last accessed 28 Oct. 2015.

17. 'All According to Plan', Human Rights Watch, 12 Aug, 2014, https://www.hrw.org/report/2014/08/12/all-according-plan/raba-massacre-and-mass-killings-protesters-egypt, last accessed 28 Oct 2015.

18. Ibid.

19. Ibid.

20. 'Weeks of Killing', EIPR.

21. Ibid.

22. 'Egypt: No Acknowledgement or Justice for Mass Protester Killings', by a grouping of human rights groups, including Human Rights Watch, EIPR and the Cairo Institute for Human Rights Studies, 10 Dec. 2013, https://www.hrw.org/news/2013/12/10/egypt-no-acknowledgment-or-justice-mass-protester-killings, last accessed 28 Oct. 2015.

23. David Kirkpatrick, 'Hundreds dies as Egyptian forces attack Islamist protestors', *New York Times*, 14 Aug. 2013.

24. Patrick Kingsley, 'Alaa Al Aswany on why he had to support Egypt's military crackdown', *The Guardian*, 29 Oct 2013, http://www.theguardian.com/books/2013/oct/29/alaa-al-aswany-egypt-muslim-brotherhood, last accessed 23 Feb. 2016.

25. H. A. Hellyer, 'Voices in and on Rabaa, one year ago in Cairo', Al Arabiya, 12 Aug. 2014, http://english.alarabiya.net/en/views/news/middle-east/2014/08/12/Voices-in-Rabaa-one-year-ago-in-Cairo-.html, last accessed 28 Oct. 2015.

8. THE RISE OF SISI

1. 'Egypt's War on Terror Takes Over Security, Law, Foreign Policy and Media', Mada Masr, 28 Oct. 2014, http://www.madamasr.com/news/egypt%E2%80%99s-war-terror-takes-over-security-law-foreign-policy-and-media, last accessed 17 Feb. 2016.
2. Omar Ashour, 'Collusion to Crackdown', Brookings Doha Centre, March 2014, http://www.brookings.edu/~/media/research/files/papers/2015/03/10-islamist-military-relations-in-egypt-ashour/collusion-to-crackdown-english.pdf, last accessed 28 Oct. 2015.
3. 'Judge Government on Respect for People's Rights', Human Rights Watch, 3 July 2013, https://www.hrw.org/news/2013/07/03/egypt-judge-government-respect-peoples-rights, last accessed 28 Oct. 2015.
4. Sara Yasin, 'Egyptian Army Shuts Down Media Outlets', Index on Censorship, 4 July 2013, https://www.indexoncensorship.org/2013/07/egyptian-army-shuts-down-media-outlets/, last accessed 17 Feb. 2016.
5. Ursula Lindsey, 'The Cult of Sisi', New York Times Latitude Blog, 12 Sept. 2013, http://latitude.blogs.nytimes.com/2013/09/12/the-cult-of-sisi/, last accessed 17 Feb. 2016.
6. 'Sisi wins presidency with 96.9% of the valid votes: Election Commission', Mada Masr, 3 June 2014, http://www.madamasr.com/news/sisi-wins-presidency-969-valid-votes-election-commission, last accessed 17 Feb. 2016.
7. Ishak Ibrahim, 'Three years after the Maspero Massacre: Where is there justice?', The Tahrir Institute for Middle East Policy, 9 Oct 2014, http://timep.org/commentary/three-years-maspero-massacre-justice/, last accessed 17 Feb. 2016.
8. Mohannad Sabry, 'How Egypt's Protest Law Brought Down the Revolution', Al-Monitor, 9 Sept. 2014, http://www.al-monitor.com/pulse/originals/2014/09/egypt-protest-law-courts-ruling-abdel-fattah.html#, last accessed 17 Feb. 2016.
9. 'El-Sisi Praises Egyptian Media's "Understanding," Defends Protest Law', AhramOnline, 1 Nov. 2014, http://english.ahram.org.eg/NewsContent/1/64/114492/Egypt/Politics/ElSisi-praises-Egyptian-medias-understanding,-defe.aspx, last accessed 17 Feb. 2016.
10. H. A. Hellyer, 'The Egyptian People demand the right to demand', Al

Arabiya, 21 Oct. 2013, http://english.alarabiya.net/en/views/news/middle-east/2013/10/21/The-Egyptian-people-demand-the-right-to-demand.html, last accessed 29 Oct. 2015.

11. Amira el-Fekki, 'Court upholds jail term for activists Maher Douma and Adel', *Daily News Egypt*, 27 Jan. 2015, http://www.dailynewsegypt.com/2015/01/27/court-upholds-jail-term-activists-douma-maher-adel/, last accessed 29 Oct. 2015.

12. Tony Gamal Gabriel and El-Sayed Gamal Eddin, 'Severe sentences for Alexandria female protesters spark Egypt outcry', AhramOnline, 28 Nov. 2013, http://english.ahram.org.eg/NewsContent/1/64/87715/Egypt/Politics-/Severe-sentences-for-Alexandria-female-protesters-.aspx, last accessed 29 Oct. 2015.

13. Omar Ashour, 'Enduring repression and insurgency in Egypt's Sinai', BBC, 13 Aug. 2015, www.bbc.com/news/world-middle-east-33905477, last accessed 29 Oct. 2015.

14. Hossam Bahgat, 'Who let the jihadis out', Mada Masr, 16 Feb. 2014, http://www.madamasr.com/sections/politics/who-let-jihadis-out, last accessed 29 Oct. 2015.

15. Kareem Farid, 'How the Egyptian Mainstream Media Cover the War on Terror', TIMEP, 23 March 2015, http://timep.org/commentary/how-egyptian-mainstream-media-cover-the-war-on-terror/, last accessed 17 Feb. 2016.

16. H. A. Hellyer, 'Is Egypt's Brotherhood choosing escalation over peace?', Al-Monitor, 6 June 2015, http://www.al-monitor.com/pulse/originals/2015/06/egypt-muslim-brotherhood-weaker-stronger-morsi-sisi.html, last accessed 29 Oct. 2015.

17. 'Egypt: Raba'a Killings Likely Crimes Against Humanity', Human Rights Watch, 12 Aug. 2014, http://www.hrw.org/news/2014/08/12/egypt-rab-killings-likely-crimes-against-humanity, last accessed 29 Oct. 2015.

18. Ashraf el-Sherif, 'What Path will Egypt's Muslim Brotherhood Choose', Carnegie Endowment for International Peace, 23 Sept. 2013, http://carnegieendowment.org/2013/09/23/what-path-will-egypt-s-muslim-brotherhood-choose, last accessed 29 Oct. 2015.

19. Mokhtar Awad and Nathan J. Brown, 'Mutual Escalation in Egypt', *Washington Post*, 9 Feb. 2015, http://www.washingtonpost.com/blogs/monkey-cage/wp/2015/02/09/mutual-escalation-in-egypt/, last accessed 29 Oct. 2015.

20. Ibid.

21. 'Muslim Brotherhood Statement Reiterates Commitment to January 25 Revolution Goals', Ikhwanweb, 29 May 2015, http://ikhwanweb.com/article.php?id=32154, last accessed 29 Oct. 2015.

22. 'April 6 condemns call for revenge against Egyptian authorities', AhramOnline, 2 June 2015, http://english.ahram.org.eg/News/1317 66.aspx, last accessed 29 Oct. 2015.

23. Ibrahim el-Hodaiby, 'The Muslim Brotherhood in transition', Mada Masr, 18 March 2015, http://www.madamasr.com/opinion/politics/muslim-brotherhood-transition, last accessed 29 Oct. 2015.

24. Amelia Cooper, 'United Nations reviews Egypt's human rights failures', Egypt Solidarity Initiative, 25 March 2015, http://egyptsolidarityinitiative.org/2015/03/25/united-nations-reviews-egypts-human-rights-failures/, last accessed 29 Oct. 2015.

25. Ibid.

26. 'Egypt receives 300 recommendations in UN human rights review', *Daily News Egypt*, 8 Nov. 2014, http://www.dailynewsegypt.com/2014/11/08/egypt-receives-300-recommendations-un-human-rights-review/, last accessed 29 Oct. 2015.

27. 'UN Human Rights Council: Adoption of the UPR Report on Egypt', Human Rights Watch, 20 March 2015, http://www.hrw.org/news/2015/03/20/un-human-rights-council-adoption-upr-report-egypt, last accessed 29 Oct. 2015.

28. 'Two years since Rabaa Masscare Impunity Still Reigns in Egypt', Press Release, Federation Internationale de Driots de l'homme, 8 July 2015, last accessed 17 Feb. 2016.

29. Jack Shenker, 'Sharm El Sheikh rumbles with grand promises of the international elite', *The Guardian*, 15 March 2015, http://www.the-guardian.com/world/2015/mar/15/egyot-sharma-el-sheikh-rumbles-grand-promises, last accessed 17 Feb. 2016.

30. Zeinab Abul Magd, 'The General's Secret: Egypt's Ambivalent Market', Sada, 9 Feb. 2012, http://carnegieendowment.org/sada/?fa=47137 4 May 2016.

31. Mona Said and Kathleen O'Neill, 'The "Youth Bulge" in Egypt: Is Labor Migration the Solution?', Middle East Institute, 20 April 2010, http://www.mei.edu/content/%E2%80%9Cyouth-bulge%E2%80%9D-egypt-labor-migration-solution, last accessed 29 Oct. 2015.

32. Michael Wahid Hanna, 'Egypt's Next Phase: Sustainable Instability', The Century Foundation, 1 July 2015, https://tcf.org/content/report/egypts-next-phase-sustainable-instability/, last accessed 29 Oct. 2015.

33. *Ibid*.

CONCLUSION: THE GENIE IS OUT

1. 'Al-Monitor mourns Bassem Sabry', Al-Monitor, 29 April 2014, http://

www.al-monitor.com/pulse/originals/2014/04/bassem-sabry-death-mourned.html#ixzz3lDWhFXMA, last accessed 29 Oct. 2015.

2. H. A. Hellyer, 'Youth need vision, not revolt, in the Muslim world', *The National*, 24 Jan. 2011, http://www.thenational.ae/thenational-conversation/comment/youth-need-vision-not-revolt-in-the-muslim-world, last accessed 2 Nov. 2015.

3. Ibid.

4. 'April 6's Ahmed Maher on Egypt under Sisi', a published translation by The Arabist of an interview done by Huffington Post Arabic, 17 Aug. 2015, http://arabist.net/blog/2015/8/17/in-translation-april-6s-ahmed-maher-on-egypt-under-sisi, last accessed 21 Oct. 2015.

5. Ibid.

6. Adapted from H. A. Hellyer, 'Where are they', *Daily News Egypt*, 1 Oct. 2013, http://www.dailynewsegypt.com/2013/10/01/where-are-they/, last accessed 21 Oct. 2015.

7. 'April 6's Ahmed Maher on Egypt under Sisi', The Arabist.

8. John Beck, 'Anatomy of a Killing: How Shaimaa al-Sabbagh Was Shot Dead at a Cairo Protest', Vice News, 24 February 2015, https://news.vice.com/article/anatomy-of-a-killing-how-shaimaa-al-sabbagh-was-shot-dead-at-a-cairo-protest, last accessed 2 Oct. 2015.

9. 'Egypt: Retrial for Policeman Accused of Killing Shaimaa El-Sabbagh', BBC, 14 Feb. 2016, http://www.bbc.co.uk/news/world-middle-east-35574004, last accessed 17 Feb. 2016.

10. George Orwell, *Homage to Catalonia*, New York: Mariner Books, 1980.

11. Linda Wertheimer, 'A Final Word With President's Faithul Speechwriter', NPR, 21 June 2006, http://www.npr.org/templates/story/story.php?storyId=5499701, last accessed 17 Feb. 2016.

SELECTED BIBLIOGRAPHY

Abaza, Mona, 'The Revolution's Barometer', *Jadaliyya*, 2012, online at: http://www.jadaliyya.com/pages/index/5978/the-revolutions-barometer-

Abou El-Fadl, Reem, 'Between Cairo and Washington: Sectarianism and Counter-revolution in Post-Mubarak Egypt.' In Reem Abou El-Fadl, ed., *Revolutionary Egypt: Connecting Domestic and International Struggles*, New York: Routledge, 2015.

Abul-Magd Z., *Imagined Empires: A history of revolt in Egypt, Berkeley*, CA: University of California Press, 2013.

Achcar, Gilbert, *The People Want: A Radical Exploration of the Arab Uprising*, Berkeley, CA: University of California Press, 2013.

al-Anani, Khalil and Malik, Maszlee, 'Pious Way to Politics: The Rise of Political Salafism in Post-Mubarak Egypt', *Digest of Middle East Studies*, 22, 1 (2013), pp. 57–73.

Albo, Moshe, 'Al Azhar Sufism in Post Revolutionary Egypt', *Journal of Sufi Studies*, 1,2 (2012), pp. 224–244.

Alexander, Anne, 'Brothers-in-arms? The Egyptian military, the Ikhwan and the revolutions of 1952 and 2011', *Journal of North African Studies*, 16, 4 (2011), pp. 533–554.

Alexander, Anne, 'Egypt's Rebels', *The Socialist Review*, 382 (2013), http://socialistreview.org.uk/382/egypts-rebels

Alterman, Jon B., 'The Revolution Will not Be Tweeted', *Washington Quarterly*, 34,4 (2011), pp. 104–116.

Amin, Galal, *Egypt in the Era of Hosni Mubarak, 1981–2011*, Cairo: AUC Press, 2012.

Anani, Khalil and Malik, Maszlee, 'Pious Way to Politics: The Rise of Political Salafism in Post-Mubarak Egypt', *Digest of Middle East Politics*, 22, 1 (2013), pp. 57–73.

Anderson, Lisa, 'Demystifying the Arab Spring: Parsing the Differences Between Tunisia, Egypt, and Libya', *Foreign Affairs*, 90, 3 (2011), pp. 2–7.

SELECTED BIBLIOGRAPHY

Armbrust, Walter, 'The Iconic Stage: Martyrologies and Performance Frames in the January 25th Revolution.' In Reem Abou El-Fadl, ed. *Revolutionary Egypt: Connecting Domestic and International Struggles*, New York: Routledge, 2015.

Armbrust, Walter, 'The Revolution Against Neoliberalism.' In Bassam Haddad, Rosie Basher and Ziad Abu-Rish, eds., *The Dawn of the Arab Uprisings: End of an Old Order?*, London: Pluto Press, 2012.

Asad, Talal, 'Fear and the Ruptured State: Reflections on Egypt after Mubarak', *Social Research*, 79,2 (2012), pp. 271–298.

Bayat, Asef, 'Arab Revolutions and the Study of Middle Eastern Societies', *International Journal of Middle East Studies*, 43,3 (2011), p. 386.

Bayoumi, Mustafa, 'Men Behaving Badly', Middle East Report and Information Project, 2012, http://www.merip.org/mero/interventions/menbehaving-badly, (accessed 19 Sept. 2012).

Berger, Miriam, 'A Revolutionary Role or a Remnant of the Past? The Future of the Egyptian Journalist Syndicate after the January 25th Revolution', *Arab Media and Society*, 18 (2013), http://www.arabmediasociety.com/articles/downloads/20130612130820_Berger_Miriam.pdf

Bowker, Robert, 'Egypt: Diplomacy and the Politics of Change', *The Middle East Journal*, 67,4 (2013), pp. 581–591.

British Council, 'The Revolutionary Promise: Youth Perceptions in Egypt', Tunisia, and Libya', 2013, Cairo.

Brown, Nathan J., 'Egypt's Failed Transition', *Journal of Democracy*, 24, 4 (2013), pp. 45–58.

Brown, Nathan J., 'Egypt's daring constitutional gang of 50', *Foreign Policy*, 20 September, 2013.

Brown, Nathan J., 'When Victory Becomes an Option: Egypt's Muslim MB Confronts Success', The Carnegie Papers, Carnegie Endowment for International Peace, 2012.

Brown, Nathan J., 'Cairo's Judicial Coup', *Foreign Policy*, 14 June 2012.

Brownlee, Jason, Tarek E. Masoud, Andrew Reynolds, *Pathways of Repression and Reform*, Oxford: Oxford University Press, 2015.

Brownlee, Jason, Tarek E. Masoud, Andrew Reynolds, 'Why the Modest Harvest?', *Journal of Democracy*, 24, 4 (2013), pp. 29–44.

Brumberg, D., 'Will Egypt's agony save the Arab spring?', *Foreign Policy*, 21 August, 2013.

Cole, Juan, 'Egypt's Modern Revolutions and the Fall of Mubarak.' In Gerges, Fawaz A., ed., *The New Middle East: protest and revolution in the Arab world*, Cambridge: Cambridge University Press, 2014, pp. 60–79.

Cook, Steven A., *The Struggle for Egypt: From Nasser to Tahrir Square*, Oxford, Oxford University Press, 2011.

Dabashi, Hamid, *The Arab Spring: The End of Postcolonialism*, New York: Palgrave/Macmillan, 2012.

SELECTED BIBLIOGRAPHY

Dadush, Uri and Dunne, Michele, 'American and European Responses to the Arab Spring: What's the Big Idea?', *The Washington Quarterly*, 34,4 (2011), pp. 131–145.

Dorsey, James, 'Pitched Battles: The role of Ultra soccer fans in the Arab Spring', *Mobilization*, 17,4 (2012), pp. 411–418.

Dunne, Michele, 'US Policy Struggles with an Egypt in Turmoil', Arab Reform Initiative, May, 2014.

Dunne, Michele and Radwan, Tarek, 'Egypt: Why Liberalism Still Matters', *Journal of Democracy*, 24,1 (2013), pp. 86–100.

El Dahshan, Mohamed, 'Does General Sisi Have a Plan for Egypt's Economy?' *Foreign Policy*, 18 April 2014.

El-Ghobashy, Mona, 'The Praxis of the Egyptian Revolution', *Middle East Report*, 258 (2011), http://merip.org/mer/mer258/praxis-egyptian-revolution

Elgindy, Khaled, 'Egypt's Troubled Transition: Elections without Democracy', *Journal of Democracy*, 35,2 (2012), pp. 89–104.

El-Mahdi, Rabab, 'Labor protests in Egypt: causes and meanings', *Review of African Political Economy*, 38, 129 (2011), pp. 387–402.

El-Mahdi, Rabab, 'Enough! Egypt's quest for democracy', *Comparative Political Studies*, 42 (2009), pp. 1011–1039.

Elmasry, Mohamad Hamas, 'Producing News in Mubarak's Egypt: An analysis of Egyptian newspaper production during the late Hosni Mubarak era', *Journal of Arab & Muslim Media Research*, 4, 2–3 (2012), pp. 121–144.

El-Sherif, Ashraf, 'Islamism after the Arab Spring', *Current History*, 111, 741 (2011), pp. 358–363.

El-Shimy, Yasser M, 'The Arab Spring Gathers Clouds: Why the Revolts for Change Have Stalled', *Insight Turkey*, 13,4 (2011), pp. 39–54.

Fadel, Mohammed, 'Judicial institutions, the legitimacy of Islamic state law and democratic transition in Egypt: Can a shift toward a common law model of adjudication improve the prospects of a successful democratic transition?', *International Journal Of Constitutional Law*, 11,3 (2013), pp. 646–665.

Fadel, Mohammed, 'Modernist Political Thought and the Egyptian and Tunisian Revolutions of 2011', *Middle East Law and Governance*, 3 (2011), pp. 94–104.

Filiu, Jean-Pierre, *The Arab Revolution: Ten Lessons From the Democratic Uprising*, London: Hurst & Co, 2011.

Frampton, Martyn and Rosen, Ehud, 'Reading the Runes: The United States and the Muslim MB as Seen Through the Wikileaks Cables', *The Historical Journal*, 56,3 (2013), pp. 827–856.

Gallup Center for Muslim Studies, 'Snapshot: Rural Egyptians Are Engaged in Political Process', *Gallup*, 7 June 2012.

Gause, F. Gregory, III., 'Why Middle East Studies Missed the Arab Spring: The Myth of Authoritarian Stability', *Foreign Affairs*, 90,4 (2011), pp. 81–90.

231

SELECTED BIBLIOGRAPHY

Gerhart Center for Philanthropy and Civic Engagement, 'Youth activism and public space in Egypt', Cairo: American University in Cairo Press, 2011.

Gerges, Fawaz A., ed., *The New Middle East: protest and revolution in the Arab world*, Cambridge: Cambridge University Press, 2014.

Ghoneim, Wael, *Revolution 2.0: The Power of the People Is Greater Than the People in Power: A Memoir*, New York: Houghton Mifflin, 2011.

Gröndahl, Mia, *Tahrir Square: The Heart of the Egyptian Revolution*, Cairo: The American University in Cairo Press, 2011.

Hanna, Michael Wahid, 'Public Order and Egypt's Statist Tradition', *The Review of Faith & International Affairs*, 13,1 (2015), pp. 23–30.

Hellyer, H.A., 'Revolution in the Arab world: Egypt and its Challenges', *Middle East Law and Governance Journal*, 3, 1–2 (2011), pp.118–125.

Hellyer, H. A., 'The Chance for Change in the Arab World: Egypt's uprising', *International Affairs*, 87,6 (2011), pp. 1313–1322.

Hesham Sallam, 'The Egyptian Revolution and the Politics of Histories', *Political Science & Politics*, 46,2 (2013), pp. 248–258.

Holmes, Amy Austin, 'There are weeks when decades happen: Structure and strategy in the Egyptian revolution', *Mobilization*, 17, 4 (2012), pp. 391–410.

Iskander, Adel, 'Teaching the Arab Uprisings: Between Media Maelstrom and Pedantic Pedagogy', *Political Science & Politics*, 46,2 (2013), pp. 244–247.

Iskander, Adel, *Egypt in Flux: Essays on an Unfinished Revolution*, Oxford: Oxford University Press, 2013.

Joffé, George, ed., *North Africa's Arab Spring*, New York: Routledge, 2012.

Joffé, George, 'The Arab Spring in North Africa: Origins and Prospects', *The Journal of North African Studies*, 16, 4 (2011), pp. 507–532.

Joshi, Shashank, 'Reflections on the Arab Revolutions', *The RUSI Journal*, 156,2 (2011), pp. 60–67.

Joya, Angela, 'The Egyptian revolution: crisis of neoliberalism and the potential for democratic politics', *Review of African Political Economy*, 38, 129 (2011), pp. 367–386.

Kahl, Colin H. and Lynch, Marc, 'U.S. Strategy after the Arab Uprisings: Toward Progressive Engagement', *The Washington Quarterly*, 36,2 (2013), pp. 39–60.

Kamrava, Mehran, 'The Arab Spring and the Saudi-Led Counterrevolution', *Orbis*, 56,1 (2012), pp. 96–104.

Kandil, Hazem, *Soldiers, Spies and Statesmen: Egypt's Road to Revolt*, London: Verso, 2013.

Kandil, Hazem, 'Soldiers Without Generals: Whither the Egyptian Revolution?', *Dissent*, 59,3 (2012), pp. 11–17.

Kandil, Hazem, 'Why did the Egyptian Middle Class March to Tahrir Square?', *Mediterranean Politics*, 17,2 (2012), pp. 197–215.

SELECTED BIBLIOGRAPHY

Keddie, Nikki R., 'Arab and Iranian Revolts 1979–2011: Influences or Similar Causes?', *International Journal of Middle East Studies*, 44,1 (2012), pp.150–152.

Khalil, Ashraf, *Liberation Square: Inside the Egyptian Revolution and the Rebirth of a Nation*, New York: St. Martin's Press, 2012.

Khalil, Karima, 'New Texts Out Now: Karima Khalil, Messages from Tahrir', *Cultural Anthropology*, 2012, in the series: 'Hotspots: Revolution and Counter-Revolution in Egypt a Year after January 25th', ed. by Julia Elyachar and Jessica Winegar, https://culanth.org/fieldsights/225-new-texts-out-now-karima-khalil-messages-from-tahrir

Khamis, Sahar, 'Islamic feminism in new Arab media: platforms for self-expression and sites for multiple resistances', *Journal of Arab and Muslim Media Research*, 3, 3 (2010), pp. 237–255.

Khatib, Lina, *Image Politics in the Middle East: The Role of the Visual in Political Struggle*, London: I.B. Tauris, 2012.

Khosrokhavar, Farhad, *The New Arab Revolutions That Shook the World*, Colorado: Paradigm Press, 2013.

Kurzman, Charles, 'The Arab Spring: Ideals of the Iranian Green Movement, Methods of the Iranian Revolution', *International Journal of Middle East Studies*, 44,1 (2012), pp. 162–165.

Lesch, Ann M., 'Troubled Political transitions: Tunisia, Egypt, Libya', *Middle East Policy*, 21,1 (2014), pp. 62–74.

Lesch, Ann M., 'Egypt's Spring: Causes of the Revolution', *Middle East Policy*, 18, 3 (2011), pp. 35–48.

Levine, Mark, 'Theorizing revolutionary practice: Agendas for research on the Arab uprisings', *Middle East Critique*, 22 (2013), pp. 191–212.

Lindsey, Ursula, 'Saving the Middle East's Past With Twitter and Other Online Tools', *Chronicle of Higher Education*, 21 Aug. 2014, http://chronicle.com/article/Saving-the-Middle-Easts-Past/148373/

Lindsey, Ursula, 'Art in Egypt's Revolutionary Square', Middle East Research and Information Project, 2012, http://www.merip.org/mero/interventions/art-egypts-revolutionary-square

Lynch, Marc, *The Arab Uprising: The Unfinished Revolutions of the New Middle East, 2nd edition*, New York: Public Affairs, 2013.

Mady, Abdel-Fattah, 'Popular Discontent, Revolution, and Democratization in Egypt in a Globalizing World', *Indiana Journal of Global Legal Studies*, 20,1 (2013), pp. 313–337.

Mahmood, Saba, 'Religious Freedom, the Minority Question, and Geopolitics in the Middle East', *Comparative Studies in Society and History*, 54,2 (2012), pp. 418–446.

Mahmood, Saba, 'The Architects of the Egyptian Uprising and the Challenges Ahead.' In Bassam Haddad, Rosie Basher and Ziad Abu-Rish eds., *The Dawn of the Arab Uprisings: End of an Old Order?*, London: Pluto Press, 2012.

SELECTED BIBLIOGRAPHY

Makar, Farida, '"Let Them Have Some Fun": Political and Artistic Forms of Expression in the Egyptian Revolution', *Mediterranean Politics*, 16, 2 (2011), pp. 307–312.

Mallat, Chibli, 'The Philosophy of the Mideast Revolution, Take One: Non Violence', *Middle East Law and Governance*, 3 (2011), pp. 136–147.

Mandaville, Peter, 'Islam and Exceptionalism in American Political Discourse', *Political Science & Politics*, 46, 2 (2013), pp. 235–239.

Masoud, Tarek, *Counting Islam: religion, class and politics in Egypt*, Cambridge: Cambridge University Press, 2014.

Masoud, Tarek, 'Liberty, Democracy, and Discord in Egypt', *The Washington Quarterly*, 34,4 (2011), pp. 117–129.

Masoud, Tarek, 'The Road to (and from) Liberation Square', *Journal of Democracy*, 22,3 (2011), pp. 20–34.

Moll, Yasmin, 'Conversation on the Egyptian Revolution', *Cultural Anthropology*, 2012, in the series: 'Hotspots: Revolution and Counter-Revolution in Egypt a Year after January 25th', ed. by Julia Elyachar and Jessica Winegar, https://culanth.org/fieldsights/240-conversation-on-the-egyptian-revolution-fieldwork-in-revolutionary-times

Moll, Yasmin, 'Building the New Egypt: Islamic Televangelists, Revolutionary Ethics, and "Productive" Citizenship', *Cultural Anthropology*, 2012, in the series: 'Hotspots: Revolution and Counter-Revolution in Egypt a Year after January 25th', ed. by Julia Elyachar and Jessica Winegar, https://culanth.org/fieldsights/231-building-the-new-egypt-islamic-televangelists-revolutionary-ethics-and-productive-citizenship

Moustafa, Tamir, 'Law in the Egyptian Revolt', *Middle East Law and Governance Journal*, 3, 1–2 (2011), pp. 181–191.

Muasher, Marwan, *The Second Arab Awakening and the Battle for Pluralism*, New Haven, CT: Yale University Press, 2014.

Osman, Tarek, *Egypt on the Brink: From Nasser to Mubarak*, New York: Yale University Press, 2010.

Owen, Roger, 'Egypt and Tunisia: From the Revolutionary Overthrow of Dictatorships to the Struggle to Establish a New Constitutional Order.' In Fawaz A. Gerges ed., *The New Middle East: protest and revolution in the Arab world*, Cambridge: Cambridge University Press, 2014.

Owen, Roger, 'The Arab "demonstration" effect and the revival of Arab unity in the Arab Spring', *Contemporary Arab Affairs*, 5,3 (2013), pp. 372–381.

Owen, Roger, 'Jadaliyya: Documenting the Revolution.' In Bassam Haddad, Rosie Basher and Ziad Abu-Rish, eds. *The Dawn of the Arab Uprisings: End of an Old Order?*, London: Pluto Press, 2012.

Özhan, Taha, 'The Arab Spring and Turkey: The Camp David Order vs. the New Middle East', *Insight Turkey*, 13, 4 (2011), pp. 55–64.

Rizzo, Helen, Price, Anne and Meyer Katherine, 'Anti-Sexual Harrassment Campaign in Egypt', *Mobilization*, 17,4 (2012), pp. 457–475.

Roy, Olivier, 'There Will Be No Islamist Revolution', *Journal of Democracy*, 24,1 (2013), pp. 14–19.

Roy, Olivier, 'The Transformation of the Arab World', *Journal of Democracy*, 23,3 (2012), p.5.

Saad, Reem, 'The Egyptian revolution: A triumph of poetry', *American Ethnologist*, 39,1 (2012), pp. 63–66.

Saad, Reem, 'Reflections on the Egyptian Revolution', *Cultural Anthropology*, 2012, in the series: 'Hotspots: Revolution and Counter-Revolution in Egypt a Year after January 25th', ed. by Julia Elyachar and Jessica Winegar, https://culanth.org/fieldsights/241-reflections-on-the-egyptian-revolution

Sabry, Mohannad, *Sinai*, Cairo: American University in Cairo Press, 2015.

Said, Atef, 'We ought to be here: Historicizing space and mobilization in Tahrir Square', *International Sociology*, (2014), pp.1–19.

Said, Atef, 'The Paradox of Transition to "Democracy" under Military Rule', *Social Research*, 79, 2 (2012), pp. 397–434.

Saikal, Amin, 'Authoritarianism, revolution and democracy: Egypt and beyond', *Australian Journal of International Affairs*, 65, 5 (2011), pp. 530–544.

Salaita, Steven, 'Corporate American media coverage of Arab revolutions: the contradictory messages of modernity', *Interface*, 4, 1 (2012), pp. 131–145. Online at: http://www.interfacejournal.net/wordpress/wp-content/uploads/2012/05/Interface-4–1-Salaita.pdf

Sallam, Hesham, 'The Egyptian Revolution and the Politics of Histories', *Political Science & Politics*, 46,2 (2013), pp. 248–258.

Sallam, Hesham, 'Striking Back at Egyptian Workers', *Middle East Report* 259, 41, 2 (2011), pp. 20–25.

Sayigh, Yezid, 'Above the State: The Officers' Republic in Egypt', Washington D.C: Carnegie Endowment for International Peace, 2012, http://carnegieendowment.org/2012/08/01/above-state-officers-republic-in-egypt-pub-48972

Sayigh, Yezid, 'Agencies of Coercion: Armies and Internal Security Forces', *International Journal of Middle East Studies*, 43,3 (2011), pp. 403–405.

Sedra, Paul, 'Reconstituting the Coptic Community amidst revolution', *Middle East Report*, 42, 265 (2012).

Shahin, Emad El-Din, 'Egypt: The Power of Mass Mobilization and the Spirit of Tahrir Square', *Journal of the Middle East and Africa*, 3,1 (2012).

Shahine, Selim H., 'Youth and the revolution in Egypt', *Anthropology Today*, 27, 2 (2011), pp. 1–3.

Shalaby, Nadia A., 'A multimodal analysis of selected Cairokee songs of the Egyptian revolution and their representation of women', *Journal for Cultural Research*, 19,2 (2015), pp. 176–198.

Sharp, Jeremy M., Egypt: *The January 25 Revolution and Implications for U. S. Foreign Policy*, Darby, PA: DIANE Publishing Company, 2010.

SELECTED BIBLIOGRAPHY

Shehata, Dina, 'The Fall of the Pharaoh: How Hosni Mubarak's Reign Came to an End', *Foreign Affairs*, 90,3 (2011), pp. 26–32.

Shenoda, Anthony, 'Public Christianity in a Revolutionary Egypt', *Cultural Anthropology*, 2012, in the series: 'Hotspots: Revolution and Counter-Revolution in Egypt a Year after January 25th', ed. by Julia Elyachar and Jessica Winegar, https://culanth.org/fieldsights/234-public-christianity-in-a-revolutionary-egypt

Shenoda, Anthony, 'Reflections on the (In)Visibility of Copts in Egypt', *Jadaliyya*, 18 May 2011.

Shokr, Ahmad, 'Reflections on Two Revolutions', *Middle East Report*, 42, 265 (2013), http://www.merip.org/mer/mer265/reflections-two-revolutions

Shokr, Ahmad, 'The 18 Days of Tahrir', *Middle East Report*, 258 (2011), pp.14–19.

Snider, Erin A. and Faris, David.M, 'The Arab Spring: U.S. Democracy Promotion in Egypt', *Middle East Policy*, 18,3 (2011), pp. 49–62.

Sonnenschein, Jan and Younis, Mohamed, 'U.S. Approval Eroding in MENA Before Film Controversy: Two in 10 adults across 12 countries express approval', *Gallup*, 24 Sept. 2012.

Sorbera, Lucia, 'Challenges of thinking feminism and revolution in Egypt between 2011 and 2014', *Postcolonial Studies*, 17,1 (2014), pp. 63–75.

Soueif, Ahdaf, *Cairo: My City, Our Revolution*, London: Bloomsbury, 2012.

Springborg, Robert, 'Whither the Arab Spring? 1989 or 1848?', *The International Spectator: Italian Journal of International Affairs*, 4, 3 (2011), pp. 5–12.

Stacher, Joshua, 'Establishment Mursi', *Middle East Report*, 42, 265 (2012).

Stacher, Joshua, *Adaptable Autocrats: Regime Power in Egypt and Syria*, Stanford, CA: Stanford University Press, 2012.

Stacher, Josha, 'Egypt Without Mubarak', Middle East Research and Information Project, 2011, http://www.merip.org/mero/mero040711

Stork, Joe, 'Egypt: Human Rights in Transition', *Social Research*, 79,2 (2012), pp.463–486.

Sullivan, Earl (Tim), 'Youth power and the revolution.' In Dan Tschirgi, Walid Kazziha and Sean F. McMahon, eds., *Egypt's Tahrir Revolution*, Boulder, CO: Lynne Rienner, 2012.

Swedenburg, Ted, 'Egypt's Music of Protest: From Sayyid Darwish to DJ Haha', *Middle East Report*, 42, 265 (2012), http://www.merip.org/mer/mer265/egypts-music-protest

Tadros, Mariz, 'Sectarianism and Its Discontents in Post-Mubarak Egypt', *Middle East Report*, 41, 259, pp. 26–31.

Teti, Andrea and Gennaro Gervasio, 'The Unbearable Lightness of Authoritarianism: Lessons from the Arab Uprisings', *Mediterranean Politics*,16,2 (2011), pp. 321–27.

SELECTED BIBLIOGRAPHY

Tripp, Charles, *The Power and the People: Paths of Resistance in the Middle East*, Cambridge: Cambridge University Press, 2013.

Tschirgi, Dan, Kazziha, Walid and McMahon F., Sean, eds., *Egypt's Tahrir Revolution*, Boulder: Lynne Rienner, 2012.

Wedady, Nasser and Ahmari, Sohrab, Arab Spring Dreams: *The Next Generation Speaks Out for Freedom and Justice from North Africa to Iran*, New York: St Martin's Press, 2012.

Werbner, Pnina, Webb, Martin, and Spellman-Poots, Kathryn, eds., *The Political Aesthetics of Global Protest: The Arab Spring and Beyond*, Edinburgh: University of Edinburgh Press, 2014.

Wickham, Carrie Rosefsky, 'The Muslim MB and Democratic Transition in Egypt', Middle East Law and Governance Journal, 3, 1–2 (2011), pp. 204–223.

Yahya, Maha, Dina Tannir, Oussama Safa, Jamil Mouawad, Vivienne Baadan, 'The Promises of Spring: Citizenship and Civic Engagement in Democratic Transitions', Social Participatory Development Section of the Economic and Social Commission for Western Asia (ESCWA), http://www.escwa. un.org/information/publications/edit/upload/E_ESCWA_ SDD_13_3_E.pdf

Youmans, William Lafi and Jillian C. York, 'Social Media and the Activist Toolkit: User Agreements, Corporate Interests, and the Information Infrastructure of Modern Social Movements', Journal of Communication, 62,2 (2012), pp. 315–329.

Younis, Ahmed, and Mohamed Younis, 'Egyptian Opposition to U.S. and Other Foreign Aid Increases: Majority now also opposes aid from international organizations', *Gallup*, 29 March 2012.

Younis, Ahmed, and Mohamed Younis, 'Support for Islamists Declines as Egypt's Election Nears: Muslim MB, Salafis, and FJP have all lost support', *Gallup*, 18 May 2012.

Younis, Ahmed, and Mohamed Younis, 'Most Egyptians Expect a Fair, Honest Election: Nearly three in four believe military will hand over power post-election', *Gallup*, 22 May 2012.

Younis, Ahmed, and Mohamed Younis, 'Most Egyptians oppose U.S. economic aid', *Gallup*, 2012.

Younis, James, Brian K. Barber and Rhett M. Billen, 'Children In the Garden of Democracy: The Meaning of Civic Egypt', *Journal of Social Science Education*, 12,1 (2013), pp. 6–13.

Younis, Mohamed, 'Majority of Egyptians Want Military Out of Politics: Most believed military would cede power', *Gallup*, 22 June 2012.

Younis, Mohamed, 'Egyptians to Government: Focus on Jobs', *Gallup*, 16 July 2012.

Youssef, C.M., 'Recent events in Egypt and the Middle East', *Organizational Dynamics*, 40, 3 (2011), pp. 222–234.

SELECTED BIBLIOGRAPHY

Zaher, Maged, *The Tahrir of Poems: Seven Contemporary Egyptian Poets*, Seattle: Alice Blue Books, 2015.

Zahid, Mohammed, *The Muslim Brotherhood and Egypt's Succession Crisis: The Politics of Liberalization and Reform in the Middle East*, London: I.B. Tauris, 2012.

Zaki, Hoda M., 'From Montgomery to Tahrir Square: The Transnational Journeys of Nonviolence and Utopia', *Utopian Studies*, 26, 1 (2015), pp. 203–219.

Zeghal, Malika, 'Resistance Movements, the State, and National Identities', *International Journal of Middle East Studies*, 43, 3 (2011), p. 390.

Zemni, Sami, Brecht De Smet, Koenraad Bogaert, 'Luxemburg on Tahrir Square: Reading the Arab Revolutions with Rosa Luxemburg's The Mass Strike', *Antipode*, 45, 4 (2012), pp. 888–907.

Zevnik, Andreja, 'Maze of Resistance: Crowd, Space and the Politics of Resisting Subjectivity', *Globalizations*, 12, 1 (2015), pp. 101–115.

Zguric, Borna, 'Challenges for democracy in countries affected by the "Arab Spring"', *Islam and Christian–Muslim Relations*, 23,4 (2012), pp. 417–434.

Zubaida, Sami, 'The Arab spring in the historical context of Middle East politics', *Economy and Society*, 41, 4 (2012), pp. 568–579.

Zuckerman, E., 'The first Twitter revolution?' *Foreign Policy*, 14 Jan. 2011, http://www.foreignpolicy.com/articles/2011/01/14/the_first_twitter_revolution

INDEX

239

INDEX

INDEX

constitutional referendum
(2011), 30, 43–5, 52–4, 56,
63–4, 106
ousting of Mursi (2013), xxxi,
xxxiii, 32, 34–6, 55, 76–7,
82–3, 88, 109, 111, 125–7,
130–4, 141–54, 158–9, 172,
175, 186, 196
and dissolution of parliament
(2012), 63, 65, 96, 107
Gamal Mubarak, relations with,
19, 51
January 25 Uprising (2011), 8,
9, 12, 20, 52
Maspero massacre (2011), 64,
89, 168, 175
and media, 37, 53
presidential election (2012), 59,
60, 63, 66, 75, 96, 98
protest law (2013), 74, 175–7
Rab'a al-Adawiyya massacre
(2013), xxxiii, 141, 145,
164–9, 174, 179–80, 199
resignation of Mubarak (2011),
xxvii, 17, 21, 22, 23–4, 25,
29–30, 41, 43, 49–52, 63,
103, 105, 106, 172–3, 186
SCAF, xxviii, 24, 26, 30, 43, 47,
50–4, 56, 59, 63, 66, 98, 100,
102, 103, 104, 106, 107, 110,
177
Suez intervention (2013), 128,
141
Tantawi, removal of (2012), 63,
83, 99–101, 102
trial of Mubarak (2011–), 52
virginity tests, 99
Egyptian Initiative for Personal
Rights, 28, 50–1, 164–7
Egyptian Movement for Change
(*Kifaya*), 5, 27–8
Egyptian National Police

anti-Morsi protests (2013), 126,
128–30
brutality, 5–7, 36, 61, 129, 154,
159, 164–8, 177, 181, 183,
201–2
constitutional decree protests
(2012), 111, 117, 124, 146
January 25 Uprising (2011),
5–12, 17, 22, 150
June 30 protests (2013), 143,
150
Rab'a and Nahda sit-ins (2013),
164–6
Egyptian Popular Current, 111
Egyptian Revolutionary Council,
180
Eid al-Shurta, 5
Eid, Gamal, 177
Englishness, xxvi
Ennahdha, 69, 86, 87, 95, 98,
195–6, 197
Erdogan, Recep Tayyip, 178
al-Erian, Essam, 39, 117
European Union (EU), 135, 137,
163

Facebook, 7, 19, 21, 61, 121
Fadl, Belal, 29, 150
Fairmont Group, 60–1
fascism, 81
Fatah, xxxi, 88
fatawa, 92
faux liberals, 151, 153
fellahin (country provincials), 6
felool (leftovers), 59, 102, 132
feminism, 15
Festival of the Police, 5
Foreign Policy, xxxii, 113
France, 81
Free Egyptians, 55
Freedom and Justice Party (FJP),

INDEX

INDEX

INDEX

INDEX